AF601386

Maps as Media

Digital Media and Society Series

Giota Alevizou, *The Web of Knowledge*
Nancy Baym, *Personal Connections in the Digital Age*, 2nd edition
Taina Bucher, *Facebook*
Mercedes Bunz and Graham Meikle, *The Internet of Things*
Jean Burgess and Joshua Green, *YouTube*, 2nd edition
Mark Deuze, *Media Work*
Andrew Dubber, *Radio in the Digital Age*
Quinn DuPont, *Cryptocurrencies and Blockchains*
Charles Ess, *Digital Media Ethics*, 3rd edition
Terry Flew, *Regulating Platforms*
Jordan Frith, *Smartphones as Locative Media*
Alex Gekker, *Maps as Media*
Gerard Goggin, *Apps: From Mobile Phones to Digital Lives*
Alexander Halavais, *Search Engine Society*, 2nd edition
Martin Hand, *Ubiquitous Photography*
Robert Hassan, *The Information Society*
Kylie Jarrett, *Digital Labor*
Amelia Johns, Ariadna Matamoros-Fernández, and Emma Baulch, *WhatsApp: From a One-to-One Messaging App to a Global Communication Platform*
Mark R. Johnson, *Twitch*
Tim Jordan, *Hacking*
D. Bondy Valdovinos Kaye, Jing Zeng and Patrik Wikström, *TikTok: Creativity and Culture in Short Video*
Graeme Kirkpatrick, *Computer Games and the Social Imaginary*
Tama Leaver, Tim Highfield and Crystal Abidin, *Instagram*
Leah A. Lievrouw, *Alternative and Activist New Media*, 2nd edition
Rich Ling and Jonathan Donner, *Mobile Communication*
Donald Matheson and Stuart Allan, *Digital War Reporting*
Nick Monaco and Samuel Woolley, *Bots*
Jeremy Wade Morris, *Podcasting*
Dhiraj Murthy, *Twitter*, 2nd edition
Zizi A. Papacharissi, *A Private Sphere: Democracy in a Digital Age*
Julian Thomas, Rowan Wilken and Ellie Rennie, *Wi-Fi*
Katrin Tiidenberg, Natalie Ann Hendry and Crystal Abidin, *tumblr*
Jill Walker Rettberg, *Blogging*, 2nd edition
Patrik Wikström, *The Music Industry*, 3rd edition

Maps as Media

ALEX GEKKER

polity

First published in 2026 by Polity Press Ltd.

Polity Press Ltd.
65 Bridge Street
Cambridge CB2 1UR, UK

Polity Press Ltd.
111 River Street
Hoboken, NJ 07030, USA

ISBN-13: 978-1-5095-5012-8
ISBN-13: 978-1-5095-5013-5 (pb)

A catalogue record for this book is available from the British Library.

Library of Congress Control Number: 2026932649

Typeset in 10.25 on 13pt Scala
by Fakenham Prepress Solutions, Fakenham, Norfolk NR21 8NL
Printed and bound in Great Britain by Ashford Colour Ltd

For further information on Polity, visit our website:
politybooks.com

Contents

Figures and Tables

Figures

Tables

Acknowledgements

Three people deserve special credit for the fruition of this book project. First and foremost, it would not exist without Sybille Lammes, who has been a steadfast mentor since my MA days, and under whose supervision my original interest in maps formed and took shape. Richard Rogers consistently pushed me to come up with the main organizing idea of the book, and recommended Polity as a potential publisher. Finally, Mary Savigar has proven herself to be a focused, details-oriented, and – importantly! – very patient editor.

A special thanks also to Shannon Mattern, whose work has been an inspiration for a long time, and who graciously gave her blessing to my use of the title 'Maps as Media' after teaching a course by that name for many years at The New School.

This book is the result of more than a decade of thinking and doing digital maps, and I am grateful to the many people with whom I have had the privilege to do so, particularly at the Charting The Digital project. Thank you, Chris Perkins, Clancy Wilmott, Emma Fraser, Naomi Bueno de Mesquita and Jana Wendler and to all the seagulls on Gozo. And of course, to Sam Hind, for friendship and collaboration lasting fourteen(!) years and counting. Much of the thinking in this book was shaped by talking and writing with you, and I'm looking forward to doing so for many years to come!

Thanks also, in no particular order, to all the wonderful friends and colleagues who inspired me to think about maps and media differently over time. To Natalia Sanchez-Querubin, Bernhard Rieder, Stefania Milan, Michael Stevenson, Anne Helmond, Daniel de Zeeuw, Ester Weltevrede, Lonneke van der Velden, Stijn Peeters, Lucia Bainnotti, Steve Jankowski, Idil Galip, Marc Tuters, Maryn Wilkinson, Gabriel Pereira, Fernando van der Vlist, Blandine Joret, Niels van Doorn, Carolyn Birdsall, Claudio Celis Bueno, Bharath Ganesh, Linda Kopitz, Jernej Markelj, Marloes Geboers, Niels ten Oever, Fieke Janssen, Anat Ben-David, Dan Kotliar, Tamar Ashuri, Shira Dvir-Gvirsman, Elad Segev, Tzlil Sharon, and Jean-Christophe Plantin. To Misha Kavka for making my return to the Media Studies department much smoother. And to my BA and MA students who made me a better media scholar. Apologies to anyone missing from the list: you have my full permission to scold me on this in person or writing.

Earlier versions of material in this book have appeared elsewhere. Chapters 1, 2 and 5 draw on the theoretical chapter and some fieldwork of my 2016 PhD 'Uniquitous Cartography' (Utrecht University). Chapter 1 also refines some conceptualization from my 2023 paper 'Google Maps' COVID-19 Layer as an Interface for Pandemic Life', in *Mobile Media & Communication* 11 (2): 193–212. Chapter 2 reuses a case study and the main concept from the 2016 paper 'Casual Power: Understanding User Interfaces through Quantification', in *Digital Culture & Society* 2 (1): 107–22. Chapter 3's Mobileye section summarizes the paper co-authored with Sam Hind in 2022 called 'Automotive Parasitism: Examining Mobileye's "Car-Agnostic" Platformisation', in *New Media & Society* 26 (7): 3707–27. Chapter 4 has a short section reworked from my 2016 book chapter '(Mini) Mapping the Game-Space: A Taxonomy of Control', *Playful Mapping in the Digital Age*, Amsterdam: Institute for Network Culture, 134–55. Chapter 6 revisits and re-examines core concepts of the infrastructural surveillance framework, from a 2019 paper co-written with Sam Hind, 'Infrastructural Surveillance', in *New Media & Society* 22 (8): 1414–36. All of them have been changed and updated, and so any errors, issues, and outlandish ideas should not reflect badly on my co-author and/or reviewers in the original pieces.

The book benefitted tremendously from the time and discussions allowed by the NWO Open Competition SSH grant 406.20.CW.005, ‘Playing Politics: Media Platforms, Making Worlds’. Keep playing, team!

Thanks to Maddie Hazelden and everyone else on Polity’s publishing team for helping make this book great! To the anonymous reviewers for the proposal and final manuscript of this book who made really great suggestions which were kind and thoughtful.

Finally – and as always – thanks to Neta, Alma, and Lavie, who make me remap the world anew, every day.

1

Introducing Digital Maps

There is a (now-defunct) Twitter bot account I have followed for years, titled 'Uncharted Atlas', made by the artist and designer Martin O'Leary. Using synthetic terrain and language generation, it produces – every single hour – a unique 'fantasy' map, of the kind you might find on the inside cover of a speculative fiction novel. O'Leary notes how he strived for perceived believability in generating maps informed by knowledge of physical and political geography (O'Leary 2016a), while adhering to linguistic rules that would create places 'a step above the usual alphabetic soup of generated placenames, and which was capable of producing recognizably distinct languages' (O'Leary 2016b). The resulting black-and-white relief maps seem quite real at a cursory glance through a twitter feed, with mountain ridges and river contours subscribing to that of real-world geomorphology; and provinces and cities where you expect to find such. A decade ago this was a striking achievement, since even contemporary models are having trouble generating consistent and unique maps, often resulting in something like the one illustrated in figure 1.1. O'Leary's maps are believable because of the research and effort he has put into his lines of code, but also because of how prevalent maps are on our screens and how often we use them to see the world around us.

A very different digital map has led to a tragedy. In March 2011, Rita and Albert Chertein, a Canadian couple in their mid-fifties took a road trip to Las Vegas. Somewhere along the way in Idaho, their GPS satnav system led them along a side road that became less and less traversable. They ran

Figure 1.1: An example of OpenAI's GPT-5 response to the prompt 'Generate a fantasy map in the style of sixteenth-century cartography, black and white, showing mountains, rivers, cities, realistic topography, fictional place names (but consistent and logical)'. After several follow-ups, the model still produced bland and redundant places.

out of fuel in the mountains and decided that Albert should take some of the supplies alongside the GPS device and head for the nearest town for assistance. He never made it, succumbing to hypothermia some 11 kilometres from their van. Rita drank what little water she could find and rationed her food, but she was on death's door when found by chance by hunters in an all-terrain vehicle seven weeks after their disappearance. Though she survived, both were the victims of what geospatial technologies writer Greg Milner calls 'death by GPS', a name that comes from US rangers in Death Valley national park. It describes

> what happens when your GPS fails you, not by being wrong, exactly, but often by being too right. It does such a good job of computing the most direct route from point A to point B that it takes you down roads that barely exist, or were used at one time and abandoned, or are not suitable for your car, or that require local knowledge that would make you aware that making that turn is bad news (Milner 2016).

There's a fine line connecting the computer-generated maps of O'Leary's bot to the tragic tale of the Cherteins, and this book is about it. Once upon a time, in the ancient days of the early 2000s (and beforehand), maps occupied a distinct and separate domain. They lived in road atlases, city planners' offices, and attachés of military and diplomatic personnel. They also lived inside computers, particularly since the 1970s–1980s personal computer revolution, but even then, still, they relied on professional skills and were siloed into specific use cases: a political map drawn for the ruling class to govern, a topographic battle map for the warring general, a nautical chart for the sea captain. While sharing certain attributes – mainly the generalization and simplification of terrain to convey information – maps were situational tools. If one were to use a map at all (which was not a common occurrence until the twentieth century), it would have to be a specific map: you couldn't supplement one for another. The idea of a universal map was always appealing, but absurd.

Borges's famous fable, about a 1:1 map that covered the entire kingdom and became instantly tattered, underlines this point.[1]

Yet, we are much closer to this fantasy now than we have ever been. Several key technological developments of the past three decades have made maps more similar to one another and less specialized than ever before. Gleaming at us from multiple screens of varying size, the many contemporary digital maps share functionality, underlying technologies, and aesthetics. Tapping at our screens to walk, drive, order food, hook up, play games and much more, the many maps collapse into a seemingly unified one, serving as an innocuous backdrop for our daily conduct. They have taken the properties of both platforms and infrastructures to facilitate life itself. From specialized tools, maps became media: ubiquitous, content-driven, and very affecting.

This book is about this change and what it might entail for those studying – or just interested – in the relations between digital platforms, space, and cartography. To do justice to the objects of study, it approaches digital maps from three central perspectives: media studies, human geography, and science and technology studies.

First and foremost, it is a *media studies* book, a hybrid discipline that has emerged in the last few decades. Media studies is primarily a humanities-centred endeavour: drawing much on cultural studies, it began with a focus on film and television (Hall 1980; McLuhan 1994; Silverstone 1999) before coalescing into a big-tent discipline, welcoming to mostly qualitative (with some quantitative) research on the various aspects of mediated communication and beyond. Media studies are often characterized by a potential slippage between theory and method (Stevenson and Kavka 2025), that makes defining the field difficult, but for the purpose of the book, it unpacks the medium-specific logics of both content and delivery (or containers of such content), through methodologies as diverse as political economy, content analysis, interface studies, and more. My work in the subsequent pages can best be characterized as *technography*, 'a way of describing and observing the workings of technology in order to examine the interplay between a diverse set of actors (both human and nonhuman)' (Bucher 2018, 61). This method is particularly suitable for analysing systems that rely on (personalized) algorithms to interact with human users, delivering radically different results, depending on who's approaching it. It consists of reviewing diverse materials such as technical specifications and white papers, 'about us' pages of major companies, social media posts about and within the platform in question, and the like. It results in analytical descriptions of *how* such systems work and substantiated assumptions of *why* they work like this (Rieder 2020; Hind 2024).

Cultural theorist Dominic Pettman connects the rise in popularity of media studies with what he calls the *posthumanities*, a new assemblage of thinking that is 'alert to the active role that technology and media play in structuring, presenting, and representing our thoughts to ourselves and each other' (Pettman 2019, para. 3). To him, media studies, and media theory in particular, allow the scope of what is *being mediated* in contemporary society to be expanded, with previously distinct spheres – love, religion, science, to name but a few – undergoing a continuous convergence with digital technologies and the business models that fuel them. For me, following Pettman, the main promise of media studies today lies in their historically honed ability to 'pay special attention to our relationship to *relationships*; including and especially the relationship to our tools (which themselves are conscientiously helping to reveal *new* relationships, as well as often rendering older relationships – say, with viruses or carbon – in a new light)' (Pettman 2019, para. 2). As we will see, maps fall naturally into this description. They are a set of self-referential tools, often held in recursive relations to each other through notions of scientific objectivity, data precision, and visual acuity. In other words: we tend to understand maps through our existing knowledge of other maps. To understand digital maps, then, we must unpack paper maps and then explore their ongoing digitalization and platformization. I do so mostly in chapter 2 and 4.

Following, the second field from which this book draws is *human geography*, and critical cartography as its distinct subset. Like many other scholarly fields, geography has changed and adapted in recent years in response to the penetration of digital platforms into ever more growing aspects of life. At its core, it remains about the relationship between people, space, and place. Specifically, space is used to denote the broadly 'objective' notions of where things are (for example, as they appear on city plans or nautical charts) and place to refer to the personal and subjective ways in which we infuse spaces with affect, memories, and meaning (such as the neighbourhood graffiti wall that appeared despite the pre-planned approach to the city; Lefebvre 1992; Elden 2007). For critical cartographers, the focus often lies in the mapmaking assemblage as an attempt to *distract or mislead* the reader (Crampton 2002). In particular, the field cast a hard (and often, rather suspicious) look at claims of tech companies regarding the beneficial use of digital spatial technologies for everyday life, particularly in urban settings. If, after Kitchin and Dodge (2011), spatiality today is enmeshed with and produced by computer code, then there is nothing inherently benign in such code (Eubanks 2017; Noble 2018) or its influence on our commuting or shopping habits, not to mention Airbnb-inflated rent. After all, major corporations such as IBM or Cisco work hard to sell various stakeholders the very need for 'smart city' technologies (Sadowski and Bendor 2019), while generally ignoring all the rough bits that make cities unfit for the type of quantification- and dashboard-driven administration practices they espouse (Mattern 2021a). So, if human geography offers us a broad lens into the making of space and place, critical cartography subsequently deals with how these are being represented on various flat surfaces (in maps), and how such objects reflect and construct power relations between territory and people (Counter Cartographies Collective et al. 2012; Wilmott 2020). While I will go into greater detail in the next section, a key concept in this sub-field's contribution to this book is in thinking of maps as not showing the world 'as-is' but rather encouraging a particular vision of *how it can be*. I develop this line of thinking further in chapter 5.

Thus, the third field that underpins this work is science and technology studies (STS). The field arose by taking a social-constructivist approach to the practices of scientists, engineers, and designers, recognizing the role of hierarchies, negotiations, and customs in the making of seemingly objective outcomes (Latour 1987; 2005; Law 1992). It helps me to delineate maps as more than just images that show (a proxy of) the world, and to realize them as actionable objects. Taking stock of the historical view of cartography and the critical scholarship mentioned in the previous paragraph, one notices a focus on *representation*. Alternatively from cartography scholars, the point of departure for STS literature is that technologies, and mapping technologies among them, are always suspect of taking on a life of their own after exiting the labs and workshops in which they were conceived, rendering the territory reflected by a map a 'spurious referent' (November et al. 2010, 588). Such an approach questions the necessary mimetic relationship between what is on the map and what is being mapped, and hence queries the necessary prescriptive power that cartographers wield over their readers: if the map changes with each user and use, how much can it truly be exercised as a tool of restriction and control? Moreover, when mapping is taken as a performative act involving the conscious and unconscious, cognitive, emotional and bodily aspects, how should we methodologically distinguish between the maker and the reader, user and producer? After all, digital media scholarship – and digital maps fit firmly within this scope – strongly argues for hybrid categories of 'produsage' (Bruns 2007) that take into account the growing spectrum of skills and literacies required to operate today. STS thus helps us to think of maps as techno-scientific objects, located at the praxis of contemporary digital cultures. I expand and develop on this in chapters 3 and 6.

At the start of the chapter, I hinted at the exceptionalism of digital maps as compared to both their analogue cousins, on the one hand, and other digital objects, on the other. I then briefly outlined which main fields of knowledge I draw on to further justify this position: media studies, critical cartography, and science and technology studies. While I will develop these fields' contributions in subsequent chapters, for the remainder of this one I wish to make a case for digital maps' exceptionalism; outlining what digital mapping is, what it does, how it differs from other research objects, and which approaches I take throughout the book to address it. To do so, I first present a historical overview of thinking with and about maps to establish the processual view on cartography. Then, I document the main technological developments that have occurred in the last three decades and led to massive uptake of digital maps as everyday consumer products. Subsequently, I explore recent work on digital cartography to highlight key concepts but also point out gaps which this book intends to fill, particularly regarding the role of user interfaces. I conclude with an outline of this book's remaining chapters and how each one fills the abovementioned gaps.

A brief history of maps, and thinking about them

Nothing exemplifies the profound change that mapping has brought into the world more than Google Maps. For many, it has become *the* de facto representation of the world, an 'objective' layer superimposed on reality, continuously updated on the fly through myriad varying data streams (Plantin 2018; McQuire 2019). The app – or website, though most today use it as an app (O'Beirne 2021) – has increasingly affected everyday life and specifically human decision making alongside other algorithmic technologies (Bucher 2018; Amoore 2020). Indeed, as an interface, people quite literally make sense of the world around them through it (Galloway 2012; Ash 2015; Bratton 2015). To understand these processes and the digital maps at their centre, we must first examine the ontological (those related to existing) relations between mapping and territory. In other words, I wish to show how thinking about mapping evolved from seeing maps as being in direct and fixed relation to the world they describe to challenging this assumption altogether. To this end, I will employ three chronologically successive paradigms that have been suggested for studying maps: *descriptive*, *prescriptive*, and *processual* mapping.

A key outcome for such periodization is to show that the maps that we have on our screens today are the product of modern trends that prioritize a form of geometrical-calculative (and, later, digital) sense-making. While often perceived as natural and objective by the broader public, they are not necessarily aligned historically with how mapping began. The caveat here, though, is in a general disagreement among scholars over what constitutes a map and thus pinpointing its origins. More often than not, cartography is thought to be rooted in the Classic period, or slightly earlier – within the contexts of Mesopotamian or Egyptian civilizations (Smith 1987). Early researchers into prehistoric mapping, for example, were quick to announce archaeological findings of ancient civilizations' 'maps', ignoring findings indicating these prehistoric objects may have been 'produced in a religious context, that matters of belief governed their execution, and that their function would have been abstract and symbolic rather than exclusively practical wayfinding and recording' (Smith 1987, 48). Calling such artefacts 'maps' and drawing linear continuity to the term used today is thus misguided.

The famed map historian J.B. Harley (1987) similarly warns against using the present to interpret the past. He points out how religious iconography, storytelling, and artistic depictions are often mashed together by researchers to incorporate contemporary notions of accuracy and pathfinding. He notes how, for a long time, cartographers and those interested in the history of cartography purported a teleological view of maps, wherein improving mathematical and technological methods would necessarily produce 'better' and 'more accurate' maps to determine real-world elements such as distance and direction. Imposing such normative criteria, rooted strongly in modernist-empiricist perceptions, on all (historical) maps, is thus very limiting. In a move that is popularly considered to have greatly contributed to the emergence of modern critical cartography (Edney 2005), Harley argued in a series of works that maps can be deconstructed through Foucauldian notions of power-knowledge, to unravel the biases of mapmakers (Harley 1987; 1988a; 1989). According to him:

> [a]t the very time maps were being transformed by mathematical techniques, they were also being appropriated as an intellectual weapon of the state system. If their study had become, by the end of the sixteenth century, the 'science of princes', it was because maps were by then recognized as a visual language communicating proprietorial or territorial rights in both practical and symbolic senses. In cartographic terms, however, the exercise of such power could be negative and restrictive. The map image itself was becoming increasingly subject to concealment, censorship, sometimes to abstraction or falsification (Harley 1988b, 59).

As a historian and cartographer, Harley recognized the technical limitations of paper maps, warning 'not only of the geographical limits to knowledge, but also of the technological constraints to representation, and of the silences in the historical record owing to the destruction of evidence' (Harley 1988b, 57). Making maps involves complex decisions regarding form and content, for instance whether a given resolution allows the inclusion of certain landmarks or whether to smoothen certain 'real' contours in consideration of aesthetics and readability (Monmonier 2018). Thus, Harley purposefully termed the information missing from a map 'silence', rather than 'lacunae' or 'errors'. By replacing a neutral designation with one bearing a negative connotation, he challenged the dominant perspective on mapping as an unbiased and scientifically objective practice. This latter imagination of maps had been rather entrenched in modern cartography since the mid-twentieth century, when renowned cartographer Arthur H. Robinson, while leading the US military mapping division during the Second World War, introduced user-testing and laboratory precision into the cartographer's toolbox (Crampton and Krygier 2005), which has been growing ever since with the penetration of computation into mapmaking. Yet for Harley and his followers, the map is never merely *made*; rather, it is *created by someone*, and that individual operates in a specific socio-political context, thus investing the map with certain discursive meanings and claims, which in turn shape its final form and determine what is included and what is omitted.

According to geographers Kitchin, Gleeson, and Dodge (2013), the debate outlined above reflects the *descriptive* approach to maps: the map is considered either a *true representation* (for Robinson) or a *social construction* (for Harley) of space. Even on the latter view, as a description of the world, however flawed, the map can uncover some truths about it, provided one is careful enough to peel away the ideological outer skin. Kitchin et al. contrast this perspective with the later work of such critical cartographers as Wood and Fels (2008), who reject the inherent truth of maps-as-descriptions; rather, they argue, the map delivers a series of propositions. In other words, the map is *prescriptive*, in that it effectively forms the world it set out to represent. Such a theoretical perspective aligns with the understanding of western cartography as a predominantly colonial enterprise, concerned with creating power structures on the ground much more than merely documenting them (Rankin 2016).

Critical cartographer Denis Wood goes as far as to suggest that 'there were no maps before 1500' (Wood 2010, 22). By that, he means that attributing the agency of what we today call 'maps' to pre-fifteenth century (or pre-twelfth, in China) artefacts is pointless, as the contemporary map carries within it the cumulative power of exploration, colonialism, and the emerging nation-states, able to *make* a place as much as *describe* it. This claim might be exaggerated to a point, leaning more on the rhetorical than the historical. For instance, it relies on the assertion that very few maps can be found from the Hellenistic period, despite Ptolemy's detailed instruction on making such maps. Empirical evidence might also be lacking since 'the breaking up and dispersal of once organic atlases or the disappearance of cartographic items into inaccessible private collections accentuate the problem of document survival' (Harley 1987, 6). Classical period maps may have indeed carried similar functions to modern ones.

Regardless, Wood's major point remains relevant: he argues that maps should be critically approached as *propositions and assertions*: first, regarding the very right to map territory by the one carrying out the task, and second in the specific claims presented. Those claims are rooted in the nation-state's desire to expand territory or affirm existing borders. Today, cartographic practice comes primarily from the jargon-heavy institutional academic processes of professional consolidation that took place during the mid-twentieth century, closing the field to outside practitioners and delineating cartography from fields like architecture, communications, or design (Wood 2003). Arguing against the previous work of the likes of Harley, for Wood, the map can never be 'cleansed' of its ideological overlay made of secrets and ambiguities, particularly when considering the institutional entanglement between governments, militaries, and academia in the professionalization of mapmaking. For all that, Wood and Fels are still convinced that the map is an ontologically stable entity, and that it is endowed with a 'finality' that renders it immutable. In a similar vein, STS scholar Bruno Latour viewed the map as an 'immutable mobile' (Latour 1990, 37): a *flat inscription* – one that reduces the complexity of the world to a drawn schema – which can be *reproduced, re-combined* or *super-imposed* in conjunction with other such inscriptions to generate new forms of (scientific) knowledge.

To be sure, Google Maps are different from representations on paper in that they are also a software product, personalized, and customizable. Arguably, they also lack Latour's underpinning linkage between immutable mobile and European colonial enterprise – sending out expeditions that can render the multitude of the world inert and transferable on their maps, to then be stored and studied in 'centres of calculation' such as chief admiralties and university libraries. Yet, media scholar Sybille Lammes (2016) claims that, even with the advent of digital mapping, maps still remain immutable mobiles, despite the technology that allows the image on the screen to be manipulated. In her view, this immutability of the digital map is anchored in its hidden infrastructure of computation and satellites 'that is not easily transformable and operates according to set rules' (Lammes 2016, 1030). And just like their ink-on-paper counterparts, such maps conjure up a certain kind of world.

Kitchin, Gleeson, and Dodge, for their part, subscribe to a view that is even more radical than the prescriptivist angle outlined above. They regard their own work as a logical conclusion of the succession of increasingly critical and relativistic approaches to maps. According to their emergent, or *ontogenetic* view of maps, one should examine maps as processual and ever-changing. To understand such emergence, they utilize Simondon's (1992) notion of *transduction* exemplified by his metaphor of growing crystals: each molecular layer is based and shaped on the previous one. 'In other words, the crystal grows through individuations, that cite previous individuations, to transduce elements into a crystal' (Kitchin and Dodge 2007, 341). Building on the earlier works of map theoreticians such as Jeremy Crampton (2001; 2002; 2003) and John Pickles (1994; 2004), Kitchin et al. return the map to the living world, as something that affects people and places connected to it, just as much as they affect it. They propose a conceptualization of maps as *emergent*, that is, as *processual* entities completely divested of stable ontology. Such an approach moves beyond socio-political conditions, the technological wherewithal, or the effect of a map's ideological content on reality. As the authors, themselves, put it:

> [s]uch a reconsideration necessitates a radical shift, as the conceptual bases of cartography move from being concerned with the 'rules' of map design, and techniques of cartographic production, and/or documenting and deconstructing the underlying ideologies and agendas of maps, to a processual perspective concerned with how mappings and cartographic design, technique and ideology emerge time and again through a plethora of practices framed within a complex discursive and material context, and the diverse, unfolding work of mappings in the world (Kitchin et al. 2013, 481).

This approach looks at *mapping* rather than *maps* as such. Mappings (that is, products of mapping processes) are contingent and emergent; they are affected by the context and depend on the decoder at least as much as on the creator. A processual view takes into account such pragmatic aspects as a map's navigational aims (Brown and Laurier 2005; November et al. 2010). It treats maps as spaces and performances (Del Casino and Hanna 2006); as ontogenetic entities that are constantly co-created through their use (Kitchin and Dodge 2007; Rossetto 2019); as objects of play, both inherently and as revealed through use (Perkins 2009b; Lammes et al. 2018); and as game-boards (Lammes 2011; Playful Mapping Collective 2016). Such a view of maps incorporates the complex sociotechnical infrastructure on which they are built, and involves a variety of multi-disciplinary methodologies and theoretical frameworks. It feeds into the changes in the nature of mobile media, where one can be connected to the internet continuously, day in day out, whether stationary or on the move, and where such connection-through-movement alters the types of information available to the user and the range of the user's reactions (de Souza e Silva and Sheller 2015; de Souza e Silva 2023).

This view of maps as emergent entities also highlights what mapping ontologist Tania Rossetto terms 'moments of particularization' (Rossetto 2019, 35), when mapping objects become (temporarily) stable, in part, due to an epistemic shift in research cultures: Google Maps, alongside the rise in mobile media use, has crystallized *this* particular form of map on *this* particular platform. The processual approach thus dovetails with the 'digital turn' in geography, espoused by Ash, Kitchin, and Leszczynski (2018), in that it questions maps' capacity to accurately represent geospatial data and probes the impact of this gap on the world; to use the authors' terms, the emergent approach critiques 'geographies *of* the digital' and 'geographies *produced* by the digital', respectively. None exemplifies this turn more than the rise of Google Maps in the early 2000s, and its subsequent bundling as locative media with mobile devices.

Cartographic ubiquity: Google Maps as the prototypical map-as-media

Google Maps is a representative of the current surge in popular, consumer-oriented mapping through what at different times was called web-, digital- and neo-cartography (Perkins and Dodge 2008; Farman 2010; Della Dora 2012; Bittner et al. 2013; Haklay 2013). Regardless of the term, Google Maps – and after it digital mapping as a whole – cannot be conceptualized as static or self-contained; it increasingly influences the view of the physical world even among individuals who do not actively use the app, for example, by changing road congestion through collecting driving data from a subset of road users (Hind and Gekker 2019; van der Graaf and Ballon 2019).

A key feature of digital cartography is its ability to visually adapt itself to the ever-changing requirements of the end-user, often through clever algorithms that learn and anticipate users' actions (with varied degrees of success). In such cases the emergent quality of the map is especially visible through such conditions as being inside versus outside one's home (de Souza e Silva and Hjorth 2009; Pink et al. 2018); it is contingent on the locative infrastructures of cellular towers and Wi-Fi hotspots (Farman 2015; Wilken 2019a); and above all, it posits a radical difference between a device displaying a mobile *map* and the practice of mobile *mapping* – notions that can be easily, and erroneously, conflated:

> The inequalities established through the relations of measurement become distorted through the establishment of elements: people are not made of binary codes, our places and locations lose flavour when reduced to coordinates, and so the paths and spaces between such abstracted inferences (such odd logics), journeys and space-times which are measured and calculated, are already hollow. Within mobile mapping, these discourses jar with something else – something intangible and inexpressible, *something not quite right* – as we use phones and signs to navigate but still end up lost, stare baffled down impossible inclines on roads that should never have been built, mirthfully note the numbers all around us describing slopes and trees and swells, and wonder why that bit of town *just doesn't make sense* (Wilmott 2020, 206, emphasis original).

The bewildered and frustrating attempts at sense-making described above have much to do with Google Maps' position *as just another app on a phone screen*. It amalgamates and personalizes information for the user, while still conforming to the design rules of its superordinate mobile platform. This resonates with Neil Postman's (1986) classic argument about how commercial television can never truly transmit radical ideas because, at the end of the day, a hard news story and a soap opera episode are both punctuated by the same time slot and ad-break constraints. For me, such mundanity of being yet another app translates the conceptual fluidity of *emergent mapping* into a methodological requirement that a *map should be analysed primarily as a media interface.* While I will detail in greater length what this distinction means in the next chapter, for now suffice to say that a mapping interface is a double-sided membrane between map users and map designers, which facilitates data flows for habitual spatial representation. In other words, it collects data from user actions and various other databases to serve users with a certain normalized image on the words, upon which they can act (or not). The resulting (non-)action then allows for further data collection, leading to further versions of the world presented to this and other users, in an almost recursive manner.

Of course, the centrality of interfaces – and user interfaces in particular – for mapping is not a new observation. It has been a key component in contemporary cartographic theory for at least two decades, with the growing popularization of digital, layered, consumer-oriented maps. As computers became widespread and the internet grew from a specialized military-scientific network into the popular medium it became (Castells 2001), geographers, cartographers, information visualizations specialists, and geographic information systems (GIS) practitioners (and the various intersections thereof) began exploring the different ways mapping interfaces can be used to explore geospatial data (MacEachren 1994; 1995; 1998). Notions of design and usability began to influence the discourse around such interfaces, especially in relation to facilitating collaborations between various fields and opening up spatial data to non-professionals (MacEachren and Kraak 2001; Kraak 2003; 2006; Cartwright et al. 2001). What started as a scientific community research agenda grew significantly in scope with the rapid introduction of consumer-grade geo-spatial visualization software and the spread of locative mobile devices that further enabled it.

In a special issue of *Cartography and Geographic Information Science*, guest editors Georg Gartner, David A. Bennett, and Takashi Morita (2007) offered the term 'ubiquitous cartography' as a general term for concurrent changes. To them, the main attribute of the technological and societal revolution of modern mapping is the sheer availability of specific maps tied to location-based services for growing groups of users. They pinpoint three main vectors that have allowed for this: advances in telecommunication infrastructure – mostly in the form of different bands of wireless networks; the opening of GPS and similar systems to broad commercial applications; and the distribution of mobile computing devices. As with many other contemporary innovations, Gartner et al. view ubiquitous mapping primarily as a consequence of technological improvement in relevant fields, making their article a listing of technical challenges that need to be overcome, such as smaller screen sizes, computational challenges involved in real-time navigation, and addressing the privacy concerns of the users of location-based services (LBS) through proper protocols. They acknowledge the myriad possibilities of ubiquitous cartography since '[a]t a high level of abstraction ubiquitous mapping applications are, therefore, computer applications that deliver information that is dependent on the location of the device and user, but beyond this generality, it is hard to find a consensus on the scope or definition of this new technology' (Gartner et al. 2007, 255).

The tone of the special issue is optimistic, and the authors concern themselves primarily with how to explore certain (technical) aspects of new wireless and satellite networks in mapping. The scope does not involve itself with the ontological and epistemological change that such cartography's claims might incur when removed from the once-contained professional practice and into the broader media. Certainly, they had no way of knowing the tectonic shift that ubiquitous cartography was about to undergo, with the launch of the first iPhone coming just a few months after the publication of the piece. But all this did happen, and so the academic tone changed quickly in subsequent publications, when media scholars, geographers, and artists began looking into these emerging technologies.

Artist and researcher Laura Kurgan is particularly sensitive to the changing role of digital mapping in the propagation of war and large-scale politics. For her, mapping technologies 'both necessitate and facilitate the interpretation of images at once measurable and digital, uncentred and ambiguous, yet comprehensive and authoritative' (Kurgan 2013, 13). Her work can be linked to broader trends of locative art (Tuters and Varnelis 2006; Jethani and Leorke 2013), where newly off-the-shelf availability of relatively accurate GPS transceivers made engaging with the global coordinates grid and its mapping interfaces possible. The art movement was somewhat short-lived, due to the introduction of the first iPhone in 2007 and subsequent wider integration of locative abilities into everyday devices, in a way that made purpose-made art about one's digital tracking via space progressively less prominent. But Kurgan's work nonetheless points at a crucial stage of reckoning with maps' role in spatial control by the end of the twentieth century. Military historian William Rankin (2016) similarly traces the development of the global positioning system (GPS) and other geographic technologies in the post-war period. He argues that over the latter half of the century, technologies of accuracy, measurement, and automation have transformed cartography from something concerning itself with representing space to a discipline aiming at *producing* it as a utility, not unlike water or electricity. As the mathematics of the grid-based Universal Transverse Mercator (UTM) system allowed far more accurate calculation of each point on the globe and the introduction of GPS allowed for acquiring and managing locations under this system, 'space [was made] legible by installing a full-scale, three-dimensional system of coordinates, essentially replacing the original terrain with an abstract electronic landscape' (Rankin 2011, 3).

This makes for a very different sort of mapping effort. Previous, paper-based, spatial knowledge (or 'geo-epistemology') required map-users to exert effort through calculation and orientation. This new geo-epistemology posits the map as active, drastically reducing the cognitive resources required to access the world beyond (through?) the map and shortening the translation process between map and action. Media researcher Lisa Parks (2005; 2009) connects this development also to how wars are being waged and covered in the press, through a persistent examination via satellite vision, and the deployment of both military and civilian GIS-enabled mapping. Positioning mapping as 'a mass technology that operates as a kind of scientific instrument' (Rankin 2011, 21), Rankin concludes that '[m]apping thus presents an opportunity to ask how everyday technological systems are theory-laden. In a general sense, this means analysing how different forms of mapping have influenced the ways that individuals understand, interact with, and help construct geographic space' (ibid., 24).

Kurgan, Parks, and Rankin thus view mapping primarily through a geopolitical lens, one resonating with the previously discussed prescriptive view on maps, in its emphasis on construction of space to be surveilled and/or invaded. It helps us understand, for example, the role of satellite start-up Starlink's assistance to Ukraine after the 2022 invasion by Russia (Iyengar 2022), which allowed the Ukrainian military crucial internet access while Russia targeted its civilian and military communication infrastructure (figure 1.2). While central to understanding the role of data infrastructures in facilitating digital mapping, this satellite schematic still doesn't fully explain how Google Maps became so ubiquitous globally as to also facilitate tracking troop movements during this very war (Lerman 2022).

A different type of scholarship does help with elucidating the latter point, one that deals with the mainstreaming of locative technologies. The rise of the smartphone after the lifting of

Figure 1.2: A fan-site, Starlink.sx, unaffiliated with the Starlink corporation, posts a real-time map of its wireless internet coverage. Screenshot by the author, October 2025.

GPS's 'selective availability' accuracy limitation by the Clinton administration, opened the service to wider audiences and created a growing demand for cartographic interfaces with LBS integration (Zickuhr 2013; McQuire 2019), such as navigation or sport-tracking apps. This, in turn, has resulted in the flocking of people without prior cartographic experience but with the necessary skills for devising and designing technological solutions onto the scene. New technologies simplified the process of creating a map, removing the need for massive investments in surveying and building of your own geo-databases. Central to this perspective is media scholars' approach to maps and mapping, particularly through the lens of *platforms*. Platforms are software giants that generate a market for two or more types of users (Srnicek 2016). They are often opaque in their dealings, drawing power from providing incomplete information to all participants, while hoovering-in massive amounts of user data that allow them to monopolize market arbitrage (Rieder and Sire 2014). For media scholar Tarleton Gillespie, being a platform is mainly about rhetoric: strategically positioning themselves as a type of neutral entity and then playing all sides. This way platforms can claim to simultaneously be an impartial stage for political expression, a computational facilitator on which to run your own code, a business opportunity for advertisers, and a levelling field for up-and-coming amateur content creators (Gillespie 2010; 2017).

Other scholars, however, tend to stay closer to the industry's definition of platforms, citing venture capitalist Marc Andreesen's famous quip that 'If you can program it, then it's a platform. If you can't, then it's not' (Bogost and Montfort 2009, 4). In particular, platforms facilitate a new type of power through their Application Programming Interfaces (APIs), or the ways in which they allow other types of software to link with their underlying data, while – crucially – gaining something in return. Platform theorist Anne Helmond (2015) postulates that APIs act as conduits for a new type of process, which she names 'platformization', in which various types of data are being made available to developers outside the platform to use in their own software or even to integrate into the platform's inner workings. One infamous example of this is Facebook allowing Cambridge Analytica the freedom to build its questionnaires inside its platform while providing it with the list of friends for each person taking the test (Venturini and Rogers 2019). For Helmond, this dynamic points at the double logic of platforms, where they simultaneously expand outwards into the web (and the world) while trying to convert more and more external data into a 'platform-ready' form, resulting in 'two processes of decentralizing platform features and recentralizing platform ready data ... which connect the infrastructural model of the platform to its economic aims' (Helmond 2015, 8). In urban settings, in particular, this leads to what some have called 'platform urbanism' (van der Graaf and Ballon 2019; Barns 2020; Leszczynski 2020), which extends the platform logic to how 'code, commerce, and corporeality ... engender and reshape everyday selves and spaces in vital ways' (Barns 2019, 2). As we will see, digital maps have been at the forefront of this process.

Google Maps is one of the first contemporary platforms (Plantin 2014; 2018) and – more importantly for this book – has facilitated a transition of maps *into* platforms. It introduced a superior user interface that combines satellite imagery, smooth scrolling and zooming, addresses, business search, and much more (Ćmielová and Pánek 2016) – all the while intent on absorbing as much geospatial data as possible. The originator of Google Maps was Google Earth, a free GIS platform first launched in 2005. Mobile media scholar Jason Farman (2010) ties together the popularity of Google Earth with the increased use of aerial and spatial imagery to show a realistic, and thus seemingly more objective, representation of the world. In a similar vein, Craig Dalton (2012) relays the history of Google's acquisition of Keyhole, Inc., the company behind Google Earth, and elaborates the way Google has integrated the latter's locative data into its own lucrative core business of search and advertising. After acquiring the proprietary software – then named Earth Viewer – Google opened it to a wide variety of non-GIS professionals at no cost. Comprised of multi-layered tiles combining aerial and satellite photography, the company gradually developed various features that became a mainstay in digital cartography, including a 3D virtual globe, based on technology developed for video games, complete with zooming functionality, as well as a map and 3D building models. This history reflects Helmond's dual logic by decentralizing its map for broad public use, while recentralizing the proprietary data collected (Plantin 2018). And while public and open source mapping alternatives exist – for example the Wikipedia-like Open Street Map (OSM) that is open for editing – those failed to achieve the penetration and recognition of their commercial counterparts.[2]

From the public's perspective, the easy-to-use integration of various modes of data visualization into a single cartographic interface have dramatically enhanced the perception of Google Maps – and later other digital maps – as neutral and apolitical. In the past, maps were drawn by hand by identifiable individuals, their authors, for all intents and purposes. When mechanical reproduction became available, the authorship lost its salience, and with it, also personal responsibility (Harley 2001). Digitalization of maps only further accelerated the trend. As Dalton (2012; 2015) points out, Google is interested in maintaining the ambiguity between authoritative authorship and individual personalization. Paradoxically enough, the map is popular *both* because it claims to represent the world objectively *and* because it shows the user a unique version tailored to one's search history and other preferences. We can see this through the example of Ukraine's peninsula of Crimea, as it appeared in the post-2014 annexation by Russia. Depending from which location one examined the region on Google (and Apple) maps, it would appear as belonging to Ukraine, belonging to Russia, or being disputed through a noncommittal dotted line, different than the solid line in which standard borders are depicted (Coldewey 2019). This seemingly erodes our ability to trust such maps, heralding the underlying danger of Google's 2013 promise to create 'A map for every person and place' (Badger 2013; 2014). Yet, most people won't bother to check an alternative version of the map. Instead, they would marvel at its ability to offer a relatively accurate depiction of their nearby stores and restaurants, or its turn-by-turn driving instructions (Morozov 2013). This divergence between users thus becomes invisible as digital maps perfect the naturalizing move that paper maps have always performed: the world is there at your fingertips, how can the map be anything but correct?

Evidently, a key element in this mapping experience is personalization. The option of saving My Places originated with the introduction of *mashups*, combinations of several maps. The first such instance was built in 2005 by Paul

Rademacher, creator of housingmaps.com, which overlaid the addresses of the Craigslist housing listing on a map – ironically enough, in violation of Google Maps' terms of use. Instead of stopping the practice, Google embraced mashups, opening the data underlying the map via an API to external developers. Google even hired Rademacher (after his project had become a success), and shortly after, introduced My Places (My Maps prior to 2013). This function lowered the skill bar for creating mashups by allowing any user to set routes and sites as markers on personalized Google maps, which could then be shared, collaboratively adjusted and saved (Dalton 2012).

Some scholars have argued, however, that the transformation of Google Maps into a platform has put such personalization at odds with the freedom of action afforded by the original map mashups (Plantin 2018; McQuire 2019). Google Maps' Street View component in particular appropriates the 'real estate' it displays (Alvarez León 2016), by collecting many kinds of public landscapes and offering it as its own commodity. Personalization is more difficult to achieve when each map is accompanied by Google-owned images of concomitant space, to be used for its data extraction purposes of navigation and advertising. Crucially, a single image has little power in this arrangement, but, through their massive collection and linking to other types of geodata, the platform does achieve its goal: 'Google Street View is then made into a commodity through the accumulation of millions of infinitesimally valuable properties, which are assembled into a coherent, fully interactive virtual "landscape of landscapes"' (Alvarez León 2016, 8). Google thus again 'benefits from the decentralization of cartographic knowledge production, through multiple forms of participation to feed its maps; however, it also shows that this openness simultaneously comes with new forms of recentralization' (Plantin 2018, 499), such as through controlling which types of things can even appear on the map or which additional operations can be done with the data provided (McQuire 2019). Rather than enabling a more democratic vision of the world, as early proponents of participatory GIS envisioned, it can foster geographic filter bubbles that avoid taking a stance by catering to the vision desired in specific places. The new 'Gulf of America', which replaces the 'Gulf of Mexico' when viewed from the US under the second Trump administration, is a good example of this (Treisman 2025).

This book exists in this multi-sided tension between Google Maps' monolithic presence as the ur-mapping platform, its origins in playful software experiments, the dual forces of de- and re-centralization it exerts on the world, and its competitors trying to both emulate and dethrone it. In December 2022, several key players in the software world, including tech giants Meta, Microsoft, Amazon Web Services, and the Dutch navigation provider TomTom, joined forces with the Linux foundation to offer an Open Source alternative to Google Maps (Barr 2022). While it is too early to speak of results, the sheer willingness for such collaboration showcases digital mapping's significance and Google Maps' entrenched position in this field. And while I tried very hard to not make this 'The Google Maps Book', its shadow looms large. My hope is that the next chapters will help readers to understand the platform from the outside in, by unravelling various aspects of digital maps, and by treating them simultaneously as descendants of their paper variants, participants in the process of platformization, and everyday media objects found on screens alongside other apps; inconspicuous and seemingly docile.

Rest of the book: a roadmap

In this introductory chapter of the book, I have given an overview of mapping theories that will be used throughout. I started by briefly charting the three key fields that inform my understanding: media studies, human geography, and science and technology studies, each with their unique contributions, which I will develop further in the next chapter. I proceeded to showcase a historiography of thinking *about* maps, and particularly the field's gradual shift from the ontological stability of maps as (sometimes flawed) depictions of the world to the processual view of them co-creating the world anew, depending on the contexts of design and use. I further cemented this perspective on maps in a flux through a description of central technological developments of the last two decades, and the resulting scholarship surrounding them. A key premise in this description was that of the user interface, a concept which takes centre-stage in the next chapter.

The second chapter focuses on media studies, and their particular subset, interface studies. It takes the digital interface as a double-sided membrane that simultaneously collects data on users while attempting to influence them. The interface is presented as a point of data collection, designer intent, and user resistance. Creating personalized and actionable digital maps allows for tailored versions of reality for individual users, to act and be acted upon. The chapter further dives into the idea of 'user experience' (UX) and, more broadly, experience design, as techniques to prolong our interaction with technology and extract more of our time, data, and attention. It asks what it means for digital maps to strive for user engagement, and whether it clashes with maps' utility. Recently, a growing plethora of hardware, web and mobile objects subscribe to the paradigm of experiential design. From the smooth contours of your phone to the carefully engineered sounds and colours of social media, aesthetics and interaction design are remaking interfaces into wonderous layered playgrounds that make you want to come back. Maps have not been exempted from this trend. The friendly icons on a Waze navigational screen or Snapchat's geofilters all make space into an experiential commodity. Through elevation of metrics and quantification into satisfying and even fun ways to simplify the world, digital maps are now playful and emotional objects, which further hides their ability to influence our daily conduct.

Chapter 3 presents the first of the case studies chapters that treat a particular aspect of mapping through digital interfaces. It focuses on the central premise of contemporary maps: to get people and goods to places. It examines the entanglement of spaces and maps in achieving such movement goals, arguing that the old division of map and territory is void. Due to the abundance of sensor technologies, control dashboards, fast internet, and affordable mobile phones, Borges's ridicule of the map-as-empire is no longer sustained. Instead, real-time information streams hybridize space and map so that changes in one affect the other. The chapter focuses on connected and autonomous vehicles (CAVs) as a particular class of media-enabled objects that link the physical world to data. Through them, the chapter shows how maps present the *world as data*: through continuous sensor and other types of data, maps simultaneously reflect and affect the world, for example through location and speed telemetry while driving with Google Maps or through user rankings on platforms like Uber. Increasingly, this data affects not just the user of the specific mapping interface, but also others – as in the case of crowdsourced navigational app Waze's change of traffic patterns across cities, leading to local protests. Furthermore, they are prone to *algorithmic visualization:* Maps convert this data from the world to the user and vice versa, but they do so selectively, and so resulting movement is dependent on the rules of conversion. The chapter ends with examining Mobileye, a manufacturer of safety equipment for cars turned spatial data giant and key player in the autonomous car race.

Chapter 4 focuses on playing with – and through – maps. It distinguishes between play as an *activity* and playfulness as an *attitude*, asking what happens when playing with maps hides away their actual seriousness. It shows how play has been instrumental in diffusing contemporary maps from its political power, how it *reambiguates* the world, making established objects and practices gleam with possibility. Technology companies, including those using mapping interfaces, have learned to integrate various aspects of playfulness into their offerings. Partially this is an attempt to offset the creeping monotony and sameness of incremental technological innovation. Play can thus vary from inserting pleasant aesthetic flourishes – like the ability to customize one's map colour scheme – to temporarily changing the functionality of the map, like in the case of Google's April 1st jokey Mario Kart and Pacman modes, that set the stage for *Pokémon Go*. Yet play in itself is ambiguous and context-dependent: one person's harmless joke is another's insult. While mapmakers might consider their playful flourish a welcomed addition, users might find this upsetting and exploitative. The chapter explores such manifestations of playfulness through the case study of Niantic, the company responsible for all the successful location-based games of the last decade, now engaged in building a 'large geospatial model' – their spatial answer to language models like ChatGPT.

Work is often contrasted with play, but chapter 5 shows that on maps they are more complementary. Unsurprisingly, maps are still primarily seen as 'serious' tools to get things done: getting places, monitoring space, analysing trends. However, many are unaware of the specific aspects that make digital maps indispensable for the transformation of digital labour practices. Building on the previous unpacking of play, this chapter examines various instances of work in mapping to show how the two are complementary rather than opposing. Drawing from theories of immaterial labour and playbour, I examine both the often-invisible labour that goes into *working on* making the maps and the way map users are often *working through* the mapping platforms. The advent of digital mapping has launched a gold rush of companies building their own cartographic databases, thus replacing professional paid work, similar to the drastic shifts that user generated content (UGC) introduced into other media environments. A key aspect here is the idea of platformization briefly touched on here but thoroughly expanded to accommodate the practice of platform labour. An early example is how navigation app Waze distributed 'virtual candy' across its navigational user interface to entice its users to make detours and perform 'ground-truthing' of their maps' accuracy. In parallel, the digital map allows for a transformation of previous types of labour into new forms. Much of the gig economy, from food delivery to ridesharing, is dependent on digital mapping interfaces, in linking constantly moving service providers and recipients with each other. However, this also gives enormous power to the companies involved in tracking their workers and controlling which information is visible to them, changing how work is done and labour is extracted.

In chapter 6, we return to the question of maps' overarching power by examining how many aspects of digital mapping are those of surveillance. Tech companies today emphatically envision – in a stark reversal of Borges's warning – a map that covers the entire world. Moreover, by making this map actionable and reciprocal, it is no longer a passive reflection of what's going on, and by making it engaging, one can continuously extend the type of data streams generated from it. Unlike its paper counterpart, to be using a digital map is (almost) always to be visible to the creator of said map. Furthermore, with the advent of artificial intelligence (AI) and machine learning, maps reproduce racial, social, and gendered surveillance. The chapter discusses my framework to understand such tracking, one of *infrastructural surveillance,* which differs from previously used frameworks of privacy like surveillance or capture. In its last section, it returns to re-examine the previous three empirical chapters (movement, play, and work) through this lens of surveillance.

In the final chapter, I summarize and predict the key trends of digital mapping as a medium. The chapter opens with exploration of the contradictory dualities contained in the various maps analysed throughout the book. The chapter then proceeds to examine three critical challenges that maps face in the foreseeable future. First, *the blurring of boundaries* addresses the increasingly difficult question of what constitutes a map when they become layered datasets, sensor networks, and infrastructure rather than discrete visual objects. Maps now operate as both frontend user interfaces and backend foundations, complicating attempts to study or regulate them. Second, *the disappearance of the interface* explores how maps are becoming invisible through autonomous vehicles and augmented reality technologies. As maps shift from human-readable screens to machine-to-machine communications via APIs, and as augmented reality (AR) overlays subsume cartographic representation into lived experience, the critical distance between user and map collapses. Third, *the encroachment of generative AI* examines how foundation models like ChatGPT are beginning to incorporate spatial data, raising fundamental questions about cartographic epistemology. When AI systems can generate plausible-seeming but geographically nonsensical maps, the relationship between representation and reality becomes dangerously unstable. The book ends with an embarrassing admission, a telling personal anecdote, and some bittersweet warnings.

As a final note, I tried to write the chapters in a way that would facilitate non-linear reading. The next chapter is heavy with theory, including a long discussion of the attention economy, and one obvious takeaway from it is that holding attention for longer stretches is extremely difficult. Therefore, I give the reader my full permission to skip it and go to the first empirical chapter (3) on movement or even skip to the end and read the embarrassing detail of my life I teased before. The book was written to be useful to a wide variety of audiences, and so each chapter is quite self-contained. But for those brave and focused souls who can go through it cover-to-cover, I guarantee a much deeper theoretical and practical understanding of what digital maps are, how they operate, and why we should all be alternating between being very excited and very worried about their role in our world.

2

Casual Power

To paraphrase a film quote: What does a map need with a UX designer?

This is a question that began percolating in my mind throughout 2014, as my PhD fieldwork was ending. I spent time at a national mapping agency and a private start-up company developing mapping Software-as-a-Service (SaaS) solution, with both products intended for public, non-specialist use. Informants kept referring to UX designer specialists to whom they outsource certain aspects of their two – radically different – products.

But isn't the map you are building a coherent user interface in and of itself, I asked? This is not a social app, nor a highly specialized system that requires a particularly able operator. They were making maps, reminiscent of (or layered upon) Google Maps, to advise or direct users in straightforward operations such as viewing a school's registration area or locating a specific apartment within a building complex. My respondents often hesitated in their answers, themselves caught in a transition that was not completely clear to them.

Yet, understanding UX and its implementation into maps allows for the unpacking of how notions of engagement and the economization of attention are employed by mapping interfaces within contemporary media platforms. The result is an *experiential interface*, a notion that will become central to the empirical chapters that follow. It engages the user in a playful mode that adds the notion of fun to a utilitarian interaction, altering the mode of being in the world through the map (Sicart 2014; Rossetto 2019). It relates to questions of power and resistance to such power in maps' interfaces, and further highlights how digital cartographic assemblages are undergoing rapid platformization. Such interfaces – in maps and beyond – show how Big Tech increasingly frames relations between users and their digital devices: as emotional and experiential rather than utilitarian.

Above all, the chapter's central argument is that map interfaces can be designed with the overarching goal of continuously engaging the user while reducing their self-reflexivity. Specifically, I claim that by outsourcing the tweaking of the interface under the mantle of 'user-experience design' to companies outside the field of cartography, maps conform to a larger trend in UX. By doing so, digital maps augment the traditional cartographer's ethos with that of the interaction designer, and the tech entrepreneur. Such logic postulates *attention* as the main currency of the contemporary web (Stiegler 2010; Terranova 2012; Marwick 2015). To do so, I present a unified framework of *casual power*, a theoretical prism that states that maps specifically exert power over users by spreading their influence across myriad daily actions, highlighting its own supposed objectivity, and capturing users' data. It casually slips through the screens by habituating daily conduct through imagined affordances and manifests in how mapping user interfaces (UIs) are deployed to anticipate and captivate user attention.

Casual power differs from existing frameworks for understanding cartographic power in several respects. Unlike Foucauldian surveillance, which operates through visibility and panoptic observation (Harley 1988a), casual power operates through invisibility and habituation. Where critical cartographers have emphasized maps' ideological distortions (Harley 1989; Crampton 2002), casual power focuses on how maps achieve compliance not through deception but through seamless integration into daily routines. This aligns with but extends Latour's concept of 'black-boxing' (Latour 1999) by specifically accounting for the affective and experiential dimensions of interface design that emerged with digital platforms. In the first chapter I reviewed the history of (digital) cartography and the scholarship surrounding it. I established the specificities of digital mapping, as anchored both in contemporary developments of mapping software as well as in the changes taking place in web and mobile media. This chapter further claims that modern digital cartography utilizes advanced UX design methods to nullify the critical consideration of maps, by making them seamlessly fit into the routines of the user. After all, as historian Raymond Craib argues about maps: 'No other image has enjoyed such prestige of neutrality and objectivity ... The most oppressive and dangerous of all cultural artefacts may be the ones so naturalized and presumably commonsensical as to avoid critique' (Craib 2000, 8). I define casual power by rejecting naturalization, through tracing design choices and the resulting 'interfacial envelopes' (Ash 2015). To operationalize casual power as an analytical framework, I first establish three conceptual foundations that underpin how power operates through mapping interfaces.

First and foremost, I understand maps to be designed with certain *affordances*, a concept grounded in Gibson's cognitive ecology framework (Gibson 1977; 1986; Norman 2002; Lialina 2018a) and adopted by the human–computer interaction (HCI) field and the designers operating in it (Hassenzahl and Tractinsky 2006; Lialina 2018a). By evoking certain affordances, mapmakers actively work on continuously adapting and expanding the user interface of their products. Their interests are often predominantly commercial (Perkins 2009a) and as such the framework of casual power examines mapmakers' goals in relation to the propagation of commercial appeal to their user base, which is measured in terms of performance metrics, predominantly the number of users and/or duration of use.

Second, such affordances are not scripture, but rather scripts or proscriptions: 'what the device allows or forbids of actors – humans and nonhuman – that it anticipates' (Akrich and Latour 1992, 261). This is what Nagy and Neff (2015) refer to as *imagined affordance* to emphasize the agency of the users, and Bucher and Helmond (2018) integrate into a unified framework as 'high-level affordances'. A digital 'like' button invites being pressed, but furthermore may conjure an entire platform vernacular (Gibbs et al. 2015) that infuses certain action with social meaning: what does 'liking' entail on Instagram versus on X, for instance? These affordances can be followed or circumvented, but nonetheless leave traces of designer intent (Light et al. 2018). When translating this to the context of *mapping* interfaces, it presents certain consequences for studying their power over users. Digital mapmakers engage with users through the maps, and attempt to introduce various types of perceived affordances into the UI to guide them.

Third, casual power operates within broader design trends that circulate rapidly across digital platforms. So-called human-centric design, for example, has become a central paradigm in how digital objects are made, often incorporating 'experiential' or 'fun' elements (Hassenzahl 2008; Diefenbach et al. 2014). These, however, also breed practices like 'dark pattern' – misleading and manipulative designs (Brignull 2010; Mathur et al. 2019) – and the overall rise of what gamification critic Ian Bogost calls 'exploitationware' (Bogost 2011b). Maps adopt these same UX paradigms. The designs employed, however, might be far from having the user's best interests in mind.

This chapter thus marks the relations between maps, interfaces, and power. It suggests casual power as a framework that is embedded in maps' *habitual mediation of space*. In short, digital maps show us a stripped-down approximation of the world, to benefit the economic interests of their creators. But unlike social media or shopping apps with which they share screens, their seemingly objective 'mapiness' often shields them from scrutiny that we reserve for the latter.

Having established these conceptual foundations, in the rest of the chapter I advance them in four distinct steps. First, I briefly explain the attention economy and how it manifests in maps through distraction and retention. Second, I unpack what the UI entails and posit that maps should be understood as experiential interfaces that attempt to make the ordinary unique. Third, I show how maps achieve this through the underlying structure of layering and its connection to the rising UX design paradigm. Fourth, I note the special role of metrics on the UI and its 'flattening' effect in mediating the world.

Paying attention to maps

Digital maps appeal to user attention in two opposite, but paradoxically intertwined, ways. First, through distraction: the map draws one away from the world and to the screen. Second, through retention, the map aims to keep our focus, keeping us coming back to the screen. In terms of distraction, while many other digital devices thrive on such redirection of attention (Odell 2019), maps do so differently by tacitly suggesting their own image as a *substitution* for the world unobserved. Until very recently maps 'competed' only with the physical world they aimed to substitute for the attention of the viewer. Today they compete with other digital objects (screens, apps, streams, feeds) with which they cohabit on digital platforms, also. Even more, maps take part in what Berry (2014) calls a *computational regime*, maintained by big-tech companies through algorithms that attempt to predict and influence user behaviours. Building on continuous surveillance of our actions, they create so-called 'data doubles' (Haggerty and Ericson 2000) of individual users that are then 'optimized' to account for designers' goals, such as longer session times or more spending. McKelvey and Neves (2021) demonstrate how 'optimization' has migrated from its precise mathematical origins, where it describes calculable improvements in algorithmic efficiency, into a vague corporate ideology that legitimizes practices harmful to users. In their analysis of platform labour, they show how the term obscures value judgements by cloaking preference for exploitative metrics in the language of rational engineering. Thinking about maps through this prism highlights how optimization can account for more efficient route planning for pedestrian wayfaring, on the one hand, and for a more favourable 'time-on-device' or 'monthly-active' user metric for a product manager, on the other.

Optimizing for *attention* is on the table, then. Overall, it will not surprise anyone that contemporary digital devices produce constant demand for user attention, often through active notifications and customized dashboards. The pings and nudges of social media have long since been joined by demands from travel, grocery, dating, and many more apps, to the extent that health and consumerism journalist Amanda Mulls exasperatedly laments that – unlike other types of spammy or marketing communications – they remain unregulated and prone to blanket and opaque options menus left for individual users. In essence once agreeing to receive notifications from an app, such user consent 'may be taken as a blanket yes to any or all notifications, whether functional or promotional in nature. (If you feel like you've been seeing more push-notification ads on your iPhone recently, you're probably right. Apple loosened the rules against these promotions in 2020.)' (Mull 2023, n.p.). Under such attentive configuration, 'thinking itself can be outsourced through cognitive technical devices which will supply the means to understand and process the raw information given by a new politics of access' (Berry 2014, 181), enrolled into the battle over our mind's ability to conform with how we work and play digitally (Sampson 2017). The colonization of the cognitive and even pre-cognitive by the computational is a necessary component in explaining how we pay attention to maps. I begin with the traditional critique of the way maps manifest their power on users' perceptions of the world before moving on to the specificities of the digital in mapping.

It has long been observed that maps tend to compress space and time, turning the potential into an actual. It is what the anthropologist Tim Ingold refers to as the 'cartographic illusion' (Ingold 2000, 234), whereby map users confuse the representation with the map. A central aspect of such an illusion

> lies in the assumption that the structure of the world, and so also that of the map which purports to represent it, is fixed without regard to the movement of its inhabitants. Like a theatrical stage from which all the actors have mysteriously disappeared, the world – as it is represented in the map – appears deserted, devoid of life. No-one is there; nothing is going on (Ingold 2000, 234).

My argument here is that in digital mapping, the cartographic illusion produces a more complex artifice. Unlike for Ingold, maps today do animate the world, populating it with images of people and objects that resemble actual actors in their mutability. They captivate the user's attention by manufacturing a momentary freeze that transfixes such actors through the screen on which they are displayed. With a click of a mouse or a tap of the finger (Hind and Lammes 2016), one can select a different mode of viewing or interacting with the map. Depending on the specific user interface, such modes include switching between schematic and satellite views or morph into more specialized displays, like ranking of locations. For many cartographic interfaces, it also allows switching into a navigation mode often while displaying rich information about the world, turning the map from a display to a guide for action and vice versa. The user is thus encouraged to believe that the digital map is in some ways *truer* to the world than the paper variant, because it amends the inertness of its predecessor, includes real-time updates from various data streams, and allows (the illusion of) control over what aspects of the world can be witnessed through the map (Kingsbury and Jones 2009).

Maps cohabit with myriad other types of objects on competing and complementary digital platforms. To tap on a map icon on your phone means to *not* tap on some other app. Digital maps are constructed with a certain goal in mind: to be used and to be useful. While at first those goals seem tautological, they are not. First, the map must be useful. It must be clear, quick to load, provide relevant information, be pleasing to the eye. It must cater to different types of users, imagined and real, and balance out between the financial goals of its developer and the possible frustrations of users (Ash, Anderson, et al. 2018). Often, those are developed through extensive user testing, by envisioning scenarios and specific 'personas' that account for different uses that are then integrated into the everyday operation of apps and desktop software (Woolgar 1990; Bounegru et al. 2022). For digital maps in particular, those are not new ideas but rather a direct development of the notions that historically have made maps into such effective information carriers (Krygier and Wood 2005), also involving extensive user testing. However, in the pre-digital age, maps rarely had to *compete* with non-maps. During a wayfaring exercise, navigators would only have in their hands the tools for navigation – a book lying on the desk alongside the map does not ping with notifications demanding attention. Now, the media landscape demands more and more of a user's attention and informational overload becomes the background noise through which miscellaneous signals attempt to break through (Andrejevic 2013; Crary 2014; Odell 2019).

As Dalton (2015) notes, new kinds of mapmakers have emerged when Google opened its API to independent developers, ones without a background in traditional cartography, who now build digital maps and map-like services in order to supplement existing software products. The map becomes another aspect of the merging tech and media industries. It is no longer compartmentalized into specific intended uses (the road atlas is pulled out in the car), but rather exists parallel to other maps, map-like interfaces and non-map interfaces. The new amateur mapmakers that Dalton describes are not necessarily brought into the fold of self-imposed cartographic traditions of truth or accuracy. Instead, they are more often immersed in the prevalent sociotechnical codes of conduct of 'playful fun and profit seeking' (Dalton 2015, 1029), using existing web cartography resources for pursuing projects in the hopes of eventual monetization. The 'fun' aspect of it is as much of a factor as 'profit': amateurs are encouraged to perform unpaid 'playbour' (Kücklich 2005) involving doing the things they love, where the chances of monetary gratification are slim and the main benefactor is the platform on which the digital object is hosted. In Kücklich's original analysis, these are video-game modders, investing work to improve or change their favourite pastime to the benefit of the game publisher, who gets free updates that can extend the players' interest in the game. For Google, the Maps API functions similarly in spreading the functionalities of the platform beyond what the tech company originally envisioned, but ensuring that any success still is incorporated into its broader ecosystem (figure 2.1). It continues the tradition of extracting value from unpaid labour online, by framing such labour as fun or turning it into a leisure activity (Terranova 2000; Scholz 2008).[1]

Ensuing software is thus characterized by the *experience of* maps rather than merely the *use* of them. Product developers and designers are making maps in certain ways while being told overtly that both creating and using software should be experiential (Imaoka 2021). They translate their own preconceptions about how the user should be engaging with their product into a set of interface decisions that attempt to make their maps fit seamlessly and casually into their users' routines, all the while making it unique and memorable to warrant constant engagement. They are, after all, competing in the

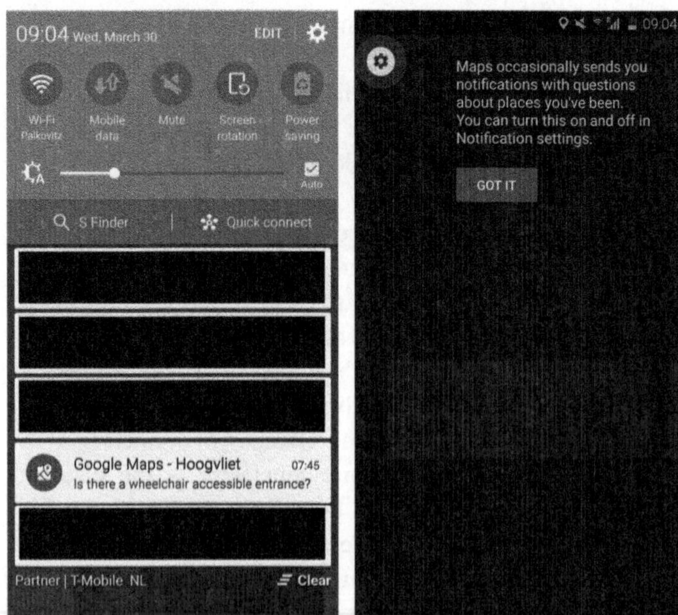

Figure 2.1: A notification from the Google Maps app prompts a user to give additional information about a supermarket they visited, while not using Maps. This is an opt-out function that appears by default and requires going into the app's settings to disable (seen on the right). Giving the information benefits the supermarket, but mostly Google, which gets free information that improves its service. Screenshot by the author, March 2016.

experience economy, as coined by authors and frequent *Harvard Business Review* contributors Pine and Gilmore (1998). The term, which was later turned into a book by the same name (Pine and Gilmore 2011), presented an argument concurrent with the then-peaking dot-com bubble: that consumers seek experiences of products that provide more than rational value. From a more critical perspective, this leads to the *attention economy*, where the computational industries are cultivating methods to capture the attention of (often young) audiences in order to maximize their future financial worth (Stiegler 2010; Crogan and Kinsley 2012; Williams 2018). Under such economy, attention is commodified and treated as value to be extracted, applying the old logic of advertising far beyond the pages of newspapers or commercial television (Celis Bueno 2017). Firms are interested in training large swathes of audiences to pay attention in specific ways that can be later turned into profits, either by subscriptions, ads, micro-payments, or otherwise. Bernard Stiegler refers to this as *neuro power* and claims that the endpoint of such a move is the gradual destruction of individuals' abilities to apply critical and reflexive attention to the world around them.

Cultural critic Tiziana Terranova (2012) suggests that this is tied to the human brain's ability to change and adapt over time – its neuroplasticity. By tapping into the shifting cognitive skills of its audiences, tech companies – those producing digital maps included – attempt to reconfigure user habits in order to domesticate and habituate beneficial ones and eradicate those that do not contribute to the economic conception of attention. Such a conception usually translates the amorphous concept into measurable and quantifiable metrics: clicks, views, likes, and shares that can be counted, packaged, and sold to advertisers or otherwise give value to the platform owner. This leads to a paradoxical state where '[t]he economic/informational plastic brain is thus caught in a double bind: on the one hand, in order to participate in the attention economy, it must enter a technological assemblage of attention; on the other hand, becoming part of this assemblage implies a dramatic cognitive loss that is translated into a subjectivity more adept at carrying out routine tasks but less capable of reasoning, reflecting and intimacy' (Terranova 2012, 6).

What results is 'a new socio-economic landscape, one in which flexibility, play, creativity, and immaterial labor – call it ludic capitalism – have taken over the old concepts of discipline, hierarchy, bureaucracy, and muscle' (Galloway 2012, 27). Since attention is valuable, yet degradable, the companies that aim at capturing it are simultaneously aiming to reduce the cognitive loads of their users while maintaining conditions in which this use is pleasant. Tony Sampson (2017) connects this with the rise of HCI's third paradigm: after designers finished conforming machines to our bodies (ergonomics) and our minds (informatics), they now aim to do so with our experiences. Yet, those are not real experiences: they are attempts to connect meaning from familiar, deeply personal events with the mundanity of digital life. A map that puts a star icon as a graphical user interface (GUI) indicator builds upon a familiar visual language in the hopes of evoking some excitement in its users – and to do so time and time again. This, according to Sampson, is an *ersatz experience*, which 'neurologically models and imitates the felt experiences of everyday life and reworks and recycles them to condition such things as worker motivation and consumer engagement' (Sampson 2017, 46). This is felt not only on screens but in the streets: geographer Sarah Barns posits that digital platforms' capacity to 'remediate experiential worlds' (Barns 2019, 8) is changing how cities operate, where personalization extends to physical shops and residents' data is captured and optimized into a single 'cognisphere' that links humans, animals and machines through computation (Hayles 2006).

As a reminder, all this does not happen 'somewhere'. Users' activities in hybrid space are mediated through various digital interfaces on their devices. After all, as predicted by Pine and Gilmore, 'New technologies, in particular, encourage whole new genres of experience' (Pine and Gilmore 1998, 99). For that we need to understand what mapping interfaces entail.

The experiential interface

'Interface' is a word with a long and complicated history. Depending on one's background, it can refer to various ways in which objects connect in a mutually fitting way ('interfacing'). The term has its origins in nineteenth-century physics and refers to how different fluid surfaces affect and push against each other (Hookway 2014). Later, it became more closely associated with the human-facing component of an intricate machine, and – with the proliferation of computers – particularly to their input/output components such as screens and keyboards. With the rise of personal desktop computing in the late 1980s, and particularly Apple's graphical operating system (OS), and Microsoft's Windows, the GUI became the focus on interfacial discussions to the extent that today 'interface' is often used as a metonym to refer specifically to the GUI on a computer or a phone, namely to the arrangement of its visual elements that aim to facilitate action and evoke reaction in human users (Drucker 2011). Ash (2015) provides an extensive literature review on interfacial theories and categorizes them into five broad categories (table 2.1). Each has its own advantages and disadvantages. For instance, seeing interfaces as primarily *computational devices* focuses on the materiality of their components (chips and screens), and highlights interfaces' dependence on other software and hardware. The GUI of Google Maps, drawing

Table 2.1: Categorization of interface theories, adapted from Ash (2015, 16–24).

Interfaces as	**Conceptualization**	**Potential issues**
1. Computational devices	Various types of connections (software/hardware, software/ software). Underscores materiality.	Ignores content and focuses on more 'real' underlying material technologies.
2. Practices	Beyond the device, there are historical and social ways that are implicated within an interface.	Same dualism as before, but instead of software/hardware (as in 1), it is body/task-scape.
3. Carriers of cultural logics and ideologies	Codifies the way to exist (societies of control). To a search engine everything looks like ranking.	A very deterministic way of linking bodies to information. Transparent (if ideologic).
4. Links between digital and analogue	Two different (irreconcilable) modalities, that need to be translated. Heat to pain to bits.	Reducing the digital to a (unified) site of possibility of the analogue's true potential.
5. Affective	Encounter between (also non-human) bodies affecting each other.	Practically, focuses on affection, or the humanist-instrumental perspective to be avoided.

on data from Google's cloud computing network, behaves differently depending on the device it runs on, and hides its location capabilities under a single 'my location' button that prompts IP address, GPS, mobile, and Wi-Fi connections from your device. At the same time, this approach runs the risk of disregarding the emotional and personal connection one makes with such an interface (sliding through a map of a town you used to live in), because such action does not leave material or infrastructural traces and thus might be deemed less 'real'.

On the other hand, looking at interfaces as *practices* (what we do with them) does highlight such personal meaning but might trap us in dualistic thinking that what happens 'on the other side of the screen' is separated from the body of the user engaged in the task. With maps, this is clearly not the case – just consider the little dance of self-orienting one does when the blue dot on the map refuses to align with one's actual location and facing. Other theories focus on interfaces as *carriers of cultural logics and ideologies*. Such theories attempt to 'read' interfaces as expressions of underlying truths, and are often rooted in Deleuze's (1992) notion that a society's machines are replicating its power structures. While exciting, such thinking encounters similar problems to Harley's and Wood's deconstructionist approach to maps: the assumption that their objects are fixed and that similar ideologies will be 'read' and incorporated by all users in identical ways. Other scholars focus on interfaces as *a link, or a meeting point, between the analogue (often organic) and digital*, presenting them as separate modalities and attempting to examine the interface as a point of impossible translation. These theories are reminiscent of those who prefer vinyl records to digital formats, confident that something intangible is lost in the conversion from a soundwave to a digital capture. While interesting conceptually, such thinking tends to reduce everything 'digital' into a singular unified field, ignoring the role of content and use-cases. Just because it is impossible to translate a digital distance into a bodily feeling both on a Google Maps screen during a road trip, and on Deliveroo's food courier tracking map, does not mean the two are the same. And conversely, some digital experience can be profoundly felt in the body, as anyone who has broken up with a partner via the internet will tell you.

Finally, Ash highlights a fairly rare category that builds on affect theory to imagine interfaces as encounters between different (types of entities) that affect each other. He himself subscribes to this view, building on Don Ihde's post-phenomenological view of technology and the philosophical tradition of flat ontologies (Bryant 2010; Harman 2010; Bogost 2012) to conceive of interfaces as linking objects that can push and pull against each other, or rather 'encounter' each other in the world. A screen of a phone is interfacing with the user through its visual components – such as displaying the Strava sports tracker app – but also interfaces differently with the phone's battery, from which it draws power depending on the specific use scenario. Here Ash warns against a common pitfall in the affective approach: one that prioritizes *affection*, i.e. the way objects appear to humans, rather than taking non-human's affecting each other with the same degree of seriousness. To him, then, interfaces are 'environments of inorganically organized objects, which communicate through processes of transduction' (Ash 2015, 16). For our technography of maps, this means paying attention to the material components of the interface (how it's made, what data infrastructures it incorporates), how it is designed and incorporated into broader platforms, and how it is being encountered by users.

This definition also fits well with the ontologically unstable nature of emergent mapping, shifting away from the traditional view of interfaces as human-centric or as a dividing binary (hardware/software, or human/non-human). In this perspective, the mapping interface is no longer seen merely as a tool for human users to operate on underlying data structures and instead incorporates its software interface with the broader app and OS ecosystem, or its modulation through the hardware of the phone on which it runs. As Ash puts it, such a theorization allows us 'to analyse [interfaces] without reducing them to a set of quantitative mathematical states on the one hand or subjective human experience on the other' (Ash 2015, 51). It also resonates with Benjamin Bratton's encompassing definition of an interface as 'any point of contact between two complex systems that governs the conditions of exchange between those systems' (Bratton 2015, 220). The two approaches complement each other: Ash zooms in on the analytic human-to-object level, while Bratton's macro approach covers the geopolitical ramifications of *interfacial regimes*.

Furthermore, echoing Galloway's (2012) conception of interfaces as unceasing effects rather than singular entities, Ash describes interfaces as 'localized foldings of space-time that work to shape human capacities to sense space and time for the explicit purpose of creating economic value' (Ash 2015, 4). Based on this concept, in later work, Ash and colleagues provide a set of guidelines for analysing UIs. They reject the notion that interfaces exert power directly or manipulate users, and instead see interface design as 'an experimental process of managing friction ... a series of bodily and technical obstacles or hesitancies that interrupt, slow or stop a user from completing a task within a digital interface, such as choosing a service or buying a product. Friction is a matter of attempting to not only produce smooth experiences, although that is part of what is being done, but of producing the possibility of a transition between thresholds at the right time' (Ash, Anderson et al. 2018, 1138).

Friction is thus understood as a design technique that attempts to either extend or diminish the range of possible actions; to either facilitate or hinder a user's transition through a key point (threshold) of a digital interface. We can thus visualize the digital mapping interface *as a probabilistic membrane between the user and the world*. In other words, we might ask, what information is given about their surrounding that informs their understanding of space? Which actions would individuals be more likely to take? And would individuals who do not use a map behave differently? To answer this we must look at the unique *layered* nature of digital mapping interfaces to create experiences.

The layered interface experience

The goal of interface designers has always been to make their products invisible, eliminating the users' consideration of the mediation and making them see 'through' the interface into the 'inside' of the computer (Norman 1988; 2002; Bolter and Gromala 2005). This is, of course a lie, as every interface comes with its own hidden logics and presumptions, but most users buy into it, at least until something in the interface breaks (Star 1999). But therein, lies its power. Consider 'We use cookies on this website to optimize your experience', a sentence that every internet user encounters multiple times a day. Remarkably, the second part of this claim is rarely scrutinized. How exactly can 'experiences' – private, subjective states – be 'optimized' through digital use (McKelvey and Neves 2021)? The recent data-turn in media studies helps us understand the *cookie* component: the creation of traceable data-bodies and their continuous surveillance, as well as the infrastructures built for trawling for, and sharing of, data between private and governmental bodies (van Dijck 2014; Cheney-Lippold 2017; Ruppert et al. 2017; Bucher 2018; Noble 2018; Amoore 2020). But the latter aspect, experience, is less evident. How can the creators of various online platforms personalize experiences for vast amounts of individual users? And what does this entail for the very notion of experience as personal, meaningful, and singular? The answer lies in the interface as a layered and *modulating* force between designer intent and user actions. By managing user friction, it opens different aspects of the experiences, allowing access to different 'depths' of the map, depending on both the specific user and the particular interface.

Often, we are being 'hypernudged' (Yeung 2017) towards taking a particular action, through the use of design elements combined with a collection of personal data from previous interactions. In UI design, making something convenient might be more powerful than outright allowing or forbidding it (Stanfill 2015; Bucher and Helmond 2018) – just consider the tediousness of clicking through the menus to reject all cookies versus the one-click acceptance of them. The entire politics of online surveillance, advertising monetization and the EU General Data Protection Regulation (GDPR) come to be decided in the moment of clicking the 'I Agree' button on a pop-up window. According to the regulation, it requires *explicit* consent – 'freely given, specific, informed and unambiguous' (Wolford 2019). Yet, as noted by Human and Cech (2021) in their research on the Western mega platforms Google, Amazon, Facebook, Apple, and Microsoft (GAFAM), all required between 7 and 10 clicks to disagree with cookies tracking, and just one to agree. This very fact of interfacial obscurity stood in the centre of the French decision to fine Google and Facebook for a record €210 million because of their obfuscation of users' choices (Rosemain 2022).

Therefore, experiential design in general – and of maps in particular – poses crucial conceptual and ethical questions about exploitation through interface, by an industry interested to monetize it, often through the use of 'dark patterns' – design techniques that work well, but harm the user (Dieter 2015; Mathur et al. 2019; Human and Cech 2021; Sinders 2022). A prime early example of such a thorny ethical issue is the 'emotional contagion study', wherein Facebook used subtle UI changes to experimentally alter the moods of approximately 700,000 users without prior consent (Verma 2014). Many other similar technologies have been deployed or developed by digital platforms (Gillespie 2017; Stark 2018;

2020) to attempt to change user behaviour incrementally through collection of data and further iterations to design. Mobile devices – for many the only access to the internet, and prominent use case for digital mapping – exacerbate those issues as the smaller screens and limited options of customization allow for even fewer options to opt out. At the time when many usability specialists convert to being UX designers (Lialina 2018b), we must be alert.

Mostly conceived so far through the lens of HCI, UX has remained a challenging concept for social science and humanities scholars. From a design perspective, multiple techniques were developed to inquire what constitutes a *good UX*: clear visual hierarchies and other usability guidelines, the creation of user personas with pre-defined needs, user-testing of workflows through hand- and eye-tracking as well as experimental implementation of multiple variants of the same interface (A/B testing) to see which ones appeal to users (Hassenzahl 2008; Diefenbach et al. 2014). Yet, rarely the same question is turned inward: *what makes UX good* (Sampson 2017; Lialina 2018b)? Or: how do the technological innovations of the user interface contribute to living a good life?

Media scholars have focused on behind-the-scenes of contemporary digital ecosystems, examining infrastructures (Parks and Starosielski 2015; Plantin and Punathambekar 2019), platforms (Helmond 2015; Plantin et al. 2018; van Dijck et al. 2018) and data (Clarke 1988; Amoore 2011; Beer 2015a). Paradoxically, this has left the actual visible portion of it all, in particular the design of the user interface, somewhat undertheorized (Hadler 2018). Yet, billions of users still encounter digital media at the level of their daily interfaces. Most of us do not understand the way convoluted algorithms combine with digital data to personalize our media use. Instead, we click and swipe, tap and scan our social feeds, and it is here where digital platforms connect with us, promising meaningful experience in every routine interaction.

Layering is a defining characteristic of the mapping interfaces encountered by map users, that helps us understand the power of UX. It alludes to both the superimposed nature of data and software structures as well as emerging hybrid relations with physical entities that such structures mediate (Manovich 2006; 2013; Parikka 2010; Galloway 2012; Verhoeff 2012; Ash 2015). For me, this is a crucial factor when discussing digital mapping, as it transfixes the logic of software, data, and code, together with the platformized political economy of their production, onto what was previously an analogue field (Dalton 2015). Displaying and comparing different visualization types on the same base map, opening and closing various layers (as in the visual information tiers of the map), clicking or tapping on a map object to access additional information about it are all examples of layered digital-map interactions. Layering can occur on the UI level, as when additional information layers are offered to the user in Google Maps (figure 2.2). But even when they are not present, the map itself is nonetheless layered, built on the underlying data drawn from

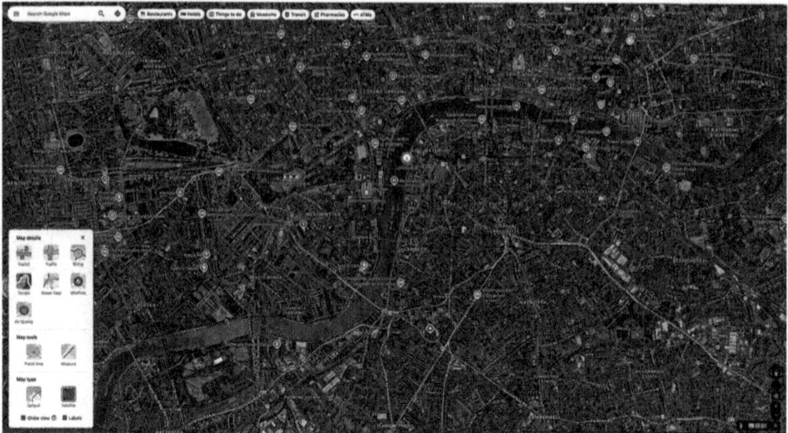

Figure 2.2: A detailed Satellite view of Google Maps on the desktop, with the layers options visible. Screenshot by the author, October 2025.

multiple sources and recombined for in-the-moment display of relevant information.

Digital map layering implies a type of interactivity which is not present in a paper map: the user is called on to actively shape and select their map (within the boundaries defined by the system's designer). Thus, the once-viral Facebook connections map that used graph theory to chart the link strength between various Facebook users based on their self-reported geographic location is not a mapping interface, even if the result (after several corrections) resembles an incomplete map of the world (figure 2.3). A static image featuring the contours of the world, even if produced by digital means, does not fit in my definition of a 'digital map' – it is a diagram or a visualization. The lack of zoom or panning options further places it firmly in the image category rather than the map category. I draw here somewhat on Richard Rogers's (2013) distinction between digitized and born-digital objects. Interfacing, after all, implies an action to be undertaken by a combination of user effort and designer intent: a *digital image* of a map, produced by digital means, is not the same as a *digital map*.

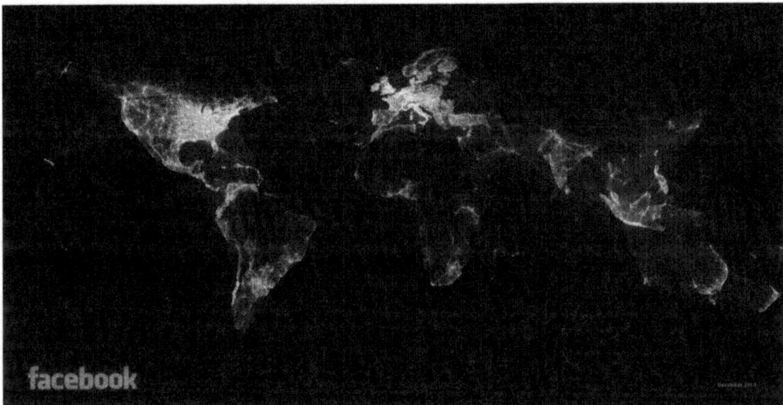

Figure 2.3: The Facebook links map forms the contours of familiar continents but is greatly lacking in places Facebook was not (yet) popular, such as Russia and China, December 2010. Source: https://www.facebook.com/notes/facebook-engineering/visualizing-friendships/469716398919.

The construction of lived spaces through interfaces becomes tangible in the tension between one's direct experience of a place, and one's simultaneous experience of it as mediated by a mobile screen (Farman 2021). Such a discontinuity is typical of the increasingly 'smart' urban space, planned and implemented based on top-down strategies (Mattern 2021a). Thus, the interface does not only depict the world for its users, but becomes enmeshed in it, and reproduces it, for example by making certain behaviours more legible and more likely than others.

The introduction of temporary, context-specific layers can dramatically reshape how users engage with maps during moments of crisis. During the COVID-19 pandemic, Google Maps introduced an infection-tracking layer that exemplified both the promise and limitations of layered mapping interfaces. Whilst ostensibly designed to help users 'navigate safely' through pandemic space, the layer's design choices revealed how the commercial imperatives of mapping platforms can conflict with public health needs. Specifically, it asserted user of certainty despite health data limitations; it treated pandemic information as separate from other spatial realities, severely limiting the maps' interactivity while in this specific mode; all presented through a frictionless interface that discouraged critical reflection about one's pandemic conduct (Gekker 2023). The layer existed for only two years before being discontinued in September 2022, yet it demonstrated how cartographic interfaces increasingly mediate not just our movements but our understanding of risk, safety, and collective crisis. A central key to this is the numerical elements of the map.

Quantification and metrics on mapping interfaces

Maps are permeated with varied forms of quantification, such as scoring (e.g., places in Google Maps), route calculations and constant (re-)evaluations of speed, directions, and ETAs. Using numerical displays, maps compress time and space for their audiences. By building these components into the maps' UIs, designers take advantage of the cognitive heuristics of the human mind, reducing reflexivity and accepting the map as more truthful. They evoke a kind of 'machine zone' (Schüll 2014), or a mechanistic engagement with an opaque interface, designed in a way to isolate the user and engross her in the immediate actions that she performs, rather than the consequences of such actions.

Anthropologist Natasha Schüll spent a decade researching gambling machine users, designers, and industry executives. Her primary finding is how they aim to get people 'into the zone'. Done through black-boxing the numerical components behind digital gambling, the zone is a psychological state of repeated interaction where the users, no longer interested in winning or losing, are engrossed in the actions themselves and the feedback loops they generate. In this state, playing to win is irrelevant, but rather the aim is, according to one gambler, 'to keep playing – to stay in that machine zone where nothing else matters' (Schüll 2014, 2).

The repetitive aspect is crucial for understanding casual power. Just like the gambling machines, digital maps are built to be operated routinely and non-reflexively, internalizing the requirements of working through a numerical user interface. The introduction of digital technologies has created a unique conjuncture of highly *traceable* and *manipulable* users, whether they are gamblers or map-users. Digitalization hides components that were previously visible and discernible behind the interface. In the case of gambling machines, the mechanical reels were gradually replaced with electronic and later digital components that created a disconnect between the game as experienced by the player and the actual outcomes, which were pre-calculated in an exact manner. Schüll concludes that by obfuscating the actual game mechanics, while giving players the illusion of control through nostalgic aesthetic elements in the design, the gambling industry aims at maintaining this aura of enchantment. The magic of the machine is intrinsically tied to the way human perception works, as '[t]here is a mismatch … between human capacities to process and respond to information and those of the digital technology. This mismatch, one could further suggest, reflects the larger asymmetry between designers and players, technologies of disenchantment and states of enchantment' (Schüll 2014, 85).

In a similar way, mapping interfaces often work to evoke a comparable unreflexively machine-zone-like state in their users. This substitutes a telic (in and of itself) use of maps for the sake of encountering the world they depict, with engaging with the map *for the sake of the map itself.* For example, in the early days of the Waze navigation app, which I further explore in the next chapter, users would be encouraged to collect points while driving, even without registering what the points are for or whether this action contributes to the overall goals of navigation (figure 2.4). Thus, a map might use vanity metrics, such as the number of times your review was read or a photo you uploaded was viewed, to convince regular users to become producers of mapped data instead of merely its consumers, making the map akin to a multi-sided market for cultural commodities – similar to how social media platforms 'sell' user attention to advertisers by making the same users generate content for their peers under the platforms' terms (Rieder and Sire 2014; Nieborg and Poell 2018).

Schüll emphasizes that the machine zone is achieved by implementing a massive tracking apparatus in the casinos. However, unlike the traditional Foucauldian surveillance of hidden cameras and guards on the casino floor, digitalization of gambling permitted the type of surveillance that Deleuze characterized as inherent to societies of control: one where the institutional gaze is internalized while the individual is turned into a 'dividual' (Deleuze 1992, 6) to be sampled, tagged, analysed, and tracked. Introduction of personalization to casino machines is reminiscent of the ongoing

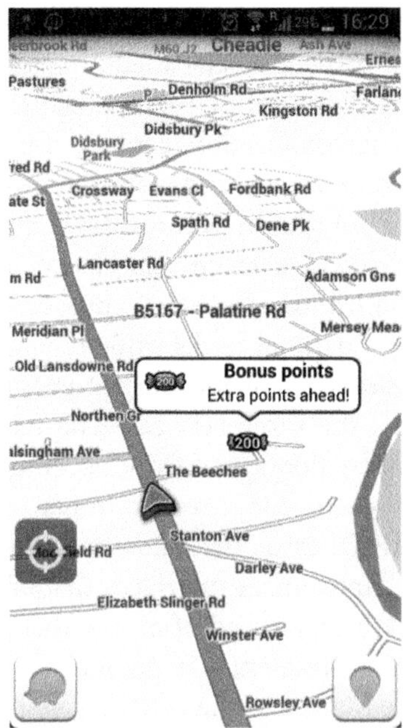

Figure 2.4: Bonus points appear on the map when no route has been selected. The only way to collect them is to 'drive over them' in the physical space. Screenshot by the author, February 2013.

personalization of Google's location services that I described in the previous chapter: both aim at reducing cognitive stress and generating a 'frictionless' (Kemper 2024) experience for the user – built for maximizing calculable interactions like clicks or shares over a period of time. After all,

> [t]he abstract quality of attention and at the same time the fact that the 'attentional assemblages' of digital media enable automated forms of measurement (as in 'clicks', 'downloads', 'likes', 'views', 'followers', and 'sharings' of digital objects) open it up to marketization and financialization (from the floating value of Internet companies to the accumulation of celebrity capital by means of a number of followers on Twitter to the changing value of 'clicks' as calculated by Google's software AdSense and AdWords) (Terranova 2012, 3).

Such quantification and commodification of attention is also an example of what social media researcher Christian Sandvig (2014) calls 'corrupt personalization' – where the users agree to personalization services for the benefit of improving their digital lives, and instead receive results based on collected data but geared towards the commercial interest of others, ensuring a skewed experience. Mapping's and gambling's digitalization processes alike offer benefits that are presented as consumer perks while relying on the private information disclosed by users who opt in to (or, commonly, fail to opt out of) the same services. The reinforced reward loops of the casino floors were not as efficient before the introduction of electronic user accounts, radio-frequency identification (RFID) cards that allow machines to recognize gamblers, and adaptive user interfaces that take into account the individual skill and speed of a user that began with the advent of digital technologies a decade ago (Schüll 2005). Similarly, Google Maps and the products built on it could not have provided effortless geolocative searches without the user agreeing to their previous searches being stored and analysed, their phone tracked (Farman 2010; Dalton 2018; Barns 2019). I will elaborate further on maps' intimate relation to surveillance in chapter 6.

While far from claiming that maps and gambling are similar, the induction of users into an attempted machine zone is nonetheless symptomatic of the larger design trends in UX. In fact, my initial interest in the machine zone came from an editorial piece by journalist and history of technology scholar Alexis Madrigal, who pointed out that Schüll's interviews with gamblers had an eerie similarity to his own experience with using social media and their coercive loops (Madrigal 2013). Such an effect can be explained in terms of *cognitive fluency*, where repeated use brings with it a sense of ease and pleasure (Jacoby et al. 1989; Whittlesea et al. 1990; Jacoby 1991; Unkelbach 2006). In gambling machines, this is achieved by a disconnect between visible mechanisms of gambling, as when machines no longer use mechanical reels, replaced by a digital interface that allows development of gambling 'skills' of precision and consistency, thus maximizing the time-on-device for the machine makers while maintaining a sense of pleasant familiarity for the user. In social media, it is through combination of ease-of-use and randomized reward that stimulate the user to 'gamble' in their feeds (Seaver 2019). Digital maps similarly allow the user to substitute complex thought processes and cognitive unease with a repeated interaction through a pleasant mantle of the familiar interface, surprising outcomes, and numeric user elements.

Maps, like Madrigal's assessment of social media, quantify basic human relations to the world, allowing one to constantly re-assess her position vis-à-vis subjective reality by answering a series of easier questions (How many friends? How many likes? How far I am?), all the while experiencing a (misleading) sense of familiarity through UI mastery. Artist and critic Benjamin Grosser, inventor of the Demetricator browser add-on on several social platforms (that deletes all quantity-related mentions from the platforms), notes on such constant numeric self-assessment:

> [o]ur need for personal worth is highly dependent on these social interactions, as both relatedness and esteem are necessarily measured in relation to others. If this essential human need can only be fulfilled within the confines of capitalism, then it stands to reason that we are subject to a deeply ingrained desire for *more*: a state of being where more exchange, more value, or more trade equals more personal worth. In other words, our evolutionarily developed desire for worth is an intrinsic need, which translates, through the 'pervasive atmosphere' of capitalist realism, into a desire for more (Grosser 2014, 5).

Grosser's argument is built on the propagation of neo-liberal managerial culture, and specifically the audit, as an evaluation method rooted in observable metrics that exceeded its original role in the financial industry and moved into domains such as higher education and public service. David Beer (2015a) suggests that measurements have a profound effect on those being measured. Using examples from professional sports, he underscores how individuals internalize the external measurements applied to them and adjust their behaviour accordingly. Beyond the realm of athletes, he connects such productive measurement to the encroachment of sensor-infused devices and the data networks that link them. According to him this results in most of us 'living in the lab' (Davies 2015; Niccolini 2018), where '[e]ven our emotions can be measured for tracking and manipulation. This "lab" is not just measuring our exercise and activities but also our emotions, well-being, health and even our sexual and reproductive properties' (Beer 2015b, n.p.). Facebook – like other social media – builds upon this culture of measurement in two ways: as a driving mode and as a data infrastructure. First, by constantly displaying metrics to the user, it aims at commodifying the social interaction into a manageable structure while playing on individuals' anxieties of missing out or losing. The numbers – most often notifications of new events – go up whether the user pays attention to them or not, maintaining constant pressure to check what is new in the feed. But the moment a user checks (i.e., clicks on the icon which displays the number), the count is gone and the user must obtain additional notifications by creating interaction opportunities, by engaging with others who are prompted if they comment or message back. Additionally, based on a list data structure, social media's databases in themselves are geared towards keeping score and assigning numerical structure; thus, '[o]n occasion, this may lead the Facebook interface programmer to include a metric simply because they can' (Grosser 2014, 11).

While not as saturated with metrics as the Facebook user interface (figure 2.5), Google Maps nonetheless has a very

Figure 2.5: Metrics locations on Facebook's user interface, reproduced from Grosser (2014) with permission.

number-heavy presence. Numbers appear independently of the user's inclinations. Selecting any point on the digital map will provide few suggestions on the possible ways to interact with it in the physical world, for example by offering quantified (time and distance) ways to reach it (figure 2.6). As I wrote elsewhere (Gekker 2016a), through its use of metrics, mapping interfaces substitute complex questions about the world and its own epistemology – How does it know where I am? Which types of places are highlighted for me? – with streamlined solutions. You are the blue dot, this route will take one minute less than the other one, and this restaurant along the way has a 7.8 ranking. The cartographic illusion (Ingold 2000) is thoroughly reinforced through the sense of datafied mastery.

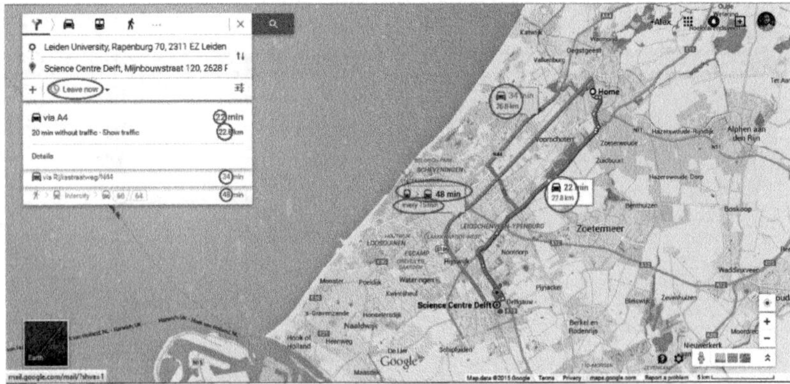

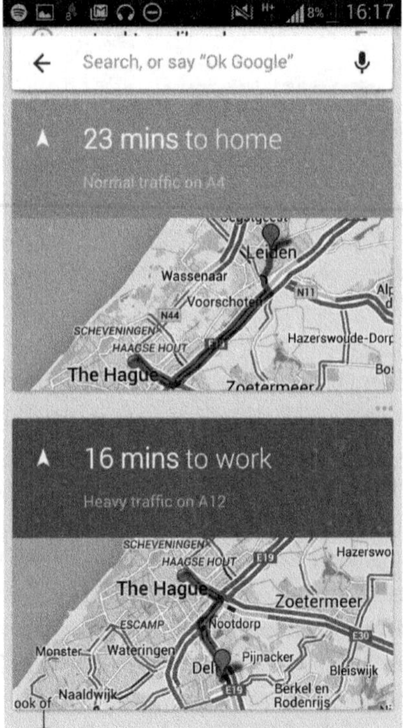

Figure 2.6: Top: Google Maps (before the 2016 redesign) metrics when navigating. Screenshot by the author. Bottom: An information card from the same era, showing quantified commuting information from the Maps app when opening the Google app on an Android phone.

Conclusion: understanding maps through casual power

This chapter has presented the main conceptual framework for the book. I positioned digital maps within the broader context of the attention economy and showed how their role as media requires mapmakers to compete for user engagement. Through the concept of casual power, I argued that maps exert influence over users by masking it through myriad daily actions, habituating conduct through imagined affordances, and operating so smoothly that they slip beneath critical scrutiny. Unlike earlier frameworks that emphasized maps' ideological distortions or state surveillance, casual power accounts for how digital cartography achieves compliance through seamless integration into everyday routines rather than through deception or visibility. This power manifests through specific interface strategies: layering additional information atop cartographic representations, and deploying quantified elements (distances, times, ratings) that simplify our engagement with the complex physical world whilst reducing reflexivity. By unpacking these mechanisms, I have established that mapping interfaces can be analysed as designed objects that modulate how we sense and navigate space.

Consider, for instance, Google Maps' star rating system for businesses. At first glance, this appears to be a neutral, user-generated metric helping people find quality establishments. Through the lens of casual power, however, we see multiple mechanisms at work: the quantified rating (7.8) substitutes for complex qualitative judgement; the star visualization creates cognitive fluency through familiarity with review conventions; the positioning of ratings alongside routing information makes them appear as factual as distance or time; and crucially, the entire system operates so smoothly that users rarely question whose interests it serves (Google's advertising clients) or what types of establishments are privileged (those that generate review data). This is casual power in action: not forcing users towards specific businesses, but shaping the informational environment in which they make choices. The map presents itself as an objective guide whilst quietly steering attention and behaviour.

Having established this theoretical lens, the subsequent chapters apply it to specific domains where digital maps have become consequential. These chapters are deliberately less theoretically laden and more empirically grounded, examining how casual power operates across movement (chapter 3), play (chapter 4), work (chapter 5), and surveillance (chapter 6). Each explores how mapping interfaces shape particular practices and relations, from autonomous vehicles to location-based games, from crowdsourced cartography to always-on tracking. In the next chapter, I use this framework to explore one of contemporary maps' primary functions: to facilitate navigational movement. There, we will see how the smooth habituation of mapping interfaces has profound consequences for how we move and think through the built environment.

3

Movement

In February 2023, the US Department of Justice (DOJ) began considering an unprecedented *third* concurrent antitrust investigation into Google's business practices – its mapping business – following legal proceedings into its search and advertising dominance (Sisco 2023). According to a Politico news report, the department representatives met with stakeholders and competitors of the search giant, to determine how much of a monopoly it is in the locative field. A key concern is Google's mapping ubiquity, which allows the company to act both as a search provider (how to get location data on a nearby pizza place) and technology infrastructure provider (how to build a food tracker that shows you how close your pizza is). Reportedly, it also bundles such capabilities when selling to vendors, forcing software developers to use both or neither, a practice the German regulator tried to restrict by forcing Google to offer car manufacturers a choice of infotainment provider (Hancock 2025). After Google dominated the search market for 'what', and Facebook and its subsidiaries monopolized the 'who', it is the 'where' of digital meaning-making that still remains open (Fisher 2013) and mapping products are the key to delivering it; ever more so with that technology's seemingly key role in the future of smart vehicles (Bergen 2018), discussed below. So, when someone looks at the screen of their phone, dropping the little stylized red pin in Google Maps (or its more realistic counterpart in Apple's mapping software), and decides where to go or how to get there, much is at stake.

This chapter explores the dynamics between mapping interfaces, location data, and movement. Various forms of navigation and wayfinding are the most common uses of popular map apps today, from everyday commuting to food delivery. The first chapter established the processual ontology of cartography (that maps are malleable and contextual) and its recent technological developments (how they are intrinsically linked with data and platforms dynamics). The second chapter extrapolated these two ideas to focus on digital maps as interfaces operating in the attention economy, claiming that map designers must navigate the line between the accessible and the exciting: depicting the world through layers of additional information, aligned with both users' needs and mapmakers' (commercial) goals. The current chapter is the first of several that explore the ramifications of these assertions across broader societal domains, specifically, the concept of 'movement'.

Under this broad umbrella I include different kinds of actions that are taken with maps to get people and/or objects from one place to another. Maps can assist *before* movement occurs, in the planning stage – think of the route planner of Google Maps that purports to assess traffic conditions or public transport schedules to predict when one must leave to arrive on time. Maps are also increasingly used *during* movement, as in how first satnav devices and now apps on mobile phones guide and direct users in real time, allowing them to re-organize their spatial knowledge on the fly. This can take various forms, like reporting a road closure via the crowdsourced driving Waze app or the appearance of a new nearby order for a Deliveroo courier. Lastly, maps can provide valuable insights *after* the movement, for example by scrutinizing one's datafied trajectory of a jog or a bike trip on the fitness tracker Strava.

A recurring case study for the chapter is the automobile. Cars co-developed alongside maps in the mid-to-late twentieth century, turning navigation from a more specialized task into a more common one. Proliferation of road atlases and A-Z maps have made long-distance navigation accessible and trained generations of drivers in the art of wayfinding (Keates 1996; Wood 2010). Both mapping and automobility can be traced back in the making of contemporary urban (and more so, suburban) living. Consider, for instance, the now infamous plan by New York City's urban planner and overall mogul Robert Moses to deliberately build low bridges over the parkways leading to Jones Beach, to supposedly impede poor and lower middle-class families from visiting it. As the story goes, Moses planned to exclude (or at least inconvenience) tall public transport from passing under the bridges, and by doing so reserve the park's use for the car-using population (figure 3.1). For our purpose, the tale shows how mapping (used for urban planning) enacts certain modes of movement, and how cars are subscribed into these modes, in deeply politicized ways. Here, both are encouraging in

Figure 3.1: A Robert Moses Parkway bridge. Photo by Adam Moss (CC BY-SA 2.0), https://www.flickr.com/photos/roadgeek/42414836211/in/photostream/.

tandem a kind of individualistic, atomized use of the city, standing in stark contrast to more communal and mixed-uses planning advocated by other urban architects: Moses' plan enacts the car-only route, and the car owners driving on it support and propagate his future's vision. Science and technology scholar Langdon Winner famously made Moses' bridges key actors in his essay 'Do Artifacts Have Politics?', where they exemplify the key tenet that '[w]hat matters is not technology itself, but the social or economic system in which it is embedded' (Winner 1980, 122). As I discussed in the previous chapters, this lesson from STS remains steadfastly true when thinking about the practices and people underpinning digital mapping. The only issue with Winner's claim is that it's built on a falsehood.

As many pointed out before, buses do in fact go under the bridges. The beaches are visited by public transport-using families and have been for some time. Scholar of US urban planning Thomas J. Campanella (2017) clarifies that originally there was no need to build lower bridges in the parkways, since heavy traffic – busses and commercial vehicles – were forbidden from entering them from the start. This had to do with the aesthetic experience Moses, and the other planners, tried to evoke, one of a rustic escape from the city into a countryside. For them, the car was a key component for opening leisure activities for the emerging middle class, a pastime reserved, up to that point in history, predominantly for higher classes. In this version of the story, the *bridge heights* are meaningless because heavier traffic was routed to the beach via the *highways* anyway, and the car-centric design looks progressive and visionary. This is one interpretation brought by Woolgar and Cooper in their exploration of both Moses' bridges and Winner's paper that is based on them. Their main claim is that despite its factual inaccuracy, the tale instead should be read as an academic urban legend, one where 'the properties of the artefact are the outcome, not the cause, of their reception' (Woolgar and Cooper 1999, 439). In other words, the bridges represent an inherent fear of technological domination, common in scholarly work as in the lives of everyday technology users: one where through a careful manipulation of an object's design, makers exert invisible power over our actions and choices. This type of fear is even more common today with the advent of pervasive digital media and is similarly reflected in the central questions surrounding digital mapping for this book.

Concluding our discussion of Moses' bridges as technological domination, Campanella refutes that Moses may *indeed* have attempted to cement in stone his vision of the car-centric parkway – just in case someone would later attempt to change the contemporaneous laws prohibiting heavy traffic on the parkway. Investigation of the bridge clearance heights across the parkways versus other modes of transportation leading to the park have shown that 'Overall, clearances are substantially lower on the Moses parkway, averaging just 107.6 inches (eastbound), against 121.6 inches on the Hutchinson and 123.2 inches on the Saw Mill' (Campanella 2017, para. 16). Langdon Winner might have been somewhat right after all, in spirit if not in fact, as stated by Woolgar and Cooper. This brings us back to the car, its role in urban imaginaries and its prominence in moving things and/or people with maps.

In explaining what urban legends are, Woolgar and Cooper use the story of a woman in a car being pursued by a male driver in another car. Growing desperate she tries to lose him in the dense traffic, until she manages to find a policeman with whom she confronts the other driver. The latter, it turns out, was only trying to warn her of the man hiding in her back seat, holding a knife. The point of urban legends, to them, is as 'moral tales of boundary transgression' (Woolgar and Cooper 1999, 440). Often in such tales, the fear of an impending transgression is subsumed by realization that it has already happened ('the call is coming from inside the house!'). The car that appears in the story is not incidental, as many similar works of urban folklore feature the automobile, as a bubble of personal autonomy in otherwise (potentially) hostile space. When combined with a car, mapping apps allow an unprecedented level of mobility, relying on the collective intelligence of spatial databases and bypassing the need for local knowledge and orientation know-how.

The contemporary promises of smart transportation and self-driving vehicles further fuel this dream of complete autonomy (Alvarez León 2019; Marx 2022). In Steven Spielberg's 2002 sci-fi thriller *Minority Report*, there is a memorable scene where the protagonist, accused of a crime he did not commit, realizes he has lost control of his car. The car's voice calmly informs him that the destination has been changed, leaving him with no choice but to escape by smashing the windshield. This depiction stands out because it portrays the vilification of the car itself, along with the infrastructural network supporting it, unlike in most other films. The personal car, particularly in the American imagination of freedom, is often seen as a means of escape, independent of public transport infrastructure (Flink 1976; Steg 2005; Cross 2018). Even when fictional characters escape from cars as unwilling prisoners, the car is usually seen as an object lacking malice and capable of redemption (Wollen and Kerr 2002) – as the urban tale invoked by Woolgar and Cooper shows. However, in *Minority Report*'s world, where cars are autonomous and potentially dominate their users, the film presents a protocological argument (Galloway 2004) that mobility leads to visibility, and visibility leads to control.

Although not as dramatic as their fictional counterparts, connected and autonomous vehicles (CAVs) are an expanding category of automobiles equipped with sensors and computational abilities (Bissell 2018; Hind 2019). These vehicles not only enable but also require the collection of substantial amounts of personal data that can be traced and attributed (Alvarez León 2019; Tennant and Stilgoe 2021). While prototypical autonomous vehicles have garnered public attention regarding their safety, connected vehicles have received less coverage (Marres 2020). This is surprising considering most contemporary vehicles exhibit a growing degree of connectivity, particularly since the European Union's ruling that all new vehicle models from 2018 must include an emergency 'eCall' service (Regulation (EU) 2015/758 2015). Similar to the impact of social navigation apps (Hind and Gekker 2014), CAVs are significant objects of study that shape our mediated lives today, as they become intrinsically tied to moving with and through digital maps.

Thus, the remainder of this chapter unpacks such movement through four moves. First, I make the case for how maps translate the world into data. Then, how such data is visualized through a series of algorithmic moves, located between designer intent and user personalization. The third section exemplifies how these two dynamics work in practice by bringing the focus back on the car, through a case study of Mobileye, a vehicle safety equipment manufacturer making forays into CAVs and mapping. I conclude by considering how the growing navigational capacities of the maps' UIs impede human agency.

Sifting the world for actionable data

In 2012, Apple's decision to replace Google Maps with their own mapping software in their mobile operating system sparked negative reactions among users (Tofel 2012). Many consumers tried the new app but eventually stopped using it due to issues with unclear and mistaken data typically associated with a new mapping database. Apple CEO Tim Cook publicly apologized for the mishap and recommended alternative mapping and navigation applications (including Google's rival Waze) while the issues were being addressed (Tozzi 2012). The executive believed to be responsible for launching the map was later dismissed (Lessin 2012). Although there were claims that Google Maps, Apple's main competitor in online mapping, lost approximately 23 million mobile users in the US (Arthur 2013), the significance of this story lies not in the user loss or gain by tech giants,[1] but in the transformative nature of the map itself for getting around.

The introduction of Apple Maps disrupted the routine use of maps and highlighted the underlying processes that support such routines. The new mapping software resulted in businesses appearing in incorrect locations, navigation instructions leading users astray, the emergence of new neighbourhoods, and various visual glitches. Users were even directed to drive onto railway tracks or airport runways (Cohan 2012; Johnson 2012; Rundle 2012). Google Maps, in contrast, had become a habitual tool for mobile users, facilitating actions like self-location and finding nearby places of interest during navigation. Importantly, this is not to say that Google's product is free from errors: in 2023 a family of a man who drowned following a car accident has sued Google Maps for directing him across a bridge that collapsed ten years prior (Gross 2023). An Indian politician has been petitioning the country to cut reliance on the platform after at least five people lost their lives in recent years in events attributed to faulty navigation (Bhattacharya 2025). These and other fatalities – not to mention less grievous outcomes – have been part of Google's map service for years. Apple's 2012 launch, while not resulting in any significant bodily harm, drew so much attention because it compounded map errors and made them very visible, shattering users' navigational routine, destabilizing their lives. Complaints shared through popular social media sources exposed Apple's map as an active agent, guiding individuals and creating various micro-realities, some amusing and others tragic. As we saw in earlier chapters, the map in this case was not an objective representation of the world, nor was it merely influenced by ideological biases or asserting a single reality. Instead, it produced contextual, faceted, and fluid worlds for individual users.

This example highlights the core principles of a processual view of mapping, particularly its situational and contingent nature when applied to movement. November, Camacho-Hübner, and Latour (2010) refer to this perspective as a 'navigational' view of the map, drawing an analogy to complex marine navigation that relies on correlating the sea chart with external conditions to orient oneself. This approach is especially pertinent when considering the haptic engagement of digital users with mobile maps, leading to what Hind and Lammes describe as the 'double-tap mode'. In this mode,

> not only is the networked process that leads to digital mapping images far more dependent on fast, and multi-directional calculations, these processes are also far more foregrounded. Being invited to give input that leads to the mapping images (e.g. velocity, movement, entering a postcode, traffic warnings), users have more of a chance to participate in the chains of productions that lead to the mapping image they engage with (Hind and Lammes 2016, 86).

This iterative and cross-pollinating process between mapmakers, users, and emerging mapping worlds highlights the dynamic nature of mapping movement. Nothing exemplifies it better than Google Street View.

Were it to launch today, Google's ambitious Street View program would probably not have been allowed (figure 3.2). We are now far more cautious in letting big tech corporations amass information over our daily routines and actions, and more suspicious of possible future uses of such data. Up until very recently, mapping something that did not 'belong' to you (a contested term as it is) was tricky, and often even criminal or grounds for accusations of spying (Wood 2010). National mapping agencies, in particular, accustomed to being the sole proprietor of a country's spatial knowledge, did not take kindly to Google's encroachment (Perkins 2009a). As noted by Alvarez León, Street View can be seen as a 'property regime', specifically here codified through a technology that is 'used to grant access to and monitor the use of the

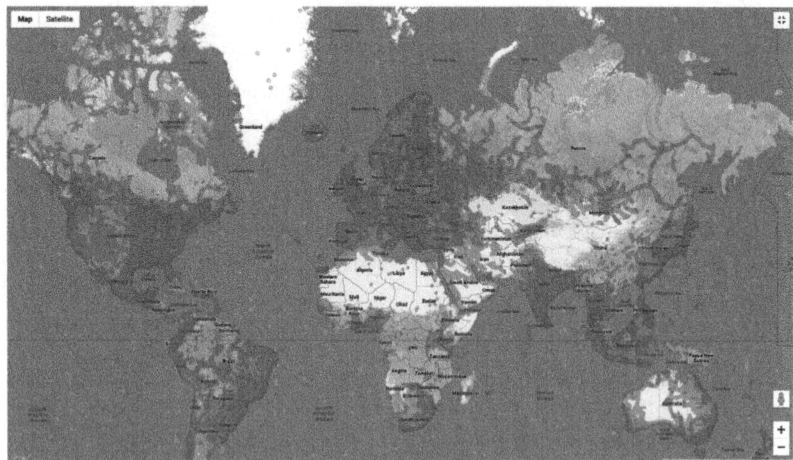

Figure 3.2: The world according to Google Street View. Darker shading represents the availability of street view imagery. Source: https://www.google.com/streetview/how-it-works/. Screenshot by the author, March 2023.

resource, as well as to define, allocate, and regulate the rights specific to each particular role. Technology thus plays a key role in the allocation of rights to a resource and therefore its management, exploitation, and commodification' (Alvarez León 2016, 2). Street View essentially asserts the right to control access to (semi-)public space and utilize it. The obvious uses are the somewhat voyeuristic pleasure of observing far-away places from the comfort of one's screen (Kingsbury and Jones 2009), or showing street imagery as part of the step-by-step navigation instructions either before or during a journey. In such a way it seems perhaps not that different from the inclusion of tricky intersection diagrams or venue invitations or visually helpful landmarks on tourist maps ('you need to turn *here*, right next to the crooked tree'). Of course, as with much else in the transition from paper to digital cartography, the scale and scope of the undertaking changes the inherent nature of older practices. Quantity becomes quality.

One obvious result is the erosion of privacy. Conceived as a navigational aid first and foremost, Street View uses specialized cars with 360° cameras mounted taller than 2.5 metres high. Mounting them closer to the ground would generate far more disruption through occlusion, although some countries, like Switzerland and Japan, did mandate this modification to the standard rig, as to not be able to photograph inside private property over fences and hedges (O'Brien and Streitfeld 2012). Privacy-cautious Germany has famously restricted the deployment of the service for over a decade (Cantrill and Bodoni 2023). Despite the company's attempt to introduce privacy controls, such as the automatic blurring of faces and licence plates, mishaps happened. In the early days of the program, controversy mounted as people were caught sunbathing in the nude on their lawns, performing (supposed) crimes or just acting silly, forever to be captured in Google's imprint of the world. After pressure from several jurisdictions, Google now allows (depending on a user's country of residence) some modicum of control over completely removing oneself or one's property from the service, but of course, screenshots were taken and shared.

Many of these photos are still in circulation appearing in clickbait-y compilations of 'funny/shocking/weird Street View images you won't believe!' (Learish 2019). A more profound exploration of the service is found in Jon Rafman's '9 Eyes' projects, where he curates and exhibits unique Street View images on a dedicated website and a Tumblr blog, depicting the image produced from unique relation to the mapped world, glitches and interfaces, as 'looking at a memory that nobody really had' (Recinos 2018). For example, Google's Street View car might encounter (and immortalize) an Apple vehicle carrying out the same task for a rival platform (figure 3.3). Here we find familiar echoes of maps' purported objectivity and the 'view from nowhere' (Perkins and Dodge 2009), translated into a supplemental feature of the mapping platform, and in line with Google's own aims of painting the world 'at the resolution of about one pixel to the inch' (Fisher 2013).

Figure 3.3: An Apple Maps Camera car, found on Google Street View. Screenshot by author.

Beyond the invasive imagery, other privacy controversy followed, as thoroughly documented in the dedicated Wikipedia page (Wikipedia 2025a). Not long after the program launched, researchers discovered that the Street View cars were also using a dragnet approach to collecting names and signal strengths of various Wi-Fi networks encountered in the wild. Google was fined and claimed to have stopped doing so, but the initial collection occurred over at least four years (Farivar 2013). This, too, had very much to do with the navigational aims of the project, as this 'wardriving' practice used specialized vans to collect unique data from routers (SSID and MAC addresses) to generate more accurate location data from WiFi networks. Google later admitted having also collected some of the information transmitted through the networks if unsecured. Mobilities scholar Rowan Wilken (2019a) unpacks this through his focus on the significance of material infrastructures in mobile communication and media studies. Through his critical reading of one of Google's competitors in this sector, Skyhook Wireless, its patents, and trade press, he highlights the complex and hidden set of overlapping infrastructures that underpin and sustain mobile communication, including Wi-Fi connectivity, location-enabled mobile communication, and various signal routing systems. Skyhook Wireless thus leveraged existing registries of WiFi networks to develop location-finding systems integrated into mobile devices, exemplifying the mutual constitution of (mapping) software and everyday spatiality.

Skyhook has been greatly diminished today after refusing to share its hotspot database with Google, which in turn pressured two of its other major customers – Samsung and Motorola – to renege on their contracts. Street View, the winner, has become massively helpful to establishing Google's dominance of location-based services in general and map interfaces in particular. It is a key feature in Google's shift from car-centric to pedestrian navigation (O'Beirne 2018) and accompanying context-aware advertising, which is the company's primary revenue source. It also had an unexpected utility when tech companies began to race for autonomous vehicles – unlike its competitors, Google had a treasure trove of visual data to train its car's machine vision (Simonite 2017; McCosker and Wilken 2020).

Street View exemplifies Google Maps' – and to a lesser extent other mapping platforms' – voracious appetite for data. There's only so much one can do with aerial and satellite imagery: you need your 'ground truthing' – using precision surveying and other means to measure it all (Gil-Fournier and Parikka 2021). According to geomedia researcher Scott McQuire (2019), Google has done the above extremely well, by developing its own mapping system through combining a range of public and purchased data with its exclusive sources. While traditional public map data from authoritative sources lacks the necessary detail for advanced services like turn-by-turn driving directions, Google enhances its maps with additional data streams. These include city-level maps, aerial and satellite imagery, proprietary data from Street

View, and non-traditional public data obtained through user contributions, tracking Android phones, donated data from Waze (purchased in 2011), and Maps-specific features like the now discontinued 'Map Maker' and its limited replacement 'Report a Missing Place' (McQuire 2019, 154). Thus, various forms of crowdsourced data have become central to mapping platforms. Things that appear visually on the map are linked to a database object, and Google has to acquire more and additional types of data to facilitate the business value its map generates. This can lead to ridiculous situations when the overall aim of the map clashes with the specific places it depicts, as in the prominent ubiquitous 'review' button that was present on Google Maps for all locations up until the redesign in 2016, applied to the user-added location of Bin Laden's Abbottabad compound after the 2011 US operation to capture him (figure 3.4). To Google, things on the map are thus primarily quantifiable locations to calculate for user's various needs.

Street View is similarly becoming a more user generated content (UGC)-oriented feature. It was opened up for outsider contribution, including uploading fully realized 360-degrees

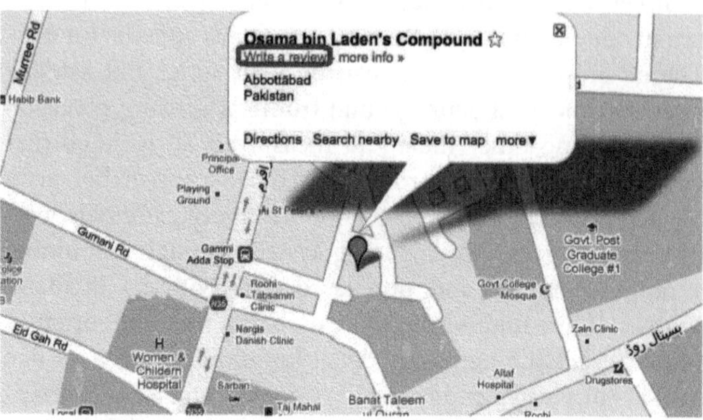

Figure 3.4: Bin Laden's compound in Pakistan, with an invitation to contribute a review. Screenshot by the author, 2011.

journeys, which up until recently was Google's prerogative alone (Google, n.d.-b). The enormous value that Street View brings to the fore is offset by the need to continuously update it (Abend 2018), least it becomes stuck in the past. Looking at the percentage of the world covered by Street View, I cannot but feel a pang of awe. Here is an idea bordering on hubris: a panoramic take on a huge swathe of public space, alongside precise mapping and measurement apparatus that supersedes any deployed historically by the most pernicious nation-state. This is the type of geo-epistemology (knowledge about the world) that erodes the boundary between representation and actuality, hinting perhaps that Google no longer *extracts* data from the world but sees it *as* data to be continuously processed and operationalized. This is a dangerous proposition since such slippage means the difference 'between knowing your neighborhood through detailed stories, a pictorial guidebook, a map, aerial photographs, the coordinates of a GPS receiver, or simply walking around. It is about trustworthy knowledge (how can I know that my world really is what I think it is?), but it is also about our everyday existence in space (how do I understand my surroundings, my mobility, my relationship to others?)' (Rankin 2016, 2).

Just like with Apple Maps' failed launch, to a mapping organization its geo-epistemology is centred around contextual location data – and the more the better. This can influence designers of digital maps to incorporate more incentives for users to provide such data. For example, map and Street View contributions have slowly evolved into the 'Local Guides' program, where users compete for points and badges to add contextual information beneficial to Google. Some people, on the other hand, reappropriate Street View into a memorial or nostalgic activity. Writing about a communal memorial art project that uses Street View, journalist Sirin Kale describes her conflicting emotions when interacting on her screen with the wall she used to lean on every day while waiting for her mother after school. Outdated imagery becomes cherished for what no longer exists, as 'Street View traps the dead and the living alike between pages of cartography, like dried flowers' (Kale 2021). After moving countries recently, I too was emotional to find an updated image of our old house on Google Maps, taken just a few weeks after our departure, and showing our old house's window depicting signs of a new family life. When looking at Google Maps' UI from the perspective of affect theory (Ash 2015), it makes sense: Street View is affected by data in the world and in turn conveys such data into human memories for specific users. But data, as the now-truism goes, is never 'raw' and should be cooked carefully (Gitelman 2013). In the case of mapping interfaces, it is done by turning data into images, selectively.

Assembling the map through algorithmic visualization

When I talk about algorithmic visualization, we need to understand both terms. Anthropologist Nick Seaver (2017) focuses on the cultural aspects of algorithms. He argues that critical scholars should approach algorithms as 'multiples', unstable objects that are enacted through the varied practices that people use to engage with them, including the practices of 'outsider' researchers. He suggests thinking of algorithms not 'in' culture, but 'as' culture: part of broad patterns of meaning and practice that can be engaged with empirically. To study algorithms one must first reject some of the mystique surrounding them, seeing them as black boxes impenetrable to an outside gaze (Bucher 2018; Christin 2020), and instead examine them simply as they are: human endeavours that attempt to create rules for complicated computerized systems (Prey 2018; Seaver 2019; Kotliar 2021). Visualization is similarly a complex notion. In a datafied world, visualization carries crucial roles of meaning-making and epistemological clarity. While often perceived as cold, rational, objective, and logical (McCosker and Wilken 2014;

McCosker 2017; Rettberg 2020), visualizations often touch upon the subjective, emotional, and affective (Drucker 2011; Niccolini 2018; Stark 2018; Kennedy and Engebretsen 2020).

Just think of the intimate link that develops with the notifications on one's phone (a data visualization of missed activity) or with various self-tracking technologies. Mapping overall is a form of data visualization and always involves selection and omission (Monmonier 2018; Krygier and Wood 2005). You simply cannot fit all the pesky details of the world onto a page. So, cartographers developed shorthands and compromises, such as showing dots instead of sprawling cities or smoothing out contours of natural phenomena for better legibility. Digital mapping does that, all the time, for each individual user. Thousands of decision points are built into every session with a map. Something as trivial as a screen size or browser selection can influence the contours of the map and thus affect which points of interest (POIs) or area names will be visible (figure 3.5).

Thus, digital mapping is a form of data visualization that changes contextually with their users. Interface scholar Alexander Galloway sees such visualizations as rooted more in the unrepresentable aesthetics of abstract numerical data rather than in any specific design rules and claims that 'any data visualization is first and foremost a visualization of the conversion rules themselves, and only secondarily a visualization of the raw data' (Galloway 2012, 83). Each mapping interface can therefore be seen primarily as a visualization of how and for what purposes its data was collected, and – through it – the kind of actions the map allows in the world. Consider, for instance, the extremely accurate maps produced by the Soviets between the 1950s and 1990s, of major global cities, much more accurate than anything produced in the West (Davies and Kent 2017). Aided by their new ability to use satellite imagery and an extensive spying network, Russia has created maps that would potentially allow extremely accurate manoeuvres for its military, had it the need to invade said

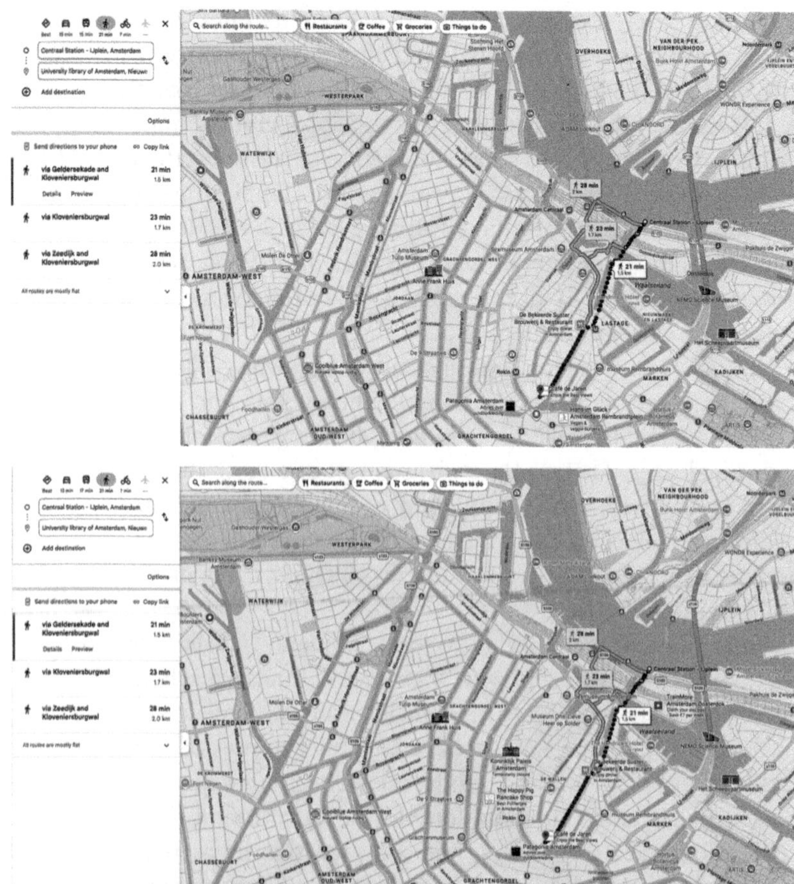

Figure 3.5: A side-by-side comparison of the same walking route request on the same laptop but from two different web browsers (Firefox, Chrome) in private/anonymous window to prevent existing user's data influencing the selection. Note the slight discrepancies: for example, the Royal Palace (Koninklijk Paleis) is only visible in the bottom image, whereas the top image features a sponsored (square) POI marker for a burger shop just below the arrival point.

cities. The maps include such seemingly trivial details as tree density in suburban areas. Trivial, that is, until you consider the need to know whether certain routes would accommodate an armoured column while others would not.

Moving with maps today is increasingly dependent on translating complex-yet-limited data collected by the mapping platform into a version of the world, uniquely tailored for the user's needs – or at the very least how they are understood through its data and algorithm schemas (Seaver 2015). This highly personalized version of the world changes our relations with it. Media scholar Chris Chesher (2012) elaborates this through a comparison of navigation in third-person computer games with that by means of a GPS (satnav) device, pointing out how both systems re-structure social space. He lists three distinct ways in which those sociotechnical spaces are similarly structured: first, by displacing ad hoc navigational practices with concrete instructions; then, by creating a subject-oriented (egocentric) consumption space where desires are gratified almost immediately through alignment of the personal point-of-view with that of the mapped world; finally, by presenting a complex information overlay on top of the mapped view (which I referred to as *map layering* in the previous chapter). Empirical experimental research around map use has similarly shown that participants' navigational habits in physical spaces do indeed correlate with their in-game behaviour, proving the transferability of digital and physical navigational perceptions, provided that they are presented through similar goal-oriented interfaces (Lange et al. 2015). As an example for how these perceptions operate in practice, let's examine algorithmic visualization central to the production of contemporary movement, by using a brief event from my own map use.

In this auto-ethnographic description, I found myself in a situation where I needed to do some grocery shopping in the Dutch city of Utrecht and sought the help of a colleague. We planned to meet at a local supermarket, and I initially suggested the nearest one that came to mind. However, just before leaving, I realized there might be another store closer to me (in the exact opposite direction). To determine the closest option, I queried Google Maps, which quickly loaded and displayed my location as a blue circle amidst three red dots representing the nearby supermarkets. Despite two options appearing to be roughly equidistant from me, the map couldn't provide a clear indication of the quickest route due to the complex layout of Utrecht's medieval centre.

I further explored the mapping interface, requesting travel time and distance for each supermarket. The map presented tentative walking paths marked by blue lines, along with estimated travel times. However, the results showed no significant difference in distance or time between the two supermarkets. It was at this point that I realized my actions were far from the self-reflexive conduct I advocated in my own academic work on maps. Additionally, I realized I was already running late for my planned meeting.

Reflecting on the situation, the map created a cartographic illusion (Ingold 2000) by compressing space and time into an algorithmically adjusted output, making the *potential* routes appear as *actual* options. This illusion arose from my focus on the map's direct output, leading me to confuse the represented landscape with the actual space. Although professionally critical of maps, I found myself substituting my own understanding of the world with the quantifiable and relational qualities provided by the mapping interface. Metrics played a decisive role in this. The map's seemingly accurate and immediate depiction of available actions in the world ('7 minutes walking') was superimposed on my perception, removing local knowledge of potentially annoying routes or busy intersections. The map took over.

To summarize this section, algorithmic visualization is central in how we move in the world through our maps. All the data continuously collected to populate mapping databases (as detailed in the previous section of the chapter) would remain inert and meaningless were it not presented to users in the ways described above. Such techniques further strengthen the cartographic illusion and lead us to confuse the map with the territory, as '[c]rucially, the map's capacity to build allies derives precisely from making absent all the work that goes into the map's crafting as a coherent account of mobility' (Ruppert and Scheel 2019, 249).

I outline in table 3.1 some of the key differences I see with the rise of algorithmic visualization interfaces for movement.[2] A necessary caveat is that I cannot (and I do not want to) have this as a totalizing claim over *all* mobility implementations, nor that this will affect each user similarly, as this negates my entire claim in the first chapter regarding the processual view of cartography. For example, a tourist map printed in a specific location could also have an egocentric orientation ('you are here, facing this way'). Rather, this is a rule-of-thumb approach to the visual component of maps that get you from A to B, such as navigation apps (e.g., Waze) and satnavs, certain public transport planners (e.g., CityMapper), and the courier- or driver-facing map interfaces of most popular gig economy apps (e.g., Deliveroo). The central difference is the orientation: new maps orient the world according to you (egocentric, 'turn right') as opposed to an external referent (allocentric, 'go east'). By doing so they shift the frame through which one perceives one's environment to one of consumption (Chesher 2012), as the world is presented as a personal resource to exploit.

New maps do not describe the world how it is, but prescribe how you should act upon it (Rankin 2016) – or shifting from geography, the description of world, to chorography, the description of place (Della Dora 2012). This also makes

Table 3.1: Comparing algorithmic visualization interfaces to older maps.

Traditional Maps	Maps Using Algorithmic Visualization
Allocentric	Egocentric
Descriptive (this is here)	Prescriptive (go there)
Draining resources	Cognitive labourer
Frictional	Frictionless
Hard to use, harder to master	Easy to use, mastery varying

the experience of using each type of map very different. The first requires you to continuously question it, orient yourself based on some external coordinates, and plan accordingly – overall draining you mentally. The other creates 'cognitive machinery' (Hayles 2002, 302) that augments the mind and does (some of the) work for you, for example through automatic orientation of the map or the calculation of remaining travel time. Note that this does not necessarily result in smoother or easier journeys – just see my own paralysed indecision in the face of two equidistant supermarkets – but rather what in the language of UX can be described as 'friction', or the propensity of certain interfaces to pause continuous interaction, or not (Ash, Anderson, et al. 2018). Ultimately, the main difference might result in the learning curve: while traditional maps were hard to use and harder to master (hope you have a compass handy), new maps are generally much easier to use. However, their simplicity is deceiving, as by taking increased agency, they might make the user more prone to mistakes and ultimately to more hazardous journeys, as described in the introduction to this book in the 'death by GPS' story.

Tying it together: Mobileye's transformation into a mapping platform

In the penultimate section of this chapter, I wish to return to Robert Moses and his bridges. Specifically, the relation between his imagined future of the car as a driver (pun not intended) of middle-class lifestyle, and his decision to plan (through maps!) Jones Beach around the parkways which conveyed rustic idyll onto the approaching drivers. Today, the car is no longer necessarily seen positively, but it still has much of the utopian imaginary expressed by Moses and his contemporaries. Particularly, this comes as part of the effort to build completely autonomous vehicles, and the role of mapping technologies in that process (Wilken and Thomas 2019).

The introduction of software and network-based media into the daily lives of users changes the way space is consumed and experienced (de Souza e Silva 2006; Kitchin and Dodge 2011). For drivers, this alters what Nigel Thrift (2004a, 2004b), via Patricia T. Clough, has called the 'technological unconscious'. The consolidation of digital screens, mapping software, and car manufacturing further changes the political economy of driving. The data streams coming from the hybridization of media-aided navigation and actual movement lead to the merger of the map and the territory, or rather the creation of a single entity called map-territory, which occupies a single ontological plane (Hind and Gekker 2019). This is not only a philosophical conjecture, but a very present one. Consider, for instance, how a driver who uses a navigational app participates in a technological assemblage that includes other similar drivers, all linking into behind-the-scenes algorithmic controls that continuously reroute traffic (Coletta and Kitchin 2017). Thus, drivers and pedestrians who are *not* part of (or even aware of) that particular app become influenced by it as 'collateral damage', often through imposing urban dashboards that operate at the precipice of public and private data (Mattern 2021a).

Thus, the car itself is becoming a central player in the world of mapping. The aforementioned Waze – one of the first popular driving apps – was instrumental in such transformation, enabling the imbrication of driving with mapping (Hind and Gekker 2014) and an actor in the governance of urban spaces (van der Graaf and Ballon 2019; Fisher 2022). And if initially it was the human-in-the-loop that participated in the mapping *through* the car, even this is beginning to change.

More recent developments in sensor systems, machine vision, computer chip design, and data processing have led to greater capacities for cars to recognize objects in the world and act upon them (Stilgoe 2017; Hind 2019; McCosker and Wilken 2020; Hind et al. 2022). Major corporate players

– both traditional car manufacturers and newcomers from the technology sector – have tested experimental vehicles on the streets in different parts of the world, from San Francisco to Beijing. Evangelists claim the autonomous vehicle to be the imminent teleological end-point of contemporary automobility, despite the persistent errors, incidents, and accidents that have placed significant doubt in their decision-making abilities (Bissell 2018). As Tennant and Stilgoe (2021) consider, different kinds of actors (such as software engineers, regulators, start-up CEOs, tech investors) see different 'problems', 'limits', or 'solutions', whether related to data collection, computer modelling, or environmental complexity. In this they can be positioned alongside similar wishful technological discourses around the Internet-of-Things (IoT) or smart cities more broadly (Ash 2018; Sadowski and Bendor 2019) that have likewise envisioned a seamless, automated, future with varying degrees of success.

Those investing in a fully autonomous future typically originate from the technology sector, such as Alphabet's Waymo, Uber ATG (now Aurora), or Tesla. Traditional automakers have also collaborated with technology companies working on stand-alone AVs, such as with General Motors and Honda's acquisition of Cruise (Thielman 2016) or Ford and Volkswagen's joint investment in Argo AI (Lawler 2020). Dedicated start-ups offering autonomous driving for specialized purposes such as taxi fleets, long-haul lorries, or urban delivery have also been founded primarily by ex-employees of major tech firms, including Aurora (co-founded by former Waymo CTO Chris Urmsom) or Kodiak (co-founded by former Google software lead, Don Burnette). In parallel, Chinese companies, such as AutoX, PonyAI, or Didi Chuxing, are following similar trajectories, even competing in machine vision challenges organized by Western counterparts such as Waymo (Zhang et al. 2021).

While all the above differ in their specific approach, they nonetheless imagine the vehicle as a new class of mobile media platform (Alvarez León 2019), able to collect and process data captured from external reality. In building (or significantly modifying) specialized vehicles, such data is used to train machine learning algorithms to recognize, and categorize, other road users. In concert with high-performance computer chips that enable real-time recognition, this entire software package ultimately becomes the 'brains' of the autonomous vehicle (Hawkins 2018). This software-led approach is already in evidence in ordinary vehicles, with the likes of Tesla and BMW releasing periodic 'over-the-air' (OTA) updates that 'unlock' additional capacities for existing cars (Halder et al. 2020).

A different approach is taken by the Israeli company Mobileye, founded in 1999 as an advanced driving assist system (ADAS) manufacturer. Typical features of ADAS include lane departure warning (LDW) and forward collision warning (FDW) systems able to alert drivers to imminent dangers. While similarly employing some purpose-built AVs, in collaboration with industry leaders such as Ford and Volkswagen (primarily as prototypes for future 'Robotaxi' deployment), Mobileye aims to achieve autonomous driving through its traditional business model of manufacturing ADAS that it claims are installed in over 200 million vehicles across fifty automaker partners (Mobileye 2022; n.d.-b). The company practises platformization (Helmond 2015; Nieborg and Poell 2018) rarely seen outside the web: its focus is on hardware, designing cameras, sensors, silicon chips, and consumer-facing physical user interfaces that provide incremental assistance to drivers, intending to 'substantially reduce fatalities and serious injuries, at a reasonable cost, while sustaining the usefulness and throughput of the road system' (Shalev-Shwartz et al. 2018a, 1).

It is this incremental approach that allows them to harness and operationalize huge amounts of driving data, further advancing their nascent platform position (Hind and Gekker 2022). Mobileye's EyeQ 'system-on-a-chip', for example, is designed to provide the computational capacity required to process huge volumes of data generated by their ADAS devices (Hawkins 2022a), striking deals with automotive OEMs (original equipment manufacturers) to access it (Korosec 2022). Its partnership with Chinese automaker Geely is intended to offer the full package of Mobileye hardware in a fully autonomous vehicle (Hawkins 2022b; Kang 2024). Combined, these technological developments in sensing, computation, and data collection have the potential to both significantly transform the automotive industry, and challenge navigational conceptions of mapping: creating maps by cars for cars (Miller 2014).

Central to this strategy is a high-definition mapping database called road experience management (REM), able to collect granular data on everything from traffic lights and curb edges to typical vehicle speeds. Rather than relying on cartographic data derived from sensor-laden vehicles, or 'dedicated mapping fleets' (Mobileye, n.d.-a), such as the Google Street View vehicles, the firm crowdsources data from Mobileye device-equipped vehicles. With coverage across private and commercial fleet markets, Mobileye claims over 60 million vehicles are equipped with Mobileye technology largely able to 'automatically collect anonymous data from the road' as users drive (Mobileye, n.d.-b). CEO Amnon Shashua further claimed that Mobileye holds the 'largest driving database in the industry', with 200PB in total, receiving 25 kilometres of data every day for a total of four billion kilometres in 2021 and an expected nine billion in 2022 (Mobileye 2022).

Mobileye aims to distinguish itself from other AV developers. Through its crowdsourcing of user data, REM is referred to as 'scalable-by-design' (Mobileye, n.d.-a) as compared to the cost of maintaining and operating a dedicated mapping fleet. Although rivals such as Waymo and Aurora have access to both dedicated fleets and user-derived sources (i.e., from Android mobile devices or Uber trips), Mobileye contends that a dedicated-fleet-led approach will result in a 'winter of autonomous driving' (Shalev-Shwartz et al. 2018b, 1) akin to earlier 'AI winters' defined by a lack of technological progress. In contrast, Mobileye's experience of building ADAS devices has enabled it to amass 'millions of harvesting agents' (Mobileye, n.d.-a) generating road data 'in every relevant region' (Intel Newsroom 2021). REM does not require full autonomy and is already built into the advanced version of Mobileye's ADAS (known as 'Level 2+'). As Shashua elaborates, REM is not a static system, instead employing OTA updates to upgrade existing functionalities and enable cloud-based uploads of REM data. In doing so, Mobileye has decentralized data collection necessary for training machine learning models, enrolling these third parties into ordinary business operations, separating data collection from data processing, and enabling scalability.

It has also used REM data 'to generalize traffic rules and driving culture' (Intel Newsroom 2021), important to establish detailed semantic understanding of how people usually drive. This crowdsourcing allows Mobileye to make associations between vehicles and road elements (traffic lights, yield and stop signs, zebra crossing locations), and non-sign-based rules like lane priority. As Shashua argues, the REM database is not a 'replacement of a navigation map' but is the 'high-resolution information that allows the car to interpret the road' (Mobileye 2022). In this, the database does not merely contain data on road types, lane dimensions, and junction layouts but of road *experiences* generated on, along, and through them. Such data becomes crucial in the ongoing merger of map-territory, and the automation of movement through and with maps.

Conclusion: From navigation to being led

This chapter has traced the evolution of mapping from a tool for understanding locations to a technology for moving through them without necessarily understanding them: 'Being glib, one could say that with representation the goal is to know about a place without having to visit. With technologies like GPS, the goal is instead to visit a place without having to know much about it' (Rankin 2016, 3). Through examining the transformation of data collection practices, algorithmic visualization, and the emergence of CAVs, we see how digital maps have fundamentally altered the relationship between movement and spatial knowledge.

The Mobileye case study exemplifies this transformation most clearly. What began as a company producing driver assistance systems has evolved into a mapping platform that treats the quotidian action of its users in the world as a data source. Through its REM system, Mobileye has effectively turned every equipped vehicle into a mapping agent, collecting granular data about road conditions rather than merely locations. This represents the culmination of trends identified throughout the chapter: the shift from allocentric to egocentric orientation, from descriptive to prescriptive mapping, and from occasional to continuous data collection. Yet this transformation raises profound questions about agency and autonomy. As mapping technologies become increasingly sophisticated at predicting and directing movement, they simultaneously reduce the need for local knowledge and spatial literacy, altering our geo-epistemology. The cartographic illusion identified in my auto-ethnographic encounter with Utrecht's supermarkets via Google Maps reveals how algorithmic visualization can paralyse rather than empower decision-making. When maps become too helpful, they risk creating dependencies that leave users vulnerable when systems fail or when the map's assumptions about optimal movement clash with lived spatial realities.

The progression from Robert Moses' bridges to Mobileye's crowdsourced mapping database illustrates how the politics of mobility have become embedded within increasingly opaque technological systems. Where Moses' vision was at least visible in concrete and steel, today's mobility politics operate through algorithms and data flows that remain largely invisible to users. The car, once imagined as a technology of individual freedom, has become a node in vast data collection networks that enable new forms of surveillance and control, which I will address more fully in chapter 6 of this book.

This evolution further challenges traditional cartographic theories that position mapmakers and map users as distinct categories. In the contemporary mapping ecosystem, every movement generates data that feeds back into the mapping platform, making users unwitting cartographers of their own spatial experiences. The double-tap mode identified by Hind and Lammes reveals how users actively participate in the continuous production of mapping realities, even as they experience maps as finished products. Looking forward, the implications extend beyond individual navigation choices to broader questions of urban governance and spatial justice. As mapping platforms accumulate more granular data about movement patterns, they gain unprecedented power to shape urban flows and, by extension, the social and economic life of cities (Barns 2020). The risk is not merely technological domination in Winner's sense, but something more subtle and pervasive: the gradual replacement of embodied spatial knowledge with platform-mediated spatial prompts. In the same way that social media have gradually rewritten the rules of our social spaces, digital mapping might do the same to our physical ones.

The challenge for critical cartographic and media scholarship is to maintain analytical clarity about these transformations whilst acknowledging their genuine benefits. Early studies show that increased practice with social media leads to greater algorithmic literacy (Oeldorf-Hirsch and Neubaum 2025). Perhaps, becoming proficient with digital maps will (partially) inoculate their users from their cartographic illusions. Digital mapping technologies have democratized access to spatial information and enabled new forms of mobility for many users. The task is not to reject these technologies wholesale but to understand how they reshape the fundamental relationship between knowledge, movement, and place. As we move through increasingly mapped worlds, the question becomes not whether we can navigate without digital assistance, but whether we can navigate with it whilst retaining some measure of spatial agency and critical self-awareness.

In the next chapter, we turn to examine how these dynamics of movement and data collection combine with digital maps' playful nature, becoming enmeshed in 'ludic capitalism' of spatial production and consumption.

4
Play

In July 2016, *Pokémon Go*, a mobile game by Niantic, launched to great fanfare. Amassing 500 million downloads by the end of that year (Gilbert 2016), it was uncharacteristically praised by educators and health professionals, due to its embodied nature. Replicating the classic Pokémon games formula, which focuses on capturing a catalogue of imaginary critters in different locales, players were required to walk around their physical surroundings, using their phones as augmented reality devices that overlaid the game world on top of the mapped environment (figure 4.1).

A central appeal made to the players of the game was one of verisimilitude: the very streets you walk on your daily commute, or the alley behind your house, can become a magical parallel reality where you are a Pokémon Trainer, trying to 'catch 'em all!'. The colour scheme and visuals of the map are similarly reminiscent of the bright geometric maps of classic Pokémon games beginning with the Nintendo Gameboy era and onwards to each new iteration of the company's gaming consoles (Wikipedia 2025c). The player's oversized avatar is strolling through styled landscapes, with green fields and blue waters representing the players' real environment to a certain extent and affecting their gameplay as well: each in-game biome is more conducive to the capture of a certain type of critter. The maps are very accurate, not in the least due to Niantic's special relationship with Google and its massive geospatial database (more on this below) which enabled an accurate real-time import of the world's physical layout into the game (Apperley and Moore 2019; Leorke

Figure 4.1: A screenshot of my own Pokémon Go gameplay, August 2016. Because I am walking on a footpath which does not appear on Google Maps, it appears as if I am walking in the field. In actuality, I am approaching an airport.

2019). Yet, the map lies, albeit in a fun and playful manner; in the screenshot in figure 4.1, I am seemingly walking through a rolling green field, when I am in fact approaching an airport (notice the arc of the access road outlining the terminal). The game converts most urban areas into a variation of rural ones, highlighting the clash between the idyllic nature of the game's imagined world and the underlying realities of its Earth infrastructure, one relying on urban presence of multiple players in tightly knit locations (Colley et al. 2017). *Pokémon Go* lies through its map – and gets away with it – because it is 'merely a game'.

If previous chapters have established digital maps' ongoing claims to seriousness, often through (perceived) objectivity gained through data extraction, this one explores their playful nature. To be sure, those are not exclusionary or even contradictory characteristics. In fact, I will show throughout the chapter how play and fun are key to the domestication of digital cartography; and how it is often through their playful aspect that they become depoliticized. Simply put, digital maps are using playful design to hide – intentionally or not – the serious things that they do. The chapter first outlines what I mean by 'playful', through engagement with play scholarship, particularly as it relates to digital maps. Then, I will dive deeper into games and their co-evolution with mapping, which I will exemplify through the case study of *Pokémon Go*. Subsequently, I will discuss cartographic play in everyday media, showing how social media are using maps to facilitate placemaking, while digital maps add social, playful, and placemaking components to its previously utilitarian offer. Finally, I will conclude by considering what kind of power structures arise at the intersection of maps and play and how they foreshadow the implications for work and surveillance discussed in the next two chapters.

Play and playfulness with and through maps

In their introduction to a co-edited collection on play and maps, Chris Perkins and Sybille Lammes (2016) declare that the relationship between mapping and play is rather strong. To them, play can be more than just a heuristic lens – it can transform mapping practices by adding experimentation and chance into it, particularly evident with the digitalization of maps. They list video games and 'fun' elements like celebrity voices in GPS navigation, alongside a longer history of treasure hunts and geocaching. Yet, they note, despite strong connections, play is still infrequently investigated in mapping research, often because of its seeming opposition to maps' aura of rationality and scientific objectivity. To them, however, playing and mapping are co-constitutive as forms of active experimentation, intersecting, and 'often legitimizing each other's existence' (Lammes and Perkins 2016, 12).

To fully appreciate the statement, we must define what play is (and, perhaps more importantly, what it is *not*). But therein lies the problem. The scope of this chapter – or of this book for that matter – would not allow me to fully commit to unpacking play. It is a fascinating and multifaceted cultural phenomenon that entails various activities – from sports to make-believe to competition. It is also always at risk of becoming a catch-all term, covering everything and nothing. If play is pervasive and undefined, it loses its analytical meaning. In my work, following Lammes and Perkins, I always tried to look at play as an *outcome of a process* on the one hand, and as *a method* on the other. By that, I mean that it requires distinguishing between play as *something that is present in the world* through a series of actions performed by humans and other things, and play *as a mode of thinking* to challenge existing epistemologies (Lammes et al. 2016). Elsewhere, I have tackled play as pertaining resistance to participation (Gekker 2018), political campaigning (Gekker 2019), TikTok's affordance for propaganda (Vijay and Gekker 2021), or world-building of the QAnon conspiracy movement (De Zeeuw and Gekker 2023). In this chapter, I'd like to focus entirely on its relation to digital (mapping) software, particularly as a form of enacting engagement. To start, let us conduct an extremely brief review of pre-digital foundational scholarship on play.

The origins of contemporary play studies lie in the works of Johan Huizinga, a Dutch historian who wrote his magnum opus *Homo Ludens* (Huizinga 1970) in 1938, which was subsequently translated into English and became a foundational work on play in/of culture.[1] In it, he defines play as bounded and reserved, something separated from real life and thus able to allow for a temporal suspension of existing societal norms, yet bound by strict rules. Roger Caillois's *Man, Play and Games* (Caillois and Barash 1961) that came out a decade later refuted Huizinga's assertion by pointing, for instance, to the prevalence of gambling or professional sports in play activities. Caillois offered a structuralist approach to play that covered a spectrum between structured (*ludus*) and free (*paidia*) activities, across four distinct categories: competitions, chance or luck, simulation (which included theatrical performances), and vertigo (which covered a range of 'intoxicating' forms of play from horse riding to children spinning in place).

A third key pre-digital approach that I will incorporate is that of Brian Sutton-Smith (1997), which became particularly popular in the game makers community through an abbreviated reprint published in a designer-oriented theory book by MIT Press (Sutton-Smith 2005). As opposed to the previous two approaches, Sutton-Smith argues that play should not be categorized according to types of activities, but rather as forms of speech – what he calls *rhetorics*. The same playful activity can be viewed from different angles, depending on the specific rhetoric used to culturally associate play with certain aspects of society or culture. Thus, seeing children play football on the street might be used in the rhetoric of *play as progress*, where play is seen as developmental and enriching; but also, and opposite, by evoking the rhetoric of *play as frivolity*, associating it with unseriousness and wasting time. He names seven such rhetorics and shows how they are applied across different domains and activities. The key takeaway from this is to recognize that – like mapping – play can be deployed strategically by various actors to make claims about the world. They do so particularly well through enrolling play into digital objects and their interfaces.

As I claimed in chapter 2, casual power lies in extrapolating the logic of ludic capitalism to look at the intertwining of familiarity and uniqueness in designing maps for experiences. Understanding the way maps capture the attention of their audience calls for further examination of play and the ramifications for playing *on* and *with* the map's interface.

This approach focuses on a specific type of play, one that can be found in contemporary digital games and their player communities. Proponents of this approach say that digital games generate meaning through an emergent interaction between the rules codified by the designers and the ensuing action of the players. Moreover, such rule-bound meaning-making – *proceduralism* – is seen as a new form of rhetorical argumentation, different from other traditional forms of persuasion as text or images (Bogost 2006; 2007; 2011a). All the while, others criticize it for being overly simplistic and deterministic, failing to recognize the unique personal properties that may change the meaning embedded in the rules by virtue of a resistant reading recognized in such cultural studies traditions as the Birmingham School (Sicart 2011). Such forms of 'gamification' have become in certain circles synonymous with exploitation and disempowerment (Woodcock and Johnson 2018).

Nonetheless, both proponents and critics of this particular interpretation of play tend to draw parallels between rule-bound meaning-making in computer games to broader computer-infused modes of living where software and algorithms have increasingly dominant roles. In his breakdown of the different ways various aspects of play are discussed in contemporary discourse, designer and media scholar Sebastian Deterding calls this approach – after Sutton-Smith – 'the rhetoric of systems' (Deterding 2015). Building on Kitchin and Dodge's (2011) work on co-constructing spaces through software, he claims that 'today's code/space is the basic technological precondition for deploying algorithmic game(like) systems beyond the confines of a single gaming device and software ... Several authors have in fact argued that computers and games show such deep structural similarities, that computerization equals gamification' (Deterding 2015, 33).

Philosopher and designer Miguel Sicart (2014) offers a dissenting view on play, breaking away from formalist definitions. He attempts to re-introduce the concept beyond rule-bound game systems while keeping it as a viable operational term for the purposes of analysis. To him, play is a mode of human activity, a mode of being in the world and with the world. Play is not bound to any particular object nor does it emerge from games with fixed rule systems. Sicart's point of departure, in fact, is not games but toys, citing the wonder and creativity they evoke in children and adults alike. For him, play transforms intended activities into others – not related to the player's original goal.

This conceptualization is built upon several components. Sicart's play is *contextual*, often dependent on environmental cues embedded in (and I would say afforded by) the objects or environments facilitating play. A video-game console controller is a cue for play, but so is a football or a carnival mask. This means that play is also *carnivalesque*, in the tradition of Bakhtin (1968), who identified the need for controlled breaks of chaos in order to maintain order over time. Play is also *appropriative*. It is a mode of being that borrows from other modes, as well as taking over existing spaces and social occurrences. An office is designed for non-play, a space focused on productivity, but can nonetheless support various forms of play, superseding and sometimes even supplementing work (Mainemelis and Ronson 2006). Play is therefore *disruptive*, as when it appropriates, it often alters whatever is appropriated, for better or worse. Certain types of behaviour of sports fans at stadiums are not considered acceptable in most other situations, nor do they have anything to do with the rules of the game being played. Play is *autotelic*, pursuing a purpose disconnected from other activities. This purpose is not fixed and the negotiation of the purpose of play constitutes an integral part of such activity. Consequently, play is *creative*, requiring players to negotiate rules, appropriating contexts and skilfully disrupting life around them. And finally, play is *personal*: while often generally conceived as a group activity, the player is immersed within her own morals, ethics, and memories; play is defined against our own goals, victories, and defeats. Overall, '[p]lay is being in the world, through objects, towards others. We play not to entertain ourselves or to learn or to be alienated: we play to be, and play gives us, through its characteristics, the possibility of being' (Sicart 2014, 18).

This definition, and specifically the evocation of objects as conduits for play, brings to the fore an important distinction for discussing mapping interfaces: between *play* and *playfulness*. While often conflated, the two are quite different, since

> play is an activity, while playfulness is an attitude. An activity is a finite and coherent set of actions performed for certain purposes, while an attitude is a stance toward an activity – a psychological, physical, and emotional perspective we take on activities, people, and objects. In this sense, playfulness is projecting some of the characteristics of play into nonplay activities. It is an attempt to engage with the world in the mode of being of play but not playing (Sicart 2014, 22).

This distinction will be useful when analysing playful interface designs. Games are the medium of play, but components or elements associated with games are now to be found in other media. Through a designer's action, a digital object can be imbued with *game-like* properties as to be *playful*. This, however, does not mean that this object was created for play or designed with play in mind. Instead, it can enable even the most serious of tasks with playfulness through play's appropriation, giving an ability to see beyond the mundane, useful, accepted uses of objects and spaces, rejecting fixity and *reambiguating* the world. It disrupts existing contexts and injects play into non-play places. To Sicart, this is particularly evident when examining software objects – not necessarily video games – which can act as 'playthings' (Sicart 2022), where new material forms of play emerge ontologically through practices such as coding and using software.

Before examining what this means for maps, I want to bring one last definition of play into the mix. Or, more specifically, a meta-definition. In their review of articles from various disciplines published between 2014 to 2019, Masek and Stenros (2021) have collected 346 papers and book chapters that included the definition of 'playfulness'. They then divide them not according to disciplines or methodologies but based on the types of engagement one envisions the player doing. This is both reminiscent of Sicart's distinction between activity and attitude, while also maintaining some of Sutton-Smith's and Deterding's approaches to rhetorics of play. Distilling all six main themes of their meta-analysis, they propose that despite the differences, a common thread can be summarized: 'Playfulness prioritizes *engagement* over external consequence, realness, or convention' (Masek and Stenros 2021, 23, emphasis added). It is with this definition in mind that we turn to a specific type of playing with maps: one through games.

The shared origins of digital gaming and mapping

The following section explores in concrete terms how mapping has been intertwined with the rise of video games for a particular form of play. It exemplifies this relation through the chief case study of Niantic's widely popular map-based location game *Pokémon Go*. As discussed previously, maps have been instrumental for navigation, trade, and conquest since the early renaissance era (Crampton 2001; Crampton and Krygier 2005). The complete, and culturally implicit, proliferation of the map as a 'representation' of physical space has, unsurprisingly, ensured its adoption by video-game designers for similar purposes in their fictional worlds. If all mapping is playful to some extent (Playful Mapping Collective 2016), then nowhere is this link more substantial than in the daily encounters of millions of users with imagined spaces on the screens of personal computers and games consoles. Therefore, to understand how play is present in the real-world digital application of quotidian mapping interfaces, we must first understand their enmeshed relationships with video games.

Video games, which are particularly potent interfaces for engaging and capturing the attention of their users, have drastically changed the relation between play and maps. Injecting mapping with play opens new possibilities (Perkins 2009b) but might close others, in line with the principles of appropriation and personalization of play advocated by Sicart. If play is foremost a *focused engagement*, and mapping is an *emergent and processual practice*, play can be subverted in order to facilitate certain ways of being in the world that benefit the mapmaker rather than the map user. This is done by occluding and enhancing certain elements of the map's digital user interface. In the case of many location-based games, the distinction between map and game board essentially disappears (de Souza e Silva and Hjorth 2009; Lammes 2011). In non-game maps, the same techniques can be used to reambiguate the world and change users' perceptions of it.

One interesting way to examine this is through the research done on video games and game development, particularly by following Ash (2010; 2012; 2015) in recognizing games' interface as an experiential spatiotemporal effect rather than one of informatics. As games ethnographer Casey O'Donnell (2012) points out, this industry is often conflated with the software industry, but this is a misguided notion. Game developers build software intended for artists and designers to create interactive experiences for gamers. Game interfaces are renowned for guiding those experiences for users, immersing them in processual engagement. Here again I return to the 'balancing act' of casual power: the inscription of affordances that make a digital object feel both familiar and exciting, to evoke repeated use. O'Donnell offers a solution to such a predicament: turning the learning and retraining process into something that is compelling in itself. He notes how video game designers excel at introducing new elements into the user interface, game mechanics, and progression systems of video games, turning the process of failure into an integral and fun part of experiencing the game (Juul 2013). This learning-as-fun, or the introduction of intrinsic motivation to the learning process, has long been hailed as the main potential of games in more 'serious' domains such as education, healthcare, and the corporate world (Abt 2002; Michael and Chen 2005; McGonigal 2011).[2]

For maps, this means that mapmaking has become more open than ever before, allowing for changes in how maps look and behave throughout its entire product cycle. This affords the introduction of elements that evoke a sense of playfulness as a mode of experiencing for the sake of engagement, disconnected from broader user goals (Masek and Stenros 2021). In other words, this makes it easier to design them for the attention economy in a way that evokes 'getting lost in the map' for users. Again, I wish to stress that this is not a necessary effect, and that it would be a generalization to assert some linear process of design-inscription-reaction. However, as I will show in my case study of Niantic, attention is harnessed in a way not dissimilar to how Ash's (2015) video-game interface envelopes affect users' spatiotemporal perception and for analogous economic purposes. This is evident by briefly tracing how video games historically represented space that culminated in *Pokémon Go*.

In the classic staple of early web culture Homestar Runner, the Flash-based video-game spoof *Thy Dungeonman* makes fun of the primordial video game: the text-based adventure. Simulating, on a screen-within-a-screen, the greenish glow of 1980s CRT monitors, the game presents to the player the snippet shown in figure 4.2.

'YOU ARE THY DUNGEONMAN!' the screen gleefully exclaims 'Ye find yeself in yon dungeon. Ye see a SCROLL. Behind ye SCROLL is a FLASK.' Here the game uses block letters to highlight potentially interactive objects, in a way that later html conventions would use blue underlined text as links (Landow 2006). The game ends with indication of how

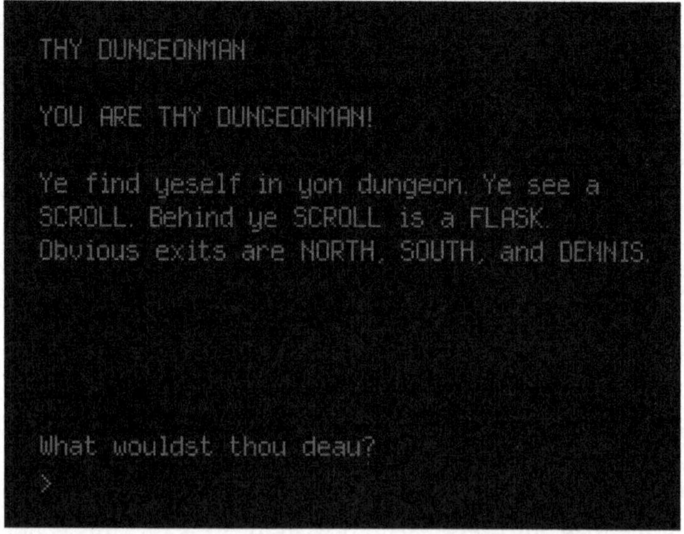

Figure 4.2: An introductory screen from the 'Thy Dungeonman', a Flash-powered parody of early 1980s text adventures. Screenshot by the author, 2016.

to traverse into the next possible area of the game (referred to as 'rooms' in early video-game parlance, but currently more associated with 'levels'), before prompting the player for action: 'Obvious exits are NORTH, SOUTH and DENNIS.'

Parodying many things, from the gaming community's fascination with High Fantasy settings and dungeons, to the common – and often inaccurate – evocation of Middle English for 'realism', the game's starting screen provides a good indication of the change maps made in later games. An inherently spatial medium (Jenkins 2004), early games lacked the necessary visual components and thus relied on text to evoke one. Like the prototypical Zork (released in 1980), text adventures often left the players wandering never-ending textual screens through typing commands like 'go north', 'enter house', 'cross stream', etc. *Thy Dungeonman* evokes an immediate sense of abstract absurdity through the addition of a third option to the possible exists: North, South, and Dennis.[3] Ironically, 'Dennis' arguably has as much of a right to exist on this list of cardinal directions as North and South. Hailing from an artificial world, and one without any graphical representation, *Thy Dungeonman*'s orientation is moored in non-diegetic indexicality, different from our own history of navigation and movement. The lack of a map renders the directionality unlinked from any common coordinate system. North and South are referential to our physical world with its magnetic poles and the curvature of the globe. In the world of *Thy Dungeonman*, and the early text games it parodies, there is no such reference, and the transition between various areas exists only as pointers in the code. Thus, the later introduction of maps into games helped cement the symbolic copying of the spatiality from our world to that of the game.

In his rundown of video-games history, Frans Mäyrä (2008) notes how the introduction of world-building graphics into games came in the form of top-down ASCII symbols maps. Those types of games bridged the gap between text-only depictions and graphical representation of space by using the limited resources available to computers of the time to evoke familiar mapping tropes from the real world, integrating elements such as legends and generalization. Thus, the progenitor of the genre, A.I. Design's 1980 *Rogue* used symbols that already existed on the computer to draw a map and populate it with various beasts and treasures (figure 4.3) in what came to be known as 'rogue-like' games. From this point on in early video-game history, the map slowly became a staple of video games' rising complexity and narrative-building ambitions, exemplified in the inclusion of a separate cloth map in 1990's *Ultima VI*'s game box (figure 4.4). In the late 1980s and early 1990s, advances in computer hardware allowed for strategy management and simulation games in the venues of *Civilization*, *SimCity*, or *StarCraft* to prosper, by making the map-based, top-down (or isometric) view an integral component of this kind of genre. Doing so changed

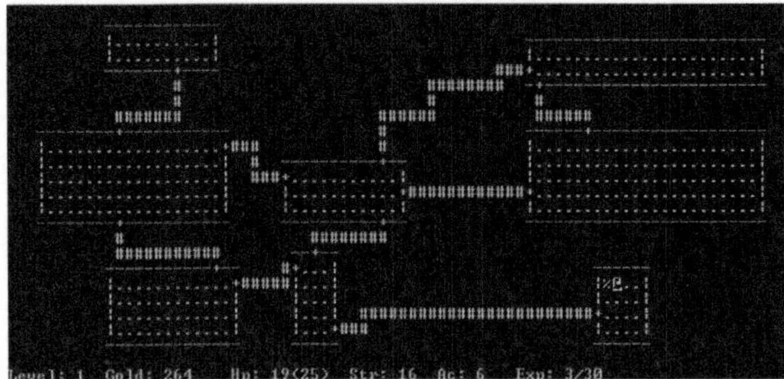

Figure 4.3: Rogue's map composed of ASCII symbols. Source: https://en.wikipedia.org/wiki/Rogue_(video_game)#/media/File:Rogue_Unix_Screenshot_CAR.PNG.

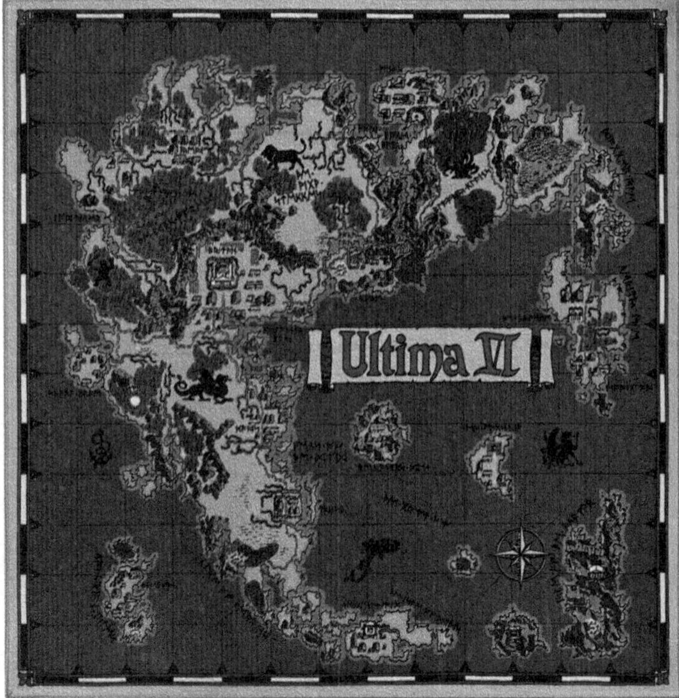

Figure 4.4: A cloth map of fictional Britannia, included in the box set of Ultima VI. Source: http://wiki.ultimacodex.com/wiki/File:U6map.jpg.

the player's perspective from one of a participant to one of a general or a manager, further impairing mapping's claim of detached objectivity.

So, if maps changed the ways games are played, what did these changes entail for moving and navigating in games? In his canonical text on game spatiality, Espen Aarseth deconstructs the relation between the player and the game to understand how rule-structures give place to emergent play. He emphasized how aspects such as level design or the use of visual cues for navigation create various perceived spatial experiences, drawing on Lefebvre's (1992) notions of triadic relations between perceived, conceived, and lived space. He highlights the ways through which designers attempt to manifest such spatial perception, but quickly conflates *game-space* with game *maps* (Aarseth 2000). Countering this, I wish to emphasize that while video games are planned and designed as spatial constructs, and while the players experience them as such, *the inclusion of a map changes this experience.* Introducing a map into a game and later designing this map as a game component means embedding certain affordances into the game's interface for the players to engage (or not) with the game in a manner that would be impossible otherwise. This is particularly cogent as digital maps in parallel made their way onto daily media devices.

While I am not arguing that all video-game screens *are* maps, or that even every top-down display constitutes one, there is an undeniable linkage between the issues of spatiality in video games, the introduction of maps as screen components and the rise of popular digital cartography outside of the gaming domain. The proliferation of technologies for geo-visualization alongside the transferability of skills between maps and games industries has led to exchange of knowledge and design concepts between the various actors involved. To illustrate, around the same time that better graphical engines allowed for maps to be included in video games, a group of GIS-trained engineers in Silicon Valley founded the start-up Keyhole. The company hired as CEO John Hancke, an entrepreneur mostly known for working within the games industry, who saw great potential in Keyhole's virtual globe technology, which cited as its inspiration science fiction and flight simulators (Dalton 2012).

The company's flagship project, Earth Viewer, meshed the functionality of 3D graphic space found in games and simulators with the accuracy and representation of virtual globes and maps. The company struggled through the 1990s, failing to find a suitable business model. However, after receiving a cash injection from In-Q-Tel, a venture capital company backed by the US intelligence community in 2003, Keyhole was acquired by Google in 2004. Earth Viewer was renamed and re-developed into Google Earth, and subsequently integrated into Google's ubiquitous Google Maps' platform (Dalton 2012). The link between maps and games goes both ways; it is in turn telling that after serving a few years as Google's Vice President of Product Management for the Geo division, Hancke subsequently set up the augmented reality games company Niantic, responsible for the augmented reality experiment *Ingress*, which became the foundation for the hit game *Pokémon Go* and (a much lesser hit) Harry Potter-themed *Wizards Unite* that shut down in 2022.

As Dale Leorke shows in his book on locative gaming, the majority of *Pokémon Go* players are not paying customers that contribute to the game's profits, but rather 'by transforming local sites into Pokéstops using the existing database created by *Ingress* players, *Pokémon Go* builds a rich repository of highly localized information that Niantic can leverage for profit' (Leorke 2019, 151). In fact, some of the early traces of Google's forays into map gamification point to Niantic's ultimate success. A series of April Fools jokes have increasingly experimented with playful design features overlaid real locations. In 2012 Google Maps web offered its users an '8-bit' version as temporary mapping layers, connecting the map to classic gaming franchises of the 1980s. 2013 featured a pirate-like treasure map layer. And 2014 brought the prototype that would become Niantic's game, spreading Pokémon critters throughout its map and exhorting users to 'catch' them in the web and mobile applications (Wikipedia 2025b). Perhaps reluctant at first to mess with the perceived seriousness of its mapping platform, the tech giant became much more confident in pushing more and more outlandish versions of it as gags (figure 4.5), showing that no matter the playful action, it is the underlying data that makes it a must for users.

This recalls the instrumentalization of maps as tools for extraction and use unpacked in chapter 1, whether for accessing space as infrastructure (Rankin 2011), its subsequent commodification (Alvarez León 2016), naturalization as calculative spaces (Wilmott 2016), locking into a platform economy (Plantin 2018), and/or regulation of global spatial data flows (McQuire 2019). In fact, as I continuously claim from this chapter onward, play is essential to understand our relations to digital mapping precisely because of their co-constitutive relationship and their neutralizing effect on one another: in evoking playfulness, digital maps reduce user anxieties around being shown a distorted version of the world they know. By bringing maps into playful objects (games and beyond), designers and makers ground them into actual 'usefulness' and give them a veneer of fact and objectivity.

Returning to the example from the chapter's introduction, you might recall how my view of *Pokémon Go*'s map looked nothing like a built environment despite being at an airport. It's worth noting that just a few months after the screenshot was taken, the map's look changed (figure 4.6). Despite its special relations to Google, in October 2022 Niantic seemingly swapped the underlying technology of its map to that of the Open Street Map (OSM), a publicly editable spatial database. While the game maker never officially admitted to the change, keen-eyed observers noticed the alterations to the game's layout and quickly correlated it to the OSM base

Figure 4.5: Examples of some of Google Maps jokes' prominence on the UI. Left: I am catching a Pokémon at Leiden University, 2014. Middle: the map changes into a 'Pac Man' layer, launching the game while using existing geography, 2015. Right: An invitation to celebrate Street View's fifteenth anniversary, with a new icon of the famous car appearing next to the 'Start' button on the Android app, 2022. Tapping it opens the option to change the display of your car into the one depicted. Screenshots by the author, and by Mark Fusco on Flickr (CC BY-SA 2.0).

Figure 4.6: A screenshot of my own Pokémon Go gameplay, November 2024, showing the OSM-based map available since October 2017. Buildings are now present (lighter shaded areas) next to open space (darker shaded).

map (Frank 2017). While we cannot know for certain why the company made the change, I propose two main likely assumptions that are tied to the key aspects of the digital map that I have detailed so far: accuracy and monetization.

First, Niantic needed a better grasp on the underlying spatial data for updating their game and growing it. If an area featured many players but was sparsely or inconsistently mapped, there was not much for them to do other than hoping Google would prioritize its update. While Google Maps incorporates suggestion features, they are quite limited and are centred on missing businesses or other usable information rather than underlying geography. On the other hand, OSM works in a similar way to Wikipedia: ostensibly it allows for anyone to edit complex features of its map; even if in practice the data shows gender and class biases (Gerlach 2015). For *Pokémon Go*, this means the ability to implicitly direct their players to edit OSM features and provide better game experience without being dependent on (and paying for) Google Maps access. To be fair, this is far from a rare OSM use-case. Many of the database's users are other commercial entities, operating in the open-source tech ethos: use and improve. Companies like Niantic receive access to crowdsourced geospatial information and in turn provide improvements to the database. If a popular[4] navigation app OsmAnd that specializes in offline GPS-enabled travel and is favoured by off-road drivers and bikers can use OSM and in turn solicit its outdoorsy userbase to add uncommon routes to contribute back to it – why can't *Pokémon Go* use play in the same way? Indeed, as stated by Christopher Greene-Szmadzinski, an OSM enthusiast and a player himself, despite what was perceived initially as 'vandalism' by the influx of new mappers, many of those who were contacted by the existing community eventually became valued contributors themselves (OpenStreetMap US 2022) and the organization now has guidelines to assist such newcomers (OpenStreetMap Wiki 2024).

The second issue is trickier, however. The switch to OSM is also inherently linked to digital maps' interfacial playfulness to continuously engage and monetize their users, as discussed in chapter 2. According to Greene-Szmadzinski, Niantic uses OSM for four purposes: presenting the base map (as in the appearance of buildings previously unavailable on Google); calculation of how and when the various monsters in the game 'spawn' based on unique location features like the presence of water or forests; the supply of 'nests' where multiple and rare monsters can be caught; and the similar calculation for the types of 'gifts' that a player can receive in different areas. Because the game is free to download and play, the monetization of players comes from the designers' ability to push players to spend money for 'freemium' features that speed gameplay and/or highlights status (Nieborg 2015; Evans 2016). In the case of *Pokémon Go* – as with previous location-based playful apps (Foxman 2014) – another possibility is to secure geo-fenced sponsorship or deals by selling player data to local businesses (Evans 2015; Leorke 2019).

What we see here is the same approach as Waze took when it started in 2006 as an open-source app that aimed to create community-based local spatial knowledge and real-time traffic updates. However, when Waze pivoted into a commercial entity in 2009, one of the first moves by the team was to distance themselves from the original open-source project and claim the mapped information (and concomitant intellectual property) to themselves. When sold to Google, some in the community saw this as a blatant disregard of the open-source ethos and demanded compensation for the free labour they have put into drawing the maps and testing the traffic features. The company was even sued in 2014 and 2020 on these grounds, though without much recourse for the claimants (Apelberg 2014; Goichman 2020). Interestingly enough, as Sam Hind and I showed elsewhere (Hind and Gekker 2014), the extensive use of gamification features for encouraging app drivers to 'ground truth' missing geospatial features was one key feature in the app's success (figure 4.7) that have led it to be later integrated into Google's platform. Yet, here Niantic is seemingly performing a paradoxical move: from the 'safety' of a closed proprietary mapping database (Google's) to the 'chaos' of an open one in relying on OSM. Why?

Partially, the answer lies in the *direction* of the move: while Waze aimed to *add* into Google's growing claim on cartographic data, Niantic tries to partition its data from Google. Jean-Christophe Plantin (2018) talks about how paradoxically, digital commercial cartography – with Google Maps being its chief example – has simultaneously opened participation, but re-centralized and enclosed resulting knowledge. In doing

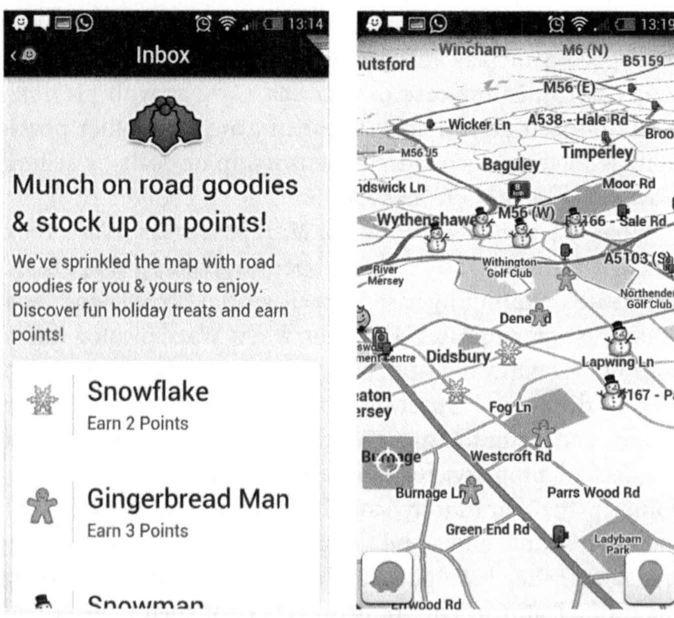

Figure 4.7: Gamification features in Waze navigation app, 2013. Screenshot by the author.

so, despite providing widely available and extremely accurate cartographic services, '*maps increasingly serve private rather than public interests*, similar to the monopoly of political elites and private patrons that characterized mapmaking for centuries before public institutes stepped in and administered mapping efforts with society in mind. The more participatory maps have become, the more enclosed they have become' (Plantin 2018, 501). Thus, if Waze used gamification features on its interface (participation) to generate proprietary *cartographic* data (enclosure) and ultimately add this data to digital mapping's biggest player, Niantic uses a mobile social game (participation) to gain unique *mobility* data, which is not available to Google (enclosure), and thus differentiate itself from the tech giant's looming shadow. A telling example is the matter-of-fact notification on *Pokémon Go*'s official blog in November 2024 about the company's intention to use its player base's repository of maps and images to build a 'large geospatial model' (LGM), which would be a spatial equivalent for what large language models (LLMs) such as ChatGPT do with language.

In the blog post, Niantic's Chief Scientist (and University of Oxford Associate Professor) Victor Adrian Prisacariu and another team member Eric Brachmann detail what they see as 'the future of spatial computing – intelligent systems that perceive, understand, and act upon the physical world' (Brachmann and Prisacariu 2024). To do so they aim to use the multiple data points provided by the movement and augmented-reality images taken by *Pokémon Go*'s (and previous games') players. Such movements represent 'the accumulation of knowledge through lived experiences and engagements with locations. Players build on their existing knowledge of urban environments gained through everyday engagements with these locations' (Moore 2015). The Niantic team wants to instrumentalize this embodied knowledge in a similar way to how OpenAI or Anthropic have harvested the written expression of billions of internet users to build their foundation – promptable – large models (Burkhardt and Rieder 2024). First, they used the data to train multiple neural networks based on specific locations, which resulted in what they call a visual positioning system (VPS), or an approach that allows the game to correlate an object's position and orientation in the world based on a single image. Their next proposed step is to combine those multiple networks into a global LGM (figure 4.8), which would allow 'implementing a shared understanding of geographic locations, and comprehending places *yet to be fully scanned*' (Brachmann and Prisacariu 2024, emphasis added). Large language or image models undergo unsupervised or self-supervised training, where through the process of tokenization and vector embedding of massive textual corpora, they achieve the ability to respond to prompts in creating data similar

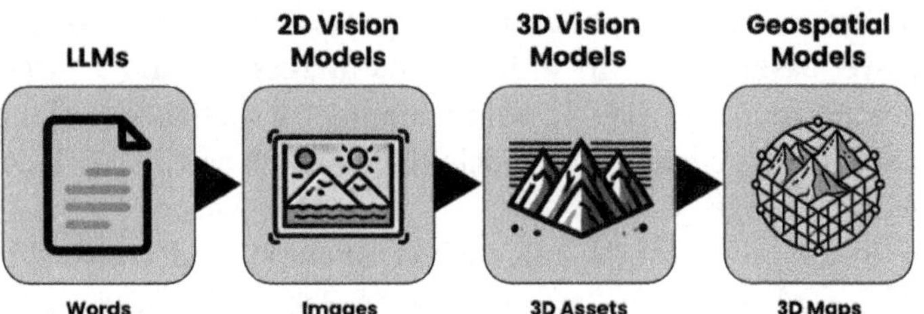

Figure 4.8: Niantic's vision for large geospatial models. Source: Brachmann and Prisacariu (2024).

to – but not found in – their original inputs (thus being 'generative' AIs). Similarly, Niantic hopes to do the same for understanding spatial relations (dimensions, distance, cultural significances) through making the connections in the corpus of already collected images, in order to 'understand' new places: 'The LGM extrapolates locally by interpolating globally' (Brachmann and Prisacariu 2024).

Just as LLMs would not have been possible without the harvesting and training models on unpaid labour of internet users and the entire available oeuvre of pirated human culture (Reisner 2024a), so is Niantic's future LGM predicated on doing the same for human movement and orientation. Interestingly it is a gaming company, rather than Google with its massive digital mapping infrastructure, that announced such an initiative. While we will have to wait and see which company (if any) succeeds in creating this model, what makes Niantic potentially leading is their unique combination of mapped knowledge coupled with AR components, while being powered by playful engagements to solicit more and unique data from users. This is reminiscent of Waze's early experimentations with gamification elements that were severely diminished with the app's incorporation into Google and therefore into the mainstream. It also hints at why the transition was made to OSM data rather than Google Maps' one – to harness the power of playing on the map, without sharing it with a potential rival. The game's reddit forum was seemingly not surprised by this announcement, although some users did show displeasure at being forced to provide training data (Edwards 2024b). In response, Niantic posted an update to the blog post a few days after publication where it stressed that moving around does not constitute training, and only through specific optional actions (scanning in a public location) does the model get updated. As in many such cases, it is hard to know what exactly constitutes training or not, and which permissions are implicitly or explicitly given by the user base who might not be at all aware of the issues at play.

Playful maps in everyday media

While *Pokémon Go* represents the most explicit gamification of cartography, the playful elements it employs have permeated many other digital map interfaces. Social media platforms increasingly incorporate mapping features that utilize similar strategies of engagement, albeit with different stated purposes. Leighton Evans (2015) approaches locative social media primarily through a theoretical lens, situating them within the historical evolution of cartography as a shift from top-down, state-controlled mapping to bottom-up, user-generated cartographies. Evans frames this shift as a tension between 'technological' revealing (treating place as a resource to be exploited) and 'poetic/dwelling' revealing (understanding place as meaningful). My approach differs in that I analyse these mapped interfaces not primarily as philosophical objects that reveal place or space, but as media objects designed to capture attention, extract data, and monetize user engagement through playful mechanisms. Where Evans sees the potential for location-based social networks (LBSN) to foster meaningful connections to place, I examine how the playful design elements of these platforms strategically obscure their extractive functions behind a veneer of fun and sociality. This alignment with casual power becomes evident when examining social media platforms that have incorporated mapping features as core components of their user experience.

The earliest example of such media is Foursquare. The prototypical placemaking app for mobile phones launched in 2009, and introduced game-like mechanics and personal touch to spaces the user visited. Using rudimentary GPS coordinates, users could 'check-in' to specific places to become their 'mayor' by frequently attending specific places. Some establishments, like bars and restaurants, even offered mayors (and their registered app friends) discounts. From 2010 to 2014 it also offered a Map view that located friends' recent check-ins on the map, attempting to utilize the growing popularity of location sharing via phones parallel to eroding notions of location privacy. As games scholar Maxwell Foxman describes in his analysis of Foursquare, the app transformed 'ordinary experiences into one of expenditure and glory' (Foxman 2014, 73) by allowing users to bring competition into their everyday existence. This form of 'proximal communication' became part of embodied experiences rather than merely an outwardly communicated act. Users would actively cultivate their movements around cities specifically to obtain badges and mayorships, often planning routes and social activities based on the game's mechanics rather than practical considerations – what I previously referred to as the reambiguating aspect of playfulness. The intensity of this engagement is exemplified by Foxman's personal anecdote of feeling 'a mixture of guilt and resentment' (2014, 85) when checking in 'off the grid' (privately) after Foursquare reduced points for private check-ins to encourage public competition. This paradox of shame and excitement is perhaps most visible in Foursquare 2014's decision to downplay the check-ins and sharing element of its app at all, focusing instead on local search. Those foundational features were in turn spun out into a separate app called Swarm. Ironically, in December 2024

Foursquare has shut down the eponymous app to focus on developing Swarm, effectively returning to its original premise, if in a much more crowded app space. In a rare feat, it also open-sourced its 'places' database, allowing others to use it freely for their geospatial goals (Proven 2024).

Most prominent among current spatial sharing social apps is Snapchat, made famous for its ephemeral 'stories' feature which was copied by every other social media,[5] with its central Snap Map feature. The AR app, particularly popular with younger audiences (Statista 2025a), has made placemaking central to its interaction. In their analysis of the platform, Wilken and Humphreys (2021) see its spatial components as part of a new 'digital wayfaring' (Hjorth and Pink 2014) in which mobile users co-construct navigational practices through apps, for example by seeing what is socially popular and then navigating to it. This is made particularly easy by how Snap makes attempts to integrate ride-hailing services such as Lyft directly into its interface. This playful visualization of space acts as what Wilken and Humphreys describe, after Marc Andrejevic, as 'digital enclosures' (Wilken and Humphreys 2021, 584) that persuade users to participate in order to generate proprietary knowledge for the company.

The look and feel of Snap Map's overall interface are derived from Zenly, a social map app that Snapchat bought in 2017. Zenly allowed users to see where their friends are, through constant GPS-tracking running in the background. Snapchat integrated the underlying technology and, for a while, allowed Zenly to run as an independent app, including developing its own property map which was not the 'most accurate map in the world, [but] it was the most playful and iconic map app on my phone. You could see animated cars, boats, rubber ducks, trucks, sea creatures, etc.' (Dillet 2022, n.p.). In an all too familiar story, Snap shut down Zenly five years after its purchase and refused to sell the company to any other potential bidder, allegedly because it saw Zenly's playful placemaking as a threat and competition to its own product. In an ironic coincidence, around the same time Google Maps restructured its Geo division, severely undercutting the independence of its own playful mapping app – Waze – after integrating some of its components into the main platform (Kabir 2022).

Snap Map is central to the app's experience and easily accessed. Despite having a dedicated tab, 'pinching' the screen – in a gesture that has become naturalized to zoom out in maps (Hind and Lammes 2016) – will also show the user on the map. When a user interacts with Snapchat in any capacity, their position on Snap Map is marked by their cartoon avatar, the Bitmoji, which changes in appearance based on geolocation (e.g., near a beach) and time of day. Using Zenly's technology and data from OSM and various other proprietary vendors, it launched the 2017 map function both to show users' friends on the map, and – perhaps more importantly – to create activity heatmaps, which are coloured areas showing social media activity at particular locations, often venues or events. These heatmaps surface algorithmic attention to 'emergent intensities of "social media life of public spaces"' (Wilken and Humphreys 2021, 586). By tagging a toggle to place snaps in 'Our Story', thus making them public, users can create hot spots on the map. Snapchat takes snaps submitted to 'Our Story' on Snap Map using Mapbox's Geocoding API to turn GPS coordinates into addresses. Mapbox also provides the OpenGL (Open Graphics Library) rendering used to create the activity heatmaps.

While coded as a fun sociability feature, the function enabled people to share testimonies from natural disasters and war zones (Sung 2023), making it another case of processual mapping transcending its original intent and offering ways to understand people and places differently. This shows that play, including mapped play, is not always fun (Malaby 2007) and that what Snap Map does perhaps relates more closely to Sicartian playful attitude than play as activity. After all, participating requires some form of disclosure, and Snap was often chastised by implicitly pressuring young users to literally disclose their location to many potential others. While the functionality changed (originally, merely opening the app would make you visible), and additional toggles were added, including a 'ghost mode' that allows one to interact with the map without being visible, the concern remains. In October 2024 the US state of New Mexico launched a lawsuit against Snapchat, highlighting how its design features made the app prime for sextortion (extortion under fear of disclosing private content), particularly with teen users (Blake and Sunderland 2024). In its goal to integrate play as a form of engagement, Snap may have inadvertently lead users to forsake other 'external consequences' (Masek and Stenros 2021) and expose themselves to danger.

In what I described so far, spatial social media are using maps to facilitate placemaking. But the process also goes in reverse: Google Maps itself is adding playful and placemaking components to its previously utilitarian offer. In 2020 the company shuffled its leadership team and hired Chris Phillips to lead its Geo division, despite him lacking any geospatial experience and coming from the world of music and entertainment technology. A year later, Phillips (2022) announced a slew of new features to Maps, that leaned more heavily on the experiential engagement with the product than its information or navigational purpose. Those included the ability to do a 'vibe check' for specific neighbourhoods based on AI-rewritten summaries of user reviews showing a Snap Map-like heatmap of popular spots; an immersive view for 250 landmarks (over 500 as of August 2025) around the world that uses aerial photography and 3D modelling to show them while predicting weather and crowdedness status; and an AR lens-like option for Street View on mobile, though these are mostly used to highlight mapped objects (like ATMs) from a ground-level camera perspective. And Street View itself has long been chockfull of various jokes and easter eggs, for instance by allowing one to 'enter' a nondescript UK police box and discovering the Tardis – a vehicle famously bigger on the inside (Kumparak 2013) – from the longstanding science fiction franchise *Dr. Who*. The map can also sometimes facilitate play from the users itself, in acts that resist and subvert the commercial logic of the platform. For instance, when a prominent Cretan cat, nicknamed 'Chonkus Maximus', attracted a rabid fanbase and a dedicated 'attraction' Google Maps pin, with hundreds of five-star ratings and reviews. However, after a short viral fame (and perhaps at the behest of local animal rights groups) Google removed the cat from the map (Kokkinidis 2025).

That is not to say that play is always and only integrated in maps by major tech platforms. Many tinkerers and small developers find clever and fun ways to experiment with maps and mapped data. One of my favourites is 'Pret-a-spider' (Jonty 2025), a simple but fun mashup, in which you can use a keyboard, mouse, or touch screen to control a five- to seven-legged 'spider' as it travels around London, each leg always anchored in a 'Pret a Manger' sandwich chain shop. As the spider gets further away from London's city centre, its strides become longer as it hops across suburban and rural Pret-less ravines. But as Dalton's (2015) ethnography of early map developers reminds us, each such playful experiment can have profit motives at its core. Another example is the 'Coffee in the Sun' app, which started as a fun idea by a Dutch student (Jacobs 2025a). He created a quick mashup that combines mapped public 3D street data with the sun's position to indicate which outside terraces are currently in the sun and not in the shade. Once the website gained traction, the developer was quick to build and launch an entire app around the concept that also promises you to 'discover hospitality around the world' (Land 2025). Overall then, playful attitudes are being incorporated into maps to keep users engaged in social activities, shopping, and navigation.

Conclusion: The extractive power of playful mapping

Digital maps function as powerful media objects precisely because of their playful qualities. As this chapter has demonstrated, the integration of play into digital cartography serves multiple functions that extend far beyond mere entertainment. Through examining the evolution of maps in games and subsequent gamification of maps themselves, we can see how playfulness has become central to the way digital maps mediate our relationship with space.

The case of *Pokémon Go* illustrates how contemporary mapping platforms leverage play to transform mundane geographies into compelling interfaces for engagement. By overlaying a fantastical game world onto physical space, Niantic created more than just entertainment – it established a powerful mechanism for data extraction disguised as fun. This exemplifies casual power in operation: users willingly provide valuable geospatial information through their movements and interactions precisely because of how the playful interface obscures the underlying commercial logic of data harvesting. This pattern extends beyond explicit games into everyday mapping interfaces. As seen in Google Maps' April Fools jokes and Snapchat's cartoonish Snap Map, playful elements have become standard features of mapping media that paradoxically serve to naturalize and depoliticize these platforms. The deliberate gamification of mapping interfaces creates a playful attitude toward space – an orientation that prioritizes engagement over critical awareness of how these maps function as media technologies.

The implications of this merger between play and cartography are profound. First, by making maps fun, developers effectively position their products as neutral or innocent tools, masking their roles in surveillance, data collection, and the commodification of movement. Second, playful interfaces encourage users to engage with space differently – prioritizing novel experiences, social connections, and fantasy over practical navigation or geographic understanding. Finally, as evidenced by Niantic's ambitions to create a 'large geospatial model', these playful engagements constitute a valuable reservoir of spatial data with potential surveillance implications. These points will be further unpacked in chapter 6.

Play, therefore, is not incidental to how digital maps function as media – it is fundamental to their operation as interfaces that mediate between users, physical space, and commercial interests. The casual power wielded through playful mapping represents a significant shift in how cartography works as a form of media, blurring boundaries between entertainment, utility, and exploitation. As we will see in the following chapter on 'Work', the playful aspects of digital maps are inextricably linked to new forms of digital labour. The same interfaces that encourage playful engagement also enable new types of spatial work, surveillance, and control that further entrench maps as powerful media technologies shaping our everyday experience of space.

5
Work

Laura is the owner and public face of the SuperHumans. Life website and YouTube channel. She does not disclose her last name nor is there a LinkedIn profile. She has been a 'freelancer and entrepreneur for more than 6 years ... a career mentor for the past 12 years' and 'worked as an advisor to Governments and Ministries of Education in 30+ European countries on topics like the future of work, the future of education, and digital nomads' (SuperHumans, n.d., pt On a Personal Note). The channel, boasting more than 390,000 subscribers at the time of writing, is seemingly part of YouTube's wide offering of get-rich-quick channels focusing on amorphous 'work-from-home', 'freelancing', or 'passive income' advice. Uncharitably, Laura may be a 'contrepreneur', a term popularized by the documentarian and video essayist Dan Olson (Folding Ideas 2022), to describe a person who's a mix of a con-artist and entrepreneur, boasting their conspicuously wealthy lifestyle while creating 'educational' content. SuperHumans.Life is no exception. The monthly 15–25 minute videos describe step-by-step how one would go about using widely accessible resources to achieve a consistent monthly income (figure 5.1) while cross promoting her other materials, calling on viewers to download her free eBooks and, ultimately, sign up for her paid courses. The most popular video on her channel is about working through Google Maps. In this chapter I argue that this is not by accident. Rather, it underscores how maps became embedded in certain types of digital labour, and acts as an entry point to understand the hidden work that goes into making them.

Figure 5.1: A screenshot from SuperHuman.Life's list of videos, taken November 2024.

SocialBlade, the popular social media database, estimates SuperHuman's channel to have received almost 300,000 views in a span of 30 days and ranks it in 1,724th place in the US (where the channel is registered) as of February 2025, with about a thousand new subscribers joining every week. Of course, as with many social media metrics, it's difficult to differentiate authenticity and interest from commercial 'engagement farms' without a thorough examination (Rogers 2018). Nonetheless, we can safely assume that at least some of the content appeals to real viewers, who watch and comment on the videos. Most of the channel's videos reach between several to tens of thousands of views. Some outperform in the hundreds of thousands. Yet the most watched video on the channel by far, with 4.1 million views (the next best one only has 1.2 million views), is about a mapping platform. Titled 'I Tried Making $800 in 4 Hours with Google Maps (To See If It Works)' (SuperHumans.Life 2023), in the video Laura takes on the challenge to make $800 in four hours, to highlight the potential of her business coaching even to those with 'no skills' and 'no experience'. She chooses Google Maps as the platform on which she'll earn money and proceeds by leveraging the platform to help small businesses optimize their Google Business Profiles. She selects a small town in the heart of the US, scouting it through Google Maps itself. Then, by identifying local businesses with incomplete or poorly optimized profiles, she offers them services to improve their online presence, aiming to boost visibility and attract more customers. Despite struggling to close sales quickly, she claims to have made $700, demonstrating the potential of using digital tools like Google Maps to find and serve clients in a time-sensitive business model.

SuperHumans.Life treats Google Maps as one platform among many, and specifically one to *work* on. There is very little map-specificity to her video, where she acknowledges, for instance, the spatial components of the platform, or even describes how this digital map works. Google Maps to her is an advertising platform first and foremost, and one which is open for the kind of search engine optimization (SEO) that she peddles – because by not being visible (enough) on the map, businesses open themselves to the very optimization processes that she offers. Her approach is far from surprising. As I have shown in previous chapters, the dual move of naturalization and commercialization of various digital maps has rendered them prone to 'backgrounding' in various daily conducts. Early studies of developers building geospatial applications for Google's then-rising API-enabled platform have shown that many gravitate to it due to perceived fun and potential of earning something (Dalton 2015), not dissimilar to Laura's attitude in the video. Maps and mapping have been labour-intensive, and often highly regulated, practices since the invention of modern cartography (Krygier and Wood 2005; Perkins 2009a; Boria and Rossetto 2017). Their liberation through APIs and widely available consumer tools shattered this rigidity.

My argument in this chapter is somewhat different, however. By tracing several different examples of work done with maps and through them, I claim that some of the widespread changes in the nature of both paid and unpaid work observed over recent decades can be attributed to the proliferation of digital mapping. Specifically, I assert that digital maps broke the traditional linkage between places and labour, and by doing so allowed for new forms of remote control that do not require a physical presence that characterized work before. Recalling Rankin's (2011) assertion about how GPS allows one to visit a place without knowing it, I posit that – combined with an intuitive navigational interface – it would also allow you to work in such an unknown place. While far from being the only contributor to the shift in remote and detached labour practices, mapping is nonetheless a central and oft overlooked component of it.

The chapter progresses through three sections. First, I review theories of digital labour with an eye to how some of the more popular scholarly ways to talk about work being done through the internet do not always fit the spatial perspective I adopt in this book. Second, I explain the work done *on maps*; or what is needed to build and maintain maps today, while juxtaposing consumer-facing with the GIS (geographic information systems) giant Esri, a distinct player in the digital mapping ecosystem that is largely unknown to consumer audiences, as it focuses on professional organizations offering advanced analysis tools. By showing how it does – and does not – participate in the domain that I defined as digital mapping, I highlight the specificity of this industry. Lastly, I present work done *through maps*; or how maps facilitate different types of working, paid or unpaid. Here I specifically zoom in on gig labour like food deliveries or ride hailing, that greatly benefitted from maps. I conclude by summarizing how working with maps works, while also coming back to the question of play from the previous chapter to show how the two are entangled.

Digital labour

A central concept that will be interrogated throughout the chapter is one of work, or labour, to be used interchangeably. In her formative text on the relations between work, digital environments, and academic research, famed STS ethnographer Lucy Suchman called the work performed by others a kind of 'black box'. Work, particularly one performed to maintain or care for something, is invisible and often unappreciated (Mattern 2018). Frustratingly, 'the better the work is done, the less visible it is to those who benefit from it' (Suchman 1995, 58). As I will elaborate in the second section of this chapter, maps are no exception to this assertion. They are a key example of the layered, multidimensional and often imperceptible work that is difficult to conceive of when using the end product. In fact, Suchman uses mapmakers' work as a key example throughout her text to ground the difficulty, at times, of giving true academic account to such production processes. After all, when I write that someone is 'maintaining a cartographic database', this entails diverse sets of activities that might include (but are not limited to): data collection and acquisition through aerial photography and photogrammetry; database management and integration of external sources, often with non-compatible formats; thus processing and standardization of data; with all the above done again and again through updates and version control under changing technologies, devices, and facts on the ground. Through this work of multiple actors, cartographic calculation thus 'entails both the capture and addition of knowledge from, and into, the world' (Hind 2020, 7).

Before understanding the specific labour enacted and demanded by maps, the notion of digital labour must be clarified. As Gandini (2021) asserts, the term has become somewhat of an 'empty signifier', evoked by different scholars for different purposes. Originally, it was a distinctly Marxist term used for critiquing the free work done by the nascent blogosphere to augment the profit of the companies providing the tools for such efforts and extracting value from the passion-driven engagement of the bloggers. The critique was subsequently expanded to account for the massive endeavour of social networking sites – and later social media platforms – in creating content for the consumption of others like them, in order to generate the possibility of ad-based revenue. Based on Dallas Smythe's (1977) audience commodification theory, this perspective saw the online audience in a similar way to how mass communication 'packaged' groups of readers, listeners, or viewers in order to then 'sell' them to advertisers. Through this approach, watching 'free' television shows can be understood as work done for the broadcaster by allowing them to further 'sell' the labour of viewing ads to the advertisers paying to position ads next to the content in question. Taking a step further, social media platforms, with their quantified *graphopticon* where 'the many watch the metrics of the many' (Grosser 2014, 1), create a perfect condition to get even *freer* labour by making selling to the advertisers audiences consuming content created for free by other users on the site.

This notion was adapted by Marxist academics as much as by internet users themselves, as noted in the oft-quoted variations on the idea that 'if you're not paying for it, you're not the customers but the product' (Belanger 2025). An early proponent of this particular interpretation was Italian cultural critic Tiziana Terranova, who first cemented the notion of free work in exchange for digital access (Terranova 2000) and later highlighted the role that quantified attention plays in such exchanges, as a resource that is progressively seen 'not only as "scarce" because limited, but also as increasingly "degraded"' (Terranova 2012, 12). Such degradation shows the 'work' done, is not only unpaid, but also dangerous through cognitive depletion (Sampson 2017). Or, to quote another favoured internet aphorism, widely attributed to visualization guru Edward Tufte: 'There are only two industries that call their customers "users": illegal drugs and software'. This approach was also present in early digital cartography, where the idea of amateurs producing 'volunteer geographic information' was lauded at first, before serious critiques of the practices emerged, focusing on, among others, the hierarchical power relations between those with the tools to build the infrastructures to harness such data and those 'volunteers' who might be expected to provide it (Haklay 2013; Kwan 2016).

However, alongside this critical totalizing lens, some noted the obvious issues in treating activities that millions do willingly for their own enjoyment as 'labour', or taking issue with the emphasis such critics put on the value of audiences' participation in the overall business models of media giants. As both Gandini (2021) and Grohmann (2025) assert in reviewing the debate, the discussion has come to an impasse due to the various ways that websites and platforms value and engage audiences. More to the point, the distinction is probably moot at this point, since the processes that took place over the last two decades have made 'digital' inseparable from 'labour' and vice versa. Through rapid digitalization, work has become intimately dependent on the internet and the web either for direct uses or as infrastructural background (Plantin et al. 2018). Moreover, instead of being a distinct category, many digital environments now routinely integrate elements of 'playbour' (Kücklich 2005; Woodcock and Johnson 2018; van Doorn and Chen 2021), or ludic capitalism as I referred to it in previous chapters. Thus, while more and more of our activities mediated by digital platforms are predicated on engagement loops, the forms of work we do on and with maps – as elsewhere – begin to resemble fun and leisure. One example of this, taken from the previous chapter, is where players of games such as *Pokémon Go* unwittingly provided accurate geospatial information to Niantic, and even helped train its unique AI model. Another one, which I will discuss further in the third section of this chapter, is the way Google's Local Guides program is deployed and monetized.

Thus, both Gandini and Grohmann in their review of digital labour research of the last decades arrive at a similar conclusion. The term 'has come to be used indistinctly to identify almost all forms of direct or indirect labouring that takes place through the mediation of a digital medium, irrespective of their adherence to [a critical] theoretical construct' (Gandini 2021, 372) where the discussion of whether 'users are exploited by social media or not' (Grohmann 2025,

116) is missing the point. Two parallel lenses serve to better understand the contemporary state of digital labour, particularly as it pertains to those using (and making) digital maps: platform labour and data labour.

Platform labour (van Doorn 2017) is a specific kind of work done through online platforms that employ workers as contractors through on-demand, and often precarious, means. Driving an Uber or delivering food via Deliveroo is a clear-cut example, although many other types exist, including performing micro-tasks on Amazon's Mechanical Turk. Unlike with social media's value extraction, there's no doubt about the employment conditions present between the platform and the worker, as the latter enters some contractual relations with the former and receives renumeration for performing certain activities. Those relations are nonetheless different from traditional employment, as many of the platforms are 'lean' companies (Srnicek 2016) that do not hold physical assets but act as mediators of arbitrage in 'multi-sided markets' (Rieder and Sire 2014; Nieborg and Poell 2018). There, a platform's position as a central repository of data between various parties allows it to show and hide different aspects of its business to facilitate, for instance, the delivery of a meal without either the restaurant or the delivery person knowing exactly how much the customer actually pays nor how the money is divided amongst the parties (van Doorn and Badger 2020).

Another example for platform labour is surge pricing, where a certain geographical area is temporarily defined as being more lucrative for platform workers. This creates a paradoxical situation where driving your own car for a ride-hailing platform means you only know enough about your route and customer from what *the platform wants you to know* while they do not own your car nor pay you steady wages. Overall, through this perspective the platforms act as 'permissive potentates' (Vallas and Schor 2020) that relegate (permit) to their semi-employed personnel some of the traditional power of the *employer*, such as setting working schedules or sometimes negotiating their rates; yet by redistributing control platforms maintain power over the key aspects of the overall labour field, by allocating the tasks and keeping the data. This is very much in line with Plantin's (2018) observation regarding the infrastructural power of Google Maps: an enclosure of *inbound data flows* alongside *distribution of data generation* creates uniquely powerful mechanisms of control, which leads us to the second approach to examine digital work.

A complementary lens to platform labour is *data labour*, a practice where free, unpaid and/or underpaid work allows for the creation of value by the capturing platform by extrapolating from human actions (Gray and Suri 2019). This is true for physical actions performed in the world through digital mediation as much as through new forms of online-specific tasks. Van Doorn and Badger (2020) note that couriers working for food delivery platforms, often precarious and migrant workers, generate value for the firm not just through the actual work done, but more so through the datafication of their routes, speeds, and actions in order to both improve the efficiency of the platform itself (e.g., by offering lower rates), but also to potentially be packaged and sold to other parties. This happens through what information scholar Philip Agre (1994) calls 'grammars of action', where discrete movements of humans are being quantified and conformed to limited patterns in a computerized workplace.

Couriers therefore are not only workers but 'data assets' that generate value by way of optimizing the platform on which they work. Through tracking and algorithmic management, they translate the quotidian skills of wayfaring, route optimization, or spatial awareness into digitalized templates that can be in turn used against them by the platforms for which they work, in a manner that Hind and Seitz (2024) call 'cynical technical practice'. Data assets are predisposed on scaling: a single courier employed on a platform might not do much, but their value increases exponentially (and their individual power reduces accordingly) as additional data points are generated from multiple delivery people. As such, they represent both immediate operational value and speculative financial one.

A recent relevant example that showcases both platform labour and data labour is the meteoric rise of ChatGPT and other generative AI foundation models (Burkhardt and Rieder 2024). Those are trained on vast amounts of human-generated text, images, and videos, breaking them down into tokenized units of meaning to enable them to be recombined into new forms (thus 'generative'). As disclosed through multiple investigations, several were trained on the 'pile', a vast collection of pirated materials of TV and film scripts, literature, and academic publications (Reisner 2024a; 2024b; 2025b). In effect, centuries of human creative labour have been processed without their authors' authorization or intent. The 'scalability' properties of the underlying transformer technology meant that the more material went into the pre-training stage of large language models (LLMs), the better the resulting generative AI agents were (Luitse and Denkena 2021), and so the large companies and frontier AI labs scraped all kinds of material they could acquire – legally or otherwise (Belanger 2025).

This rapidly changed (and is still changing) the face of the open web and required a response from various organizations, from trade bodies to government regulators across the world (Information Commissioner's Office 2025). The platform Reddit, for instance, recognized that what used to be a place for individuals to communicate with one another on a specific topic has suddenly become a growing repository of high-quality training material. Their response was to block the website for external developers, and to significantly increase the costs of using Reddit's API, which until now was used primarily by the community itself and researchers interested in the platform (Shakir 2023). In response, many of the platform's popular communities rebelled and engaged in various tactics to force the company to cancel those changes (Peters and Porters 2023) – though to little avail. Once genuine written human interaction became an asset, the company essentially started viewing their user base as data assets, showcasing the data labour perspective. At the same time, the company attempted to limit the power of its human moderators by introducing powerful AI tools that can automate some of the work done previously by volunteer human moderators and advancing personalized genAI-based content moderation filters for users. Through the platform labour lens, this can be viewed as an attempt to regulate and extract more value from existing human work. While discussing the ramifications of generative AI technologies on labour far exceeds the remit of this chapter, the example is helpful in highlighting one aspect that I will return to in the discussion of map labour: the prevalence of assetization on digital platforms.

Digital maps, like other types of digital objects, are increasingly in the double bind of *assetization* and *rentiership*, which shape their labour dynamics. The first signifies the changing form of such objects under contemporary platform and data economies, one that 'is not the commodity but the asset, and that the financial contours it entails are not those of market speculation but of capital investment' (Birch and Muniesa 2020, 1–2). This challenges the old critique of media commodification – turning consumption from something to be packaged and sold – to showing how business imagination around digital products is instead organized around long-term investment. Rather than selling products, platforms generate returns through 'pump and dump' schemes, where initial investors cash out through an exit or (rarely) an initial public offering (IPO) without the platform ever achieving profitability (van Doorn and Badger 2020). This leads to what Sadowski (2020) calls 'the internet of landlords', where the shift from one-time payment towards the production of continuous rent is the *modus operandi* of modern firms. Such rent is extracted either directly, in the form of subscription fees for digital infrastructures and services, or indirectly, by turning users into funnels for generating more data. This dynamic has been observed in fields as diverse as popular video games (Bernevega and Gekker 2022), build-to-rent properties (Nethercote 2023), and car ownership (Shapiro and Forelle 2024). Companies, in other words are 'seeing like a market' (Fourcade and Healy 2016) in that they see as their imperative to collect as much data points as possible and turn users into assets. These undercurrents are also very present in the work practices in and around digital mapping.

Working on the map

Mapping has been very labour-intensive from the very start of the profession. Eratosthenes' three-tome *Geographika*, published in the third century BC, was compiled through meticulous archival and quantitative work, consisting of one tome on previous observations, another dedicated to calculating the circumference of the Earth, and the third that laid the foundation of political geography by dividing the world into entities with recognizable borders. Ptolemy's *Geographia*, translated into Latin in the second century AD, which is widely regarded as the basis for Roman and Medieval mapmaking, consisted of both scrupulous calculations of various data points (a gazetteer), such as the Earth's circumference or longitude and latitude coordinates of key points in the Roman Empire; as well as maps drawn from various reports of travellers (Dilke 1987b). The work of producing and reproducing these maps became central to the operation of the Roman Empire (and influenced subsequent nations), by, for instance, deprioritizing mathematical accuracy championed by Ptolemy and focusing instead more on practical issues of connectivity and logistics (road and routes) than on geographical fidelity (Dilke 1987a). This work included numerous scribes, clerks, travellers, captains, and generals. Many of the maps that were used until the late Middle Ages were mistake-ridden reproductions of the original Ptolemaic maps, since it was more feasible to use them instead of surveying and correcting new ones. Ironically, Ptolemy himself criticized Marinus of Tyre, whose work he incorporated into his own Atlas, for similarly including transcription errors into his maps instead of calculating anew.

Modern digital maps might seem safe from these issues, but this is not the case. A striking example is Sandy Island, which appeared between Australia and New Caledonia in the Coral Sea on numerous maps, including Google Maps until 2012, despite not actually existing (Woods 2012). The origin of the phantom island can be traced to an 1876 report from the whaling ship *Velocity*, and the error persisted through generations of cartographic reproductions (Gayle 2012). Much like the medieval scribes who copied Ptolemaic maps without verification, modern cartographers often relied on existing datasets when creating digital maps, inadvertently perpetuating historical errors. The persistence of Sandy Island demonstrates how even in the age of satellite imagery and GPS, the fundamental challenges of verification and the tendency to rely on existing cartographic sources continue to shape our understanding of geography. It was only when the Australian research vessel *Southern Surveyor* attempted to visit the supposed location in 2012 that the error was definitively corrected, leading to its removal from Google Maps and highlighting how the work that goes into the verification of geographical data remains a crucial aspect of modern cartography.

A similar story from the same era occurred with Apple Maps' 2012 release in iOS 6, where the disputed Senkaku/ Diaoyu islands appeared twice on the map – with different coordinates depending on whether users searched for their Chinese or Japanese name. Much like medieval scribes who reproduced existing maps without verification, Apple had inadvertently merged multiple (nationally conflicting) datasets without proper reconciliation, resulting in a duplication of the islands (figure 5.2). The error likely stemmed

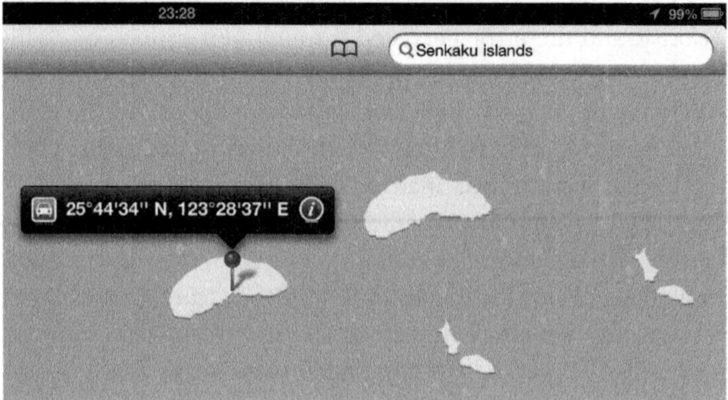

Figure 5.2: The dual view of the Diayou/Senkaku islands. Source: Geens (2012).

from incorporating both Japanese geographic data and an intentionally offset Chinese dataset, as PRC authorities have been known to deliberately introduce spatial inaccuracies in their maps to thwart GPS-based georeferencing. Google Maps faced similar challenges with these datasets but had implemented human verification processes to catch and correct such duplications (Geens 2012).

The enduring presence of such errors (ancient and digital) speaks to the persistent role of what Latour (1986, 29) terms *centres of calculation*: nodes where inscriptions are gathered, processed, and circulated to enact power at a distance. Whether in the Roman Empire's reliance on travellers' reports or Google's algorithmic synthesis of national datasets, these centres remain critical infrastructures where decisions about spatial truth are made and legitimized. Today, these centres may be housed in server farms or corporate cartography teams rather than scriptoriums, but the underlying dynamics of inscription, delegation, and epistemic authority remain. The map, far from a transparent window onto the world, emerges from a chain of automated and/or deliberate transformations where errors can be institutionalized as easily as truths. Moreover, the increasing automation of these centres, from algorithmic conflation of contradictory sources to the outsourcing of error checking to volunteer-based platforms like OpenStreetMap, complicates traditional notions of responsibility. As Hind and Lammes (2016) argue, digital mapping platforms do not simply reflect a 'double-click' logic of direct access to reality, but rather obscure the vast network of translations behind every pixel, in the haptic and embedded 'double-tap' logic of touchscreen map interaction. It is only in moments of failure, when phantom islands surface or geopolitical duplications arise, that these centres of calculation are (temporarily) laid bare, revealing the maintenance required beneath the presumed immediacy of digital cartographies.

My own previous research on contemporary mapmaking institutions highlights the work required to maintain them. The fieldwork I carried out in Israel's national cartographic agency Survey of Israel (SOI) has shown how central and influential are the efforts that go into maintaining the data structures behind the maps (Gekker 2016b). Like other national agencies, SOI was long dominant in Israel's cartographic landscape merely because it was the only organization with the resources to gather and maintain such data. The appearance of computers and geographic databases changed little, since accessing and retrieving this information still required skills and technology that the general population lacked, and it interested only specialized entities. This has changed with the introduction of the web. My main research object within the agency was the then so-called *web-server* team, a unifying term for several projects aiming to bridge SOI's closed geographic-database system and provide wide swathes of professional and non-professional audiences outside the agency with simple access to the data confined within BANTAL, the national topographic database, the backbone of many SOI's operations. When the digital map becomes merely a 'cartographic interface' (Muehrcke 1990), connecting end users with obscured databases (Plantin 2018), the work done traditionally by cartographers in the span of decades and centuries, becomes condensed into months and weeks.

The influence of BANTAL exemplifies this transformation. As a centralized topographic database, it acts as more than just a repository – it fundamentally shapes how geographic information is collected, processed, and disseminated throughout SOI. The database's rigid structure, with its predefined categories for geographic entities, creates a standardized framework that both enables and constrains the organization's cartographic practices. For instance, when the web-server team needs to implement new features for public access, they must work within the confines of BANTAL's established categories and data structures. Even seemingly straightforward additions, such as categorizing dirt paths requiring all-terrain vehicles, necessitate extensive coordination across departments to maintain the database's integrity. This standardization, while ensuring consistency, can create challenges when incorporating external data sources. The integration of utility company maps and Ministry of Construction and Housing data proved particularly challenging, as these sources lacked compatibility with BANTAL's standardized format, necessitating time-consuming manual processing. Thus, what appears as a simple interface to end-users actually represents a complex network of interdepartmental dependencies and standardization processes, all governed by the database's underlying structure.

Maintaining this structure is no simple feat. The sheer scale of operations involves multiple specialized departments working in concert – from the photogrammetry teams capturing aerial data to the quality assurance department ensuring data integrity. Each piece of geographic information undergoes a rigorous journey: from initial collection through aerial photography and ground surveys, through complex processing and standardization protocols, to final integration into the database. The challenge is magnified by the dynamic nature of the data, exemplified by the cadastral layers which – at least in 2014 – required updates every two days to maintain accuracy. This constant flux demands not only technical expertise in database management but also careful orchestration of interdepartmental workflows to prevent disruptions. These maintenance processes, while resource-intensive, are fundamental to BANTAL's role as Israel's geographic backbone, enabling it to serve as an authoritative source for a wide range of applications and services. But similar efforts are not limited to national mapping services. They are present in Google Maps' continuous quest for an all-encompassing map of the empire (Plantin 2018; McQuire 2019), navigation app Waze's reliance on gamification to perform ground truthing (Hind and Gekker 2014; Mattern 2017), Open Street Map's efforts to galvanize its community for voluntarily maintaining their open source database (Perkins and Dodge 2008; Gerlach 2010), or pandemic maps' struggle with providing equitable information to people with varying risks (Mattern 2021b).

Perhaps the clearest indication of the efforts required to build and maintain maps online lies in the somewhat murky distinction between geographic information systems (GIS) and digital maps. At face value, those are two different things: the former encompasses the suite of professional-grade tools that use spatial statistics to assist in the calculation of various use cases, from remote-sensor data for climate modelling to urban planning and design (figure 5.3). The ur-example of this is Esri, the behemoth firm of the GIS industry and seller of the ubiquitous ArcGIS tools package. The latter is the focus of this book, a variety of consumer-facing maps that require no expert knowledge or calculation, offering the familiar usability of an app in map form. Google Maps is the prominent case study here. Moreover, as noted by media researcher and critical GIS practitioner Laura Beltz Imaoka, the difference between the two has been constantly emphasized by Esri to create a product distinction and continuously sell expensive software licences to researchers, governments, and security organizations: 'The gap between "free maps" and "technology" and between "billions of people" and "enterprise consumers" are common phrases in Esri's public relations discourse. It distances and distinguishes Esri's motives and positions its clients, products, and services as "serious" endeavours against an expanding class of novice mapmakers and open-source products' (Imaoka 2021, 112).

But looking deeper into the organizational logic behind the two types of objects, and particularly their rootedness in the

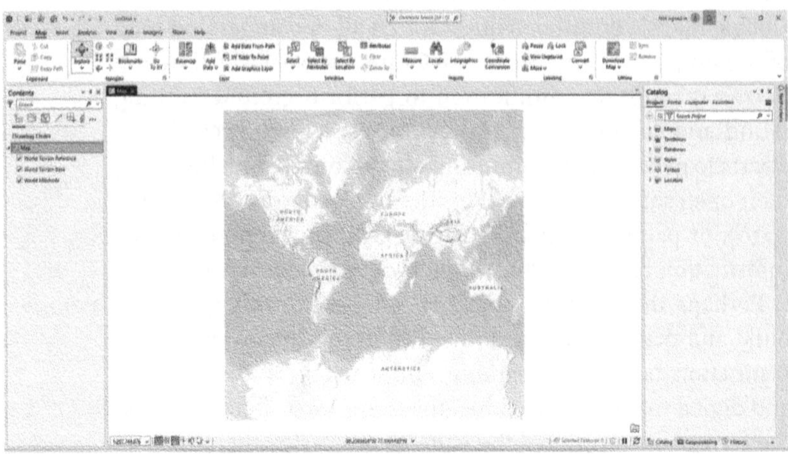

Figure 5.3: A screenshot of Esri's ArcGIS interface on Windows.

pursuit of spatial data for economic gains (Duggan 2024), one cannot ignore that they are two sides of the same labour coin. Mike Duggan, a critical cartographer, argues that at the foundation of our contemporary explosion of digital cartography lies the desire of public and commercial organizations to deploy better 'location intelligence' for tasks as distinct as fighting crime or solving land disputes between indigenous tribes and the government of Indonesia. The proliferation of GIS as a technology from the 1970s onward has democratized access to spatial calculation while creating an imagined community of GIS practitioners (and vendors) that aimed to solve problems through maps (Imaoka 2017). This resulted in a growing familiarity with such tools and their integration into various platforms (Barns 2020), which in turn led to non-reflexive deployment by those unfamiliar – or uninterested – in the cartographic gap between the map and the territory, for example developers trying to integrate 'a map' into their website or app. GIS thus became indicative of 'data-based' and clever approaches to problems.[1] In parallel, the field has become more dependent on data collected through habitual use of digital maps on mobile devices, with those using it becoming more prone to errors and miscalculations (Kwan 2002; 2016; Thatcher et al. 2016).

Consider, for instance, the work done by city planners. They create maps according to which urban development unfolds, in a process that requires both adherence to specific professional codes and communal deliberations (Carton 2007). But as Wilmott and Wood (2024) note, the deliberation is limited by the condition imposed by the *base map*, the underlying layer of basic information upon which the rest of the development is imagined. While existing before digitalization, the centrality of GIS and the workflow processes accompanying it made the base map increasingly formulaic and rigid, unable to accommodate alternative imagining of cities. This is especially true as the working conditions of those involved in mapmaking and map maintenance resembles more the ethos of the tech sector, with highly divided (if occasionally well-paid) workforce. When workers of Mapbox, one of the only (if much smaller and somewhat different in scope) competitors to Esri, tried to unionize in 2021, they lost (Love 2021), which has sent a wave of resentment and departures from the company. In a long post, one of its founding employees recounts how the discussion of social justice, including working conditions in the tech and GIS worlds, were paramount to the young company in the early 2000s but then gradually disappeared with time (Bemel-Benrud 2022).

A similar fate awaited the French mapping startup Zenly, acquired in 2017 by US tech giant Snap, which integrated its underlying technology into its Snapchat Map feature and then shut it down in 2023, mostly due to culture clashes between the companies. In an interview with a journalist, one ex-employee explained that '[Zenly's] working culture was one where, if you were moving fast enough, you'd be able to fix mistakes fast enough before they became big mistakes. But that just doesn't work in a Snap world' (Deck 2022, n.p.). As I claimed with Daniel Joseph when analysing a different media object – the independent video-game studio – it is extremely hard to maintain your claimed politics when faced with networked distribution in a globalized competition. The success brought by being 'indy' or 'resistant' falters in the face of labour and logistic challenges of measuring up to the new popularity and expectation this status brings (Gekker and Joseph 2021). Making maps today is big business, and it requires serious resources.

To illustrate this point, and conclude this section, I want to reference the data centre maps produced by Carr and colleagues (2022) for three urban areas that are central to knowledge work. In those maps, they detail known and estimated energy requirements of each data centre (displayed as large red circles to indicate impact on the urban fabric), alongside the water in the area required for cooling such construction. To me, such maps appropriately represent both the work this research team has put into making spatial realities visible and trackable, while also showing the hidden work *behind* the production of such maps, in how the data and software that make them rely on cloud infrastructures. Ironically, by 'aim[ing] to understand the human geographical and urban societal implications of data centres, (while) addressing ramifications on labor, real estate, geographies of policy and investment, and the competition for resources that DCs depend on' (Carr et al. 2022, 107), they neglect to consider how these very same data centres support their own labour in producing the map. The 'location intelligence' (Duggan 2024, 153) flowing in and out of these centres also makes other types of work possible: the work through maps.

Working through the map

Recall SuperHumans Laura's video that began this chapter. When convincing her audience to use Google Maps as a tool to secure low-effort freelance gigs, she obviously does not mention Google's data centres, the work that goes into maintaining the base map, or any other aspects that make contemporary digital mapping smoothly available at the tap of one's finger. Google Maps, like other platforms, performs a balancing act between presenting themselves as a neutral canvas (or a conduit) with minimal control, while simultaneously being full of potential to elevate content and business practices for a variety of users and partners. As presciently stated by Tarleton Gillespie (2010), platforms become such not merely by *doing* something, but mostly by *saying* that they are: simultaneously assuming control and releasing responsibility. For workers, such duality results in platforms being permissive potentates (Vallas and Schor 2020) that create the illusion of independence while dictating – through obfuscation – more and more aspects of the employment conditions.

And while Google Maps, or most other digital maps, are not labour platforms in the traditional sense, they become central in the flattening of space and time to make labour distributed and disconnected, often to the detriment of those engaging in it. Particularly in the transportation and food delivery industries, companies are no longer required to maintain a physical centre for their drivers or couriers, relying instead on algorithmic modes of control (Mohlmann and Zalmanson 2017). For spatially distributed work, the map allows workers to be signalled where (and sometimes when) they must be, while simultaneously tracking both the workers' location and their interaction through the map's user interface to continuously optimize them (mentioned above as producing 'data assets').

Gemma Newlands (2021) traces the centrality of the map for delivery platforms through her critical examination of how algorithmic surveillance restructures workplace dynamics in the gig economy. In her research on platforms like Foodora and Deliveroo, Newlands demonstrates how these organizations deploy algorithmic surveillance as their primary control mechanism, transforming traditional dyadic observer–observee relationships into a system where non-human agents perform monitoring, assessment, and decision making. Drawing on Henri Lefebvre's (1992) spatial triad theory, she reveals how platforms privilege 'conceived space' (abstract digital cartography) over 'perceived' and 'lived spaces' (material embodied reality of workers). This privileging creates a problematic epistemological gap, which she calls *cartographic dissonance,* as algorithms can only process machine-readable data whilst remaining blind to workers' contextual, embodied experiences.

When delivery workers navigate through congested urban streets, facing harsh weather, traffic, or customer interactions, these material realities become invisible within the abstract digital mapping systems that optimize their labour. While often benefitting the map-providing platform, this is not a unidirectional control. First, such resulting divergence between digital representation and physical reality limits organizational knowledge-building and disrupts the cartographic illusion of the firm. Second, it creates interstitial spaces where workers can resist algorithmic control through data obfuscation (like GPS spoofing or using third-party apps) and collective action, demonstrating the complex spatial power dynamics of platform-mediated work. Interestingly, this power can flow also in the reverse direction, as when the couriers of Grab, Singapore-based food delivery app, complained about how unusable Google Maps was in Jakarta. This prompted the company to build its own special cameras and offer its five million freelance drivers extra pay for carrying out mapping activities on top of their regular duties. It now aims to produce the ground-up GrabMap specifically for itself and similar companies, competing with Google on its home turf (Anindya 2024). Platform labour gig work is thus central to mapped work, particularly when gamification is added to the mix.

In the previous chapter, I outlined playing with maps not just as a way for map makers to facilitate engaging with space differently, but as an inherent part of digital maps' overall plea to depoliticize maps and assuage user suspicions of them. In this section I want to further extend this argument: that such depoliticization through play is central to the bidirectional transformation of regular users into free workers for mapping applications while simultaneously removing power from paid workers who are managed through them.

Niels van Doorn and Julie Chen are both researchers of gig work who carried out ethnographic studies in New York City and Beijing, respectively. When comparing notes of their independent results, they noticed how a similar process occurred in the different platforms operating in both cities. At the start of their operation, fuelled by venture capital money and/or attempts to recruit as many 'riders' as possible, all platforms offered many incentives, and often did so in language and interfaces coded as playful (Sicart 2014; Deterding 2015): using customization, various badges and game mechanics, creating random intervals for orders in New York, or challenging riders weekly by locking certain deliveries behind 'levels' and resetting them each week in Beijing. Despite their differences, for both cities and various apps the map was central in simultaneously gamifying the work experience and obfuscating it: over time, various indicators such as distance or time measurement began to disappear, and instead the map added personalized incentives that pushed the riders to work more than they intended or drive more recklessly to keep up. Performing this sort of data labour (Grohmann 2025) reinforces Newlands's cartographic dissonance, as the 'game' on the screen becomes increasingly detached from the realities of actual employment performed through it. Gamification is an excellent tool for Agre's (1994) grammars of action – making continuous worker actions discrete and sequential – and combined with digital maps' casual power makes workers less able to discern which of and how their actions are being broken down over time.

Waze, which was previously mentioned in the context of gamification techniques, was also an early pioneer of turning map users into workers. As argued elsewhere (Hind and Gekker 2014), this 'social navigation' application effectively transformed everyday drivers into unpaid cartographic labourers, through three specific dynamics: reporting road hazards, collaboratively managing vehicle flow, and addressing latent map errors. Unlike traditional satnav systems that presented the driving world as an immutable 'base map', Waze positioned the digital map on the same ontological plane as the physical road environment itself – as a fluid, manipulable object that users could actively reshape. What made this labour extraction particularly effective was its presentation through ludic mechanics: drivers earned points for contributions, collected bonus 'treats' for verifying map data, and watched their avatars 'munch' these rewards in Pacman-like fashion. This playful design masked what was essentially a 'volunteered, mass data-collection practice' (Hind and Gekker 2014, 175) as something 'fun' and socially rewarding. Through the merging of touchscreen interfaces and gamified sociable interactions, Waze naturalized this form of 'playbour' (Kücklich 2005) embedding it within drivers' everyday spatial routines while simultaneously reconfiguring the very experience of driving itself, and through it, of resulting space as drivers-mappers affected traffic and social norms (Hind and Gekker 2019; Fisher 2022). This transformation of map users into free labourers had profound implications, as it represented a shift in agency from state agencies and purpose-built satnav companies to an ostensibly 'collaborative' public – one that was nonetheless contributing to a privatized mapping database that would eventually be acquired by Google.

An even more complicated picture is presented by Gaode Map (Hu 2025), the most used Chinese map (Statista 2025b) and a super-app (Steinberg 2020) that contains multiple different seemingly unrelated services that operate in tandem under a shared brand and data collection regime extending 'appification' into everyday life (van der Vlist, Helmond, Dieter, et al. 2025). Gaode offers not merely a mapping service, but functions as a comprehensive platform that integrates ride-hailing, food delivery, and various location-based services within a single interface. As a 'host-style app' (2025, 3323), that contains multiple interfaces to sub-apps that require no additional installs, it simultaneously relies on its overall cartographic infrastructure whilst enabling third-party transactions through its intermediary model. This dual function creates a particular form of spatial power, as Gaode leverages its dominance in digital mapping to extend into ride-hailing markets through strategic partnerships with local taxi companies and drivers. Unlike Western counterparts, Gaode's aggregation model operates within China's market hierarchy (Zheng and Huang 2018), navigating between state regulation and informal labour grassroots markets. Through its 'no-commission league' and 'good taxi' programs, Gaode attempts to distinguish itself from competitors like Didi by promising greater autonomy to drivers whilst still employing the gamified mechanics of algorithmic management that characterize platform labour. Moreover, by making itself available to smaller regional ride-hailing and taxi services who lack established presence in the app market, it entrenches its position as a spatial labour infrastructure.

While being most prominent, food delivery and ride-hailing are not the only ways people work through maps. Similar to Gaode's role in China, Google's 'one map to rule them all' approach (McQuire 2019) in the rest of the world is likewise creating a multitude of ways both regular people and professionals work through it. The platform itself encourages this by promoting such aspects of it such as their 'Local Guides' program, which awards gamified points (figure 5.4) to map users who go beyond reference and add information to the map (in a classic free labour or playbour manner). Previously somewhat separated, over the years the guides UI has become directly integrated into Maps itself, which will occasionally prompt users to answer a question about a place they navigated to using Google Maps (or simply visited while having location history on). The questions are innocuous, along the lines of 'Does this place have wheelchair access?' or 'Can you buy milk here?' and you respond by pressing one of three buttons: yes, no, I don't know/skip. By participating, you gain points and levels. Google gains the data needed to maintain its advantage over competitors when it comes to spatial search, particularly combined with user reviews integrated into the map (Mathayomchan and Taecharungroj 2020). And while users ostensibly work to grow Google's epistemic dominance of physical space, according to the cheerful video posted by the GM's official channel, 'with every place added, photo taken, and review shared, local guides inspire us to explore our world' (Google Maps 2022, at 1:42).

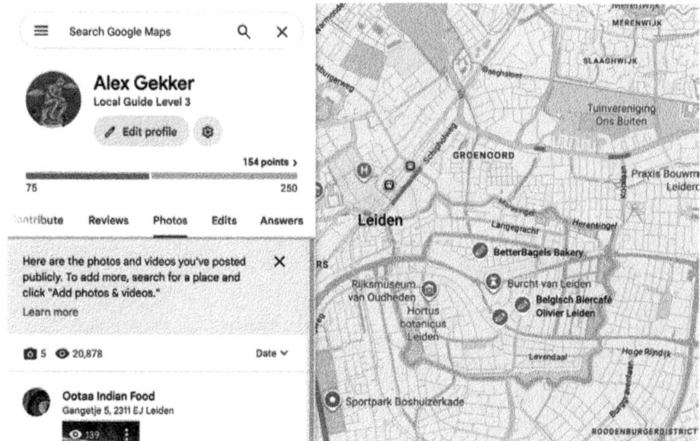

Figure 5.4: Screenshot from my local guides profile page as of 2025. Alas, after 9 years of occasional submissions, I've only gained two levels.

Through such mundane data collection, Google Maps, and particularly its Street View function, has become central to various types of work done on the platform. As discussed in chapter 3, Street View puts Google in a unique position of providing accurate mapped data alongside street-level imagery as a service through its API. Of course, other companies attempt to catch up and provide similar functionality, for example Meta-owned Mappillary, with its dedicated open-source image collection and stitching, or Apple, Bing, and Baidu Maps, which all have a version of Street View (Look Around, Streetside, and Baidu Street View, respectively). Yet, no one has the outside influence (or job opportunities) that Google Maps does. Street View commodifies geographic information by making public space beholden to the tech giant to monetize, in what geographer Luis F. Alvarez León called a new property regime (Alvarez León 2016). Still, despite its global ambition, the Street View map is far from complete. As with many 'universal' platforms, its coverage gets sparse as we move away from the Global North, echoing the colonial legacies of mapping (figure 5.5). This gap can

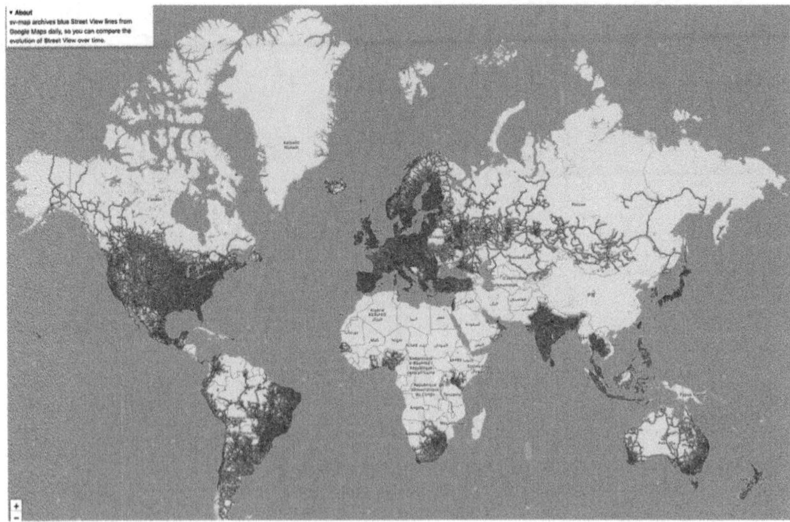

Figure 5.5: The official coverage of Google's Street View, as of April 2025. Source: screenshot by the author from https://sv-map.netlify.app/. (Compare to figure 3.2 to see changes over two years of additional photography.)

be exploited. Users equipped with the right kinds of 3D cameras can contribute their own street imagery, either as a standalone 'Photo Sphere' or stitched together through third-party applications into virtual tours (Google, n.d.-a).

An investigation by the educational vlogger Phil Edwards shows that over the last couple of years, a growing number of independent companies and individuals have set up their own Street View enterprises, that are filling the gaps left by Google. This is done for various reasons, from altruistic interest in promoting one's cultural heritage to commercial motivations in advertising a tour or safari operator, for instance. Often, such images are branded in a particular way, for instance when looking directly down, but are otherwise indistinguishable from regular Street View images to the casual user. A community centre and a realtor alike can decide to map and upload images of a relevant area to attract attention (and business) their way (figure 5.6).[2] Another

Figure 5.6: Privately uploaded Photo Sphere Street View imagery from Woodstock Community Centre and the Realtor Eugene Gank in Sydney, Australia, respectively. Screenshots from Google Street View, March 2025.

person interviewed in Edwards's video represents the Ugandan company RippleNami ('a ripple of data becomes a tsunami of information'). One of their central projects is collaborating with various state and local African governments to add street images. When they do so, there's a significant uptick of tourism in the area. In all these examples, people treat the map as a spatial search interface, and work to augment their own findability in what is called search engine optimization (SEO) while continuously contributing valuable data to the platform. As with other business practices, this can also be exploited by various unscrupulous actors, like when Canadian journalistic investigation has uncovered that half of local appliance repair companies on Google Maps were fake or fraudulent (Grundig et al. 2020).

One final example of how people work through maps comes from the same company. Unlike in its African tourism system, RippleNami captures urban data in Uganda and Gambia to feed into its rental tax compliance system (rTCS). Joining a growing fleet of surveyors and assessors making use of Google Maps and other commercial digital mapping, the company attempted to algorithmically estimate the potential revenue of rental property in a specific area, by combining existing aerial imagery with their own Street View additions. Having the ground-level images helped them check the number of storeys a specific building has, generating more accurate taxation estimation. And by publishing it to Google Maps after collection, they claim to 'promote' the community surveyed by making it more visible and searchable.

Conclusion: Making maps work

This chapter has shown what it means to work with digital maps, both in terms of the effort it takes to maintain their seemingly seamless reflection of the world, and how this results in new types of labour practices. Distinction between geographic information systems (GIS) and commercial digital mapping is becoming more tenuous as the former powers the latter, while hiding their work behind obfuscating user interfaces. New types of work are becoming available through the map, as ride-hailers and couriers ('riders') become unmoored from shared places of congregation that previously characterized logistical work. Instead, driven by the changing nature of platform labour, they can be tracked and 'activated' from anywhere to anywhere by using the map as a command-and-control structure. All the while, they are generating valuable data for the firms behind the map, allowing tighter control to be maintained by, for example, finding the precise incentive schemes that will get a courier to work on a rainy day, or the minimum payment per trip that will keep a ride-hailing presence in a city viable. More mundane uses of maps for work harken to today's ability to easily create custom maps, for instance the 'Amsterdam Valley' one, that puts the tech companies and startups of the Dutch capital on a single display, highlighting potential places for job seekers.[3]

This chapter comes after the one on maps and play, but they are more complementary than contrasting. In fact, in the introduction to a special issue on 'Work and Play' in the journal *Information, Communication & Society*, the guest editor explains how at first the submissions were to be divided into these two categories, but 'it became clear that a more complex dialectic was under way. As such, the papers begin by investigating play-structures incorporated into work, theorize play *as* work, analyse the workings of play, diagnose the new world of work and, finally, suggest ways in which a work-play dynamic might be utilized by radical pedagogy' (Darlington 2018, 1189). He further explains that one of the key examples that challenged this dichotomy was the case of *Ingress* and *Pokémon Go*, which I presented in chapter 4. Gamification with and through the map easily lends itself to merging of play with work and the masking of the serious consequences this might have. The current chapter shows its consequences for people's employment: what I throughout the book called casual power is also very much present in the way that digital maps appeal to our sense of exploration and wonder, making us potentially less suspicious of them exploiting us compared to other digital platforms (such as social media), which have become notorious in the public imagination (Zuboff 2019). This is not to say that mapmakers are *purposefully* manipulating their users. By their nature, maps are simultaneously deeply personal and extremely political, as shown by Google Maps' addition of the United States to its list of 'sensitive' countries alongside China and Russia after Trump's 2024 re-election and subsequent demands for the Gulf of Mexico to be renamed as the Gulf of America (Elias 2025). Rather, this cartographic superimposition of the past and current, fun and serious, sometimes (inadvertently) affects how work is done.

In their research on user perceptions of work and play, a group of Finnish game scholars conducted a survey of 382 YouTubers and Twitch streamers (Törhönen et al. 2019). While a very different type of labour than those working through maps, they were interested in a similar question to this chapter: When does play become work and vice versa? After examining respondents' personal attitudes, unsurprisingly those who saw what they did *primarily as work* were the most engaged and earned the most. Perhaps less intuitively, those who viewed their craft *primarily as play* earned *more* income than creators who alternated between the two approaches or saw them equally applying to their case. The researchers note how this highlights 'the increasing workification of our play activities' (Törhönen et al. 2019, 1). Taking both this and the previous chapter together, this is very much true when it comes to digital maps. And as I will show in the next chapter, this is also done through a constant surveillance of the map users.

6

Surveillance

In January 2018, the locations of multiple military bases around the world, some of them highly classified, were exposed. Not just exact positions, but troop movements and patrol routes became widely available to anyone with an internet connection. The culprit was not a determined hacker group, nor a whistle-blower à la Edward Snowden, but a popular fitness-tracking app called Strava. The app allows users to track their exercise data, via smartphones/smartwatches and optionally by connecting to dedicated devices such as Bluetooth heartrate monitors. It became popular and widely used among smartphone sports enthusiasts, more so in wealthy Global North countries. Among them were active military and security personnel stationed in countries like Syria and Afghanistan, which have far fewer Strava users. Therefore, when viewed on the new global heatmap feature launched by the platform just a few months beforehand, places where soldiers walk, run, and bike 'lit up' against the relative darkness of surrounding territory devoid of such users. The public heat map works like Snap's Snap Map discussed in chapter 5: it highlights aggregated activity from different users. While not showing individual or time-specific measurements, unlike Snap Map the heat map is structured as tracks, not amorphous areas, and thus routes that are used often and consistently (e.g., a perimeter road of a base) are visible in their fullest. Beyond exposing intimate details about soldiers' lives inside existing known bases, for instance where they sleep or eat, the 'leak' as it was called in the press (although to be fair, nothing was actually leaked) uncovered unknown or unconfirmed bases, for example a suspected NATO installation near a dam in Northern Syria or a Russian base in Hmeimim in the same country (Sly 2018) (see figure 6.1).

What happened here? Inadvertently for its users, yet common to many other digital apps, Strava's privacy settings were set to 'opt-out' rather than 'opt-in', meaning that by default, one's physical activity became visible on the global map, unless one would choose to purposefully turn it off in the settings. Collective movements of individuals were then aggregated to chart routes and paths in places where supposedly there shouldn't be any. Lack of specific identifiers was further not a guarantee of anonymity, as indicated by another prominent map-based privacy case, where a high-ranking priest in the US Catholic church resigned his position when outed through the use of the Grindr app, popular in the gay dating scene (O'Brien and Bajak 2021). Despite being supposedly anonymous, the Grindr app would sell bulk user data through third-party data brokers, that could be then resold while using geofencing to ask for users in specific locations.

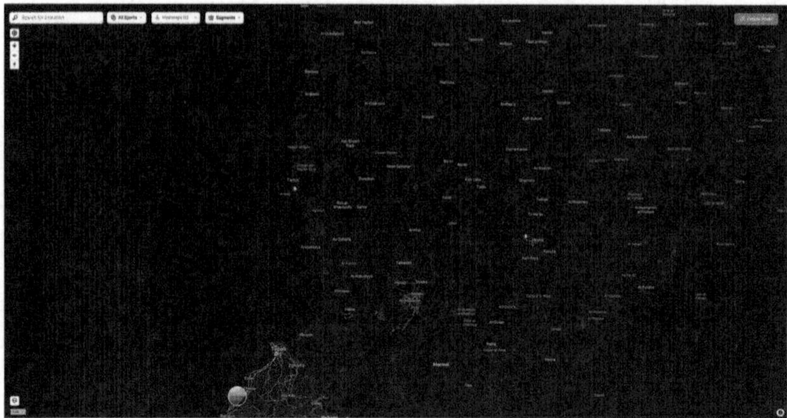

Figure 6.1: The area of Syria where military bases were disclosed in 2018, seen through the Strava heatmap feature in June 2025. The app now only shows very high-resolution tracks of activity, preventing identifying specific locales. Screenshot by the author.

Using the priest's known public movements, investigative journalists from the Catholic newspaper *The Pillar* were then able to locate his 'anonymized' unique identifier among the aggregated user data. They then determined that the user in question was inside gay bars and private residences while on Grindr. In a subsequent lawsuit he filed against the dating app, the priest contested the decision to release his private data into the public realm and failing to properly inform him of doing so (Melnick 2024).

It is tempting to discount both Strava and Grindr as merely acting out of greed to monetize their user data through what business scholar Shoshana Zuboff (2019) calls 'surveillance capitalism' and will be discussed later in this chapter. However, my argument here is different. In chapter 3, I have shown how for many users, digital maps have become indistinguishable from the act of moving in the world, particularly in cars. In chapter 4, I presented how maps integrate play into their design and use to become naturalized and non-suspicious. In chapter 5, movement and play have combined to explain how work being done through and on maps makes use of their unique attributes. In this chapter, I will return to the elements mentioned in each of these previous chapters and highlight how the attribute of surveillance is not accidental to digital map use, but central to how they are built and operated.

To start, I will review the different genealogies of surveillance in media studies, to anchor the idea of 'infrastructural surveillance' that I proposed with Sam Hind. Then I unpack the four characteristics of infrastructural surveillance: aggregation, standards, distribution, and enclosure as they apply specifically to digital maps. Next, I use this conceptual framework to return to some of the case studies examined in the three previous chapters and reflect on how the surveillance aspect of each one was central to its mapped nature. I conclude by considering the seemingly unavoidable nature of map-based surveillance.

From panopticon to infrastructural surveillance

The notion of surveillance is central to contemporary understanding of the relations between technology and society. Ever since Jeremy Bentham invented it, the Panopticon has become a central metaphor for Foucault's (Foucault 1977) organizational theory of society, where we imagine ourselves being watched by others. In a series of letters to his brother, Bentham (2017) proposed a circular prison where the inmates are visible from the central control structure, which are in turn themselves obscured from view. Driven by the moral philosophy principles of utilitarianism, the idea was for the prisoners to know that they can be watched at any moment, forcing them to always be on their best behaviour. The warden and guards would in turn be watched through occasional visits by members of the public, ensuring a just system. For Michel Foucault, this construction invoked not *justice* but *power*; specifically, the way that such watchability by higher-ups resembled the internalized fears of citizens in modern societies. To him,

> [t]his enclosed, segmented space, observed at every point, in which the individuals are inserted in a fixed place, in which the slightest movements are supervised, in which all events are recorded, in which an uninterrupted work of writing links the centre and periphery, in which power is exercised without division, according to a continuous hierarchical figure, in which each individual is constantly located, examined and distributed ... – all this constitutes a compact model of the disciplinary mechanism (Foucault 1995, 195).

The classroom, the barracks (of the conscripted), the hospital, and the factory floor all harken back to the Panopticon's configuration of being watched.

Gilles Deleuze, in an essay written as a 'postscript' to Foucault, grounded in discussions of his seminars in the late 1980s, has further specified this contemporary form of surveillance. Accordingly, we are moving from the disciplinary societies that proliferated in a series of enclosures, to societies of control that thrive in the continuous and undefined digital spaces, where you need to keep an active LinkedIn profile not because you need a job but because you *might* need one. One is being watched by ways of data segmentation and categorization, turning from individual into a 'dividual' whose data doubles are being unceasingly (re)categorized by governmental and commercial mechanisms (Cheney-Lippold 2017). This leads to an even deeper internalization of a 'liquid' surveillance (Bauman and Lyon 2013), where collaboration of the surveilled is expected – or even desirable when involving luxury items such as sports trackers or AI-enabled cameras (Gilliard and Golumbia 2021).

In turn, Shoshana Zuboff's (2015; 2019) concept of *surveillance capitalism* identifies a new economic system predicated on the extraction of human experience as raw material for behavioural data, which is then processed into predictive products that anticipate what we will do now and in the future. Surveillance capitalism operates through what Zuboff terms behavioural futures markets, creating economic imperatives for continuous data extraction that exceed the operational requirements of service provision. Meanwhile, Murakami Wood and Monahan's (2019) notion of *platform surveillance* examines how digital platforms become sites of multiple, intersecting forms of surveillance that blur traditional boundaries between state and corporate monitoring. Platform surveillance emphasizes the ways platforms mediate social relations whilst simultaneously extracting value from the data generated through these interactions, creating new forms of algorithmic governance that operate across multiple scales and contexts. For instance, Netflix's distribution of content through proprietary content delivery networks (CDNs), built separately from shared internet traffic providers, relies on predictive analytics of viewing habits to pre-load specific content onto various edge nodes (Helles and Flyverbom 2019).

In this societal configuration, harkening back to Foucault and Deleuze, one does not have *to be* surveilled in order to *feel* like one is. Such *imagined* surveillance occurs when expectations of personal and professional social media presence clash with the internalized fear of 'you never know who's looking [at your profile]' (Duffy and Chan 2019, 132). Experiencing it becomes particularly destabilizing in an algorithmic culture where users are never sure which aspects of their life are structured by computation and which merely felt such (Bucher 2017), and come up with various folk theories and remedies to become (in)visible online (Bishop 2019; 2020). These real and imagined surveillances acquire the logic of automation, where to process and make sense of the data collected – and user's changing behaviours in response to such collection – platforms deploy a *cascading* surveillance (Andrejevic 2019). The collection of more data requires more automation which in turn allows for collection of more granular data, repeat ad infinitum. To Andrejevic, this means that the Foucauldian panopticon is coming to an end: instead of internalized potential surveillance, the subject experiences omnipresent adjusting surveillance, directed towards modifying behaviours rather than punishing undesirable ones.

Coming from a different disciplinary background, computing scholar Philip Agre developed what has become a crucial distinction in understanding contemporary forms of digital control. In his influential work 'Surveillance and Capture: Two Models of Privacy', Agre (1994) contrasted two fundamentally different approaches to monitoring and regulating human behaviour. His main assertion was that what is being done through computers is not surveillance in the traditional sense. The surveillance model employs visual metaphors (e.g., 'Big Brother is watching') and emphasizes non-disruptive, surreptitious data collection that maintains territorial boundaries between 'private' and public spheres. This model derives from historical experiences of malevolent political activities of state organizations, such as the infamous

East German Stasi, creating what amounts to an adversarial relationship between watcher and watched. By contrast, the capture model employs linguistic metaphors, taking as its prototype the quasi-philosophical project of 'ontological reconstruction' undertaken by computer professionals in IT companies, where digitized data is sorted and categorized for better retrieval and further operationalization. Rather than surreptitious observation, capture describes readily apparent instrumentation that entails the reorganization of existing human activities, often for commercial benefit to the capturer.

What makes capture distinct from surveillance is its approach to protocological power (Galloway 2004). Rather than simply watching, capture operates by creating grammars of action (discussed in more detail in the previous chapter) wherein activities are divided into institutionally standardized parts and reconstructed in real time from captured ontologies. Transforming activities into sequences of 'minimum replicable units' (Quinn 1992, as cited in Agre, 1994, 108) makes them representable within computational systems, enabling what Agre termed the 'computerization of the workplace' through the sequencing and ordering of work processes. This restructuring embodies protocological power: actors become bound not by the content or intention of their actions, but by whether such actions are permissible under the sociotechnical transmission protocols of the organization. The result is a form of procedural rhetoric (Bogost 2006) that operates through the systemic level of interface design (Drucker 2011; Stanfill 2015; Ash, Anderson, et al. 2018), where possibilities are constrained through 'greyed out' buttons and predetermined pathways.

Agre's prescient analysis, written in 1994, laid the groundwork for understanding how digital technologies would come to reshape social life through the reorganization of human activities into machine-readable formats. However, his framework focused primarily on workplace reorganization and early computing practices, emphasizing locally organized activities within particular institutional contexts. The contemporary digital landscape, particularly as it relates to mapping technologies and connected autonomous vehicles, requires extending his insights beyond both the workplace focus of capture and the business model emphasis of surveillance capitalism to account for what Sam Hind and I have termed *infrastructural* surveillance.

Infrastructural surveillance represents a qualitatively different form of control that departs from Agre's classic distinction whilst also differing from both surveillance capitalism and platform surveillance in crucial ways. Unlike Zuboff's surveillance capitalism, which centres on a macroeconomic approach of value extraction from human experience, infrastructural surveillance sidesteps business models entirely by embedding surveillance directly into the technical requirements of operations. Where platform surveillance examines how platforms mediate and monitor social relations, infrastructural surveillance addresses the under-explored infrastructural requirements that certain digital technologies claim as necessary preconditions for basic functionality. Whereas *captured* actions (form-filling, box-ticking) are operationalized from existing *a priori* multitudes of life, under 'smart' technologies no actions are possible *outside of the bounds allowed by the infrastructure.* Privacy is thus not threatened after the fact but is constrained as a matter of fact. Participation is dependent on the agreement to be surveilled and immediately curtailed by such surveillance. This model emphasizes the total reformatting of privacy practices along infrastructural lines and gestures towards the largely inescapable nature of sovereign power wielded by infrastructural operators, from mobile phone network providers to map apps.

Infrastructural surveillance in digital maps

Digital mapping technologies exemplify the transition from traditional surveillance and capture models to infrastructural surveillance. Unlike the panopticon's disciplinary gaze or workplace capture systems that reorganize existing human activities, digital maps create entirely new ontologies that make machine-readability a prerequisite for spatial participation. This represents a fundamental shift in how surveillance operates within contemporary digital infrastructures (table 6.1). Drawing from my analysis in the previous chapters and extending insights from critical infrastructure studies, we can identify how digital mapping platforms embody the four key characteristics of infrastructural surveillance: the

Table 6.1: Comparing surveillance, capture, and infrastructural surveillance. Adapted from Gekker and Hind (2019).

Surveillance	**Capture**	**Infrastructural Surveillance**
Employs visual metaphors: Big Brother is watching you.	Employs linguistic metaphors by means of various grammars of action.	Employs 'totalizing' metaphor of infrastructure, omnipresent and invisible until breaks.
Emphasizes non-disruptive, surreptitious data collection.	Describes the readily apparent instrumentation that entails the reorganization of existing activities.	Reorients itself towards the facilitation of nonhuman actions rather than reorganization of human ones.
Is concerned to mark off a 'private' region by means of territorial metaphors of 'invasion' and the like.	Activities are being constructed in real time from a set of institutionally standardized parts specified by the captured ontology.	Creates new ontologies, by means of continuous training on various datasets.
Depicts the monitoring of activity as centrally organized and presumes that the resulting information is centrally stored.	Emphasizes the locally organized nature of activities within particular institutional contexts.	Entails distributed organization within infrastructural constraints and wide data sharing.
Takes as its prototype the malevolent political activities of state organizations.	Takes as its prototype the quasi-philosophical project of ontological reconstruction undertaken by computer professionals in private organizations.	Takes as its prototype the quasi-metaphysical geopolitical 'stack' of planetary computation.

aggregation of data, initialization of *protocols* limiting possible actions, the prioritization of *distributed* modes of governance, and the *enclosure* of the user in a personalized bubble of sovereign power.

Aggregation involves the systematic development of new infrastructural formations capable of capturing multiple data sources with differing regularity and granularity. As Plantin (2018) demonstrates, Google Maps derives its cartographic supremacy from aggregating diverse data sources: governmental and international satellite data, local business information, in-house projects like Street View, and passive user data from smartphones and connected devices. This aggregation creates comprehensive spatial arrangements that exceed any single platform's individual capabilities, moving beyond simple data collection to establish what Plantin sees as a shift from participatory platform to knowledge infrastructures. Unlike surveillance capitalism's focus on behavioural surplus extraction for predictive products, this infrastructural aggregation aims to achieve totalizing spatial knowledge of operational conditions across multiple scales and contexts. In effect, most digital maps defy Borges's fable that I presented in the first chapter, aiming to actually produce a map of an empire that indeed covers it in its entirety.

A clear example can be seen in the prolonged attempt by the tech giant Amazon to buy the robotic Roomba cleaners parent company iRobot before abandoning the attempt after pressure from European regulators in January 2024 (European Commission 2024). When the intention first surfaced, many pointed out that the purchase would effectively allow Amazon to access detailed layouts from millions of homes being cleaned by iRobot devices (or have been done so in the past). To function, the devices create a map of the spaces to be cleaned and optimize their movement accordingly. While it might not be exactly clear for what purpose Amazon would use floorplans and blueprints, many privacy organizations raised alarm. When asked about the potential use of such data, the company refused to respond and instead issued a general statement about keeping user data safe, with 'Customer trust is something we have worked hard to earn – and work hard to keep – every day' (Johnson 2022). Amazon ended up not buying iRobot, but will acquire the Bee device, which uses continuous audio monitoring to isolate the owner's voice and whoever they're talking to, transcribe it using generative AI and then turn it into 'insights' (Silberling 2025). This idea of totalizing collection, while not directly related to mapping, helps to understand how iRobot or other spatial technologies could serve Amazon's aggregation options (or those of other big tech firms).

Standards development represents the creation of protocological rules that force spatial data to conform and follow instructions governing their operation. Here, Galloway's (2004) concept of protocological power becomes crucial, when actors become bound not by the content of their spatial practices, but by whether such practices are permissible under the sociotechnical transmission protocols of mapping infrastructures. The control of APIs functions as what Plantin identifies as obligatory passage points for spatial data flows, constituting a new way to delimit what mapping entails and 'who is mapping, who is mapped, and who can access the map' (Plantin 2018, 495). The development of standards is always a work of classification and exertion of invisible power over what is to be accepted as the default (Woolgar 1990; Bowker and Star 2000; Lampland and Star 2009). In mapping, because of their spatial ramifications, standards acquire surveillant capacity to determine how physical spaces are being included – or not – in the map, and who gets to be seen.

For instance, a recent update to Google Maps in India (Singh and Mehta 2024) demonstrates how seemingly neutral technical standards embed particular spatial ontologies and exercise classificatory power over territorial representation. Google's deployment of an AI model to identify 'narrow roads' using satellite imagery and Street View data appears as a technical optimization yet constitutes a standardization of what qualifies as navigable space according to Western automotive mobility paradigms. The algorithm's training to recognize road width through building proximity, tree cover, and drainage infrastructure establishes a protocological hierarchy that privileges certain forms of spatial organization whilst rendering others as obstacles to be avoided. Similarly, GM changed its guidance from directing drivers to 'take a ramp' onto a specific street name (which is rarely known in India) to 'take the flyover'. This reveals how mapping standards must be continuously recalibrated to accommodate local spatial vernaculars. Yet, this accommodation occurs within predetermined algorithmic frameworks that maintain Google's gatekeeping authority. For instance, the integration of EV charging station data, including India's first mapping of two-wheeler charging spots, demonstrates how standards development anticipates and shapes future mobility patterns, embedding particular visions of sustainable transport that may not align with existing spatial practices or urban planning. Here, local spatial knowledge must be translated into standardized data formats to achieve visibility within the digital cartographic apparatus.

The *distribution* of knowledge production throughout digital mapping exemplifies what Parks and Starosielski term the foregrounding of 'processes of distribution' in media infrastructures (2015, 5) rather than just its production and consumption. Digital maps cultivate multiple, distributed knowledges by collecting various forms of data from users, secondary data markets, brokers, legacy databases, and the like. This distribution operates within a flat ontology where map and territory exist on the same plane, creating novel forms of spatial agency (Hind and Gekker 2019). As demonstrated in our analysis of social navigation platforms like Waze, users simultaneously make and use maps in ways that immediately transform territorial conditions. When a Waze user marks a traffic incident on their mobile screen, this action joins hundreds of other signals, ultimately resulting in route recalculations that directly affect traffic flows in physical space, affecting drivers *who are not actively using the app* (cf. Fisher 2022).

This process exemplifies the unified concept of the map-territory, where alterations to cartographic representations have immediate material consequences for spatial organization. As Helles and Flyverbom (2019) demonstrate with Netflix's content distribution networks, this involves tracking of user behaviour to optimize speed and quality of streaming video, for example by pre-loading certain types of content to edge devices based on machine learning of previous spikes in demand. In mapping contexts, the same approach leverages user navigation patterns to anticipate spatial data and optimize routing algorithms. The dashboard cameras company Bee Maps (not related to the Bee app acquired by Amazon) is an example of such distribution. Bee Maps captures detailed imagery every eight metres whilst instantly processing data through AI algorithms to detect street-level objects such as signage, construction zones, and billboards, using them to make highly accurate – and constantly updating – maps (Buczkowski 2025). This crowd-sourced approach demonstrates how cartographic production becomes distributed across multiple actors – drivers, AI systems, and clients – creating a hybrid assemblage where human labour, computational processing, and spatial sensing converge.

Finally, such distribution does not constitute genuine decentralization but an *enclosure* of knowledge, that Helmond identifies as efforts to 'decentralize data production while recentralizing data collection' (2015, 5). This leads to redefined sovereign relations between mapmakers and their users, which transcends the corporate-state boundaries that characterize both surveillance capitalism and platform surveillance. Such supra-national and distributed vision of sovereignty builds on Benjamin Bratton's theorization of a global geopolitical 'stack' which is 'not an already given vessel into which states intervene or markets mediate or political theologies invest with myths; rather it is generated in the confluence of platform logics' (2015, 34). Under such conditions, infrastructural surveillance is imbricated with sovereignty which is 'produced less by formal law than by shared physical postures of political subjects in relation to common infrastructure' (2015, 21). In other words, the aggregation of data through the setting of standards, even if distributed across multiple parties, *still converge within the actors who set the protocological rules* according to which such collection happens.

To exemplify: after becoming the de facto hegemon of the web for the better part of two decades, Google changed the access terms and pricing for its Maps API, requiring opening a Google Cloud account and adding a credit card to access even the free map views per developer (Dent 2018). This has caused many smaller map publishers, NGOs, academic projects and hobbyists to terminate their existing GM mashups. Some governmental agencies around the globe, often underfunded and using GM as a cheap or free alternative to make information accessible to its citizens, scrambled to respond. All this shows that opening collection to third parties does not buy them a seat at the table. Developing the platform over time, Google continuously tweaks the design of GM to blur the boundaries between *using* it and *adding* to it. From the collection of phone data for estimating public transport busyness, to the inclusion of new forms of place evaluation by using emojis (Hawkins 2023) or the integration of social reporting features that were previously unique to Waze (Shakir 2024), the map's thirst for data needs to be continuously quenched, but Google will be the one holding the keys.

Ultimately, the four modalities of aggregation, standards, distribution, and enclosure point to how maps today structure conditions of privacy rather than merely describe or report it. Consider the 'nearest neighbour attack', a new type of cyber-attack employed by sophisticated state actors using online mapping data (Goodin 2024). Instead of going directly after a 'hardened' primary target, hackers use publicly available spatial data such as map layout, satellite imagery, or Google Maps business listings and public directories to identify small businesses, contractors, or shared-space tenants that are close to the target (or have line-of-sight to it). Those are more likely to have weak security and thus be good compromise candidates to hack and then use as a proximal node for carrying out a more sophisticated attack – all without setting a foot in the physical proximity of the target.

This infrastructural surveillance model in digital mapping reveals how contemporary spatial technologies transcend both Agre's capture framework and traditional surveillance models by eliminating the map-territory distinction entirely. It is therefore not merely an extension of surveillance capitalism into spatial domains (Gentzel et al. 2021), but something else. Where capture systems reorganize existing activities through grammars of action, and where traditional surveillance maintains representational relationships between watcher and watched, infrastructural surveillance creates new ontologies where space itself becomes knowable only through machine-readable formats that serve as both representation and operational reality.

The examples from Google's API pricing changes to Amazon's attempted acquisition of iRobot demonstrate how this model creates what Keller Easterling (2016) terms *extrastatecraft*: forms of governance that operate outside traditional state sovereignty whilst wielding quasi-sovereign power over access and mobility. The result is spatial enclosure on an unprecedented scale: the transformation of geographic knowledge into a proprietary resource controlled by infrastructural operators who assume functional sovereignty over territorial conditions themselves. Unlike previous models where citizens could theoretically 'opt out' of surveillance or resist capture mechanisms, infrastructural surveillance in digital mapping

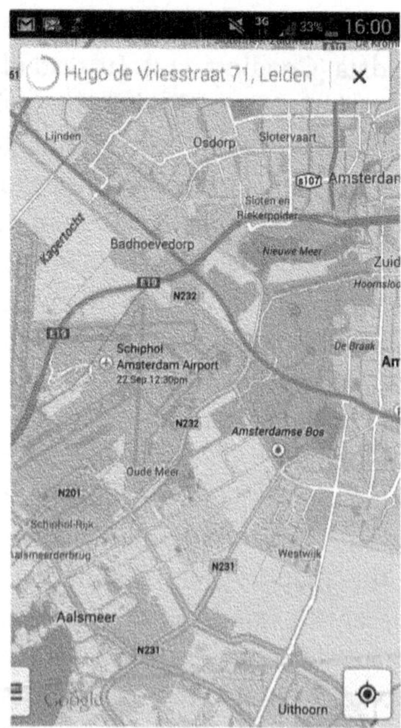

Figure 6.2: A then-new Google Maps feature, where viewing the airport would inexplicably show me the date and time of a future flight, presumably derived from my Gmail mailbox. This was not something I opted-in for. Screenshot by the author, September 2014.

renders such resistance increasingly impossible, as machine-readable spatial participation becomes a prerequisite for basic mobility, navigation, and spatial citizenship (figure 6.2). The map-territory assemblage thus represents not merely a new form of surveillance, but a fundamental reorganization of spatial power relations where the distinction between cartographic representation and territorial reality dissolves into a single, inescapable infrastructural totality.

Re-examining mapping through surveillance

After establishing how infrastructural surveillance underpins much of digital mapping today, I would like to return to the three use-cases of maps that I explored in the previous chapters: movement, play, and work. While each constitutes its own self-contained logic of how digital mapping operates in the world, they also show the overarching logic of surveillance. The Covid pandemic has further advanced and naturalized surveillance techniques, through popularization of contact tracing apps and infections maps, including a dedicated 'Covid-19 Layer' as discussed in chapter 2. While necessary and mostly beneficial measures, such 'surveillance creep' has bled into various digital aspects (Gekker and Ben David 2020), including maps. Thus, in this section I will re-examine some of the key ideas and case studies presented in each previous chapter to highlight their reliance on tracking their users in various ways, turning over the rock of mapping's surveillant underbelly.

Movement: the watched journey

A masked, shirtless man stands defiantly on top of a Waymo autonomous robotaxi, which is broken and graffitied. Another car is set in flames in the background; a crowd looks on. A set of iconic photos showing the scenes above have spread out around the world following anti-government protests in Los Angeles in June 2025. The vehicles were not simply collateral damage. While it is not fully clear, some reports suggest that rioters have summoned the cars to a specific spot and then torched at least five of them, prompting the company to pause service to parts of the city (Gregg et al. 2025). The irony of summoning a self-driving vehicle to its own demise was not lost on commentators, but that might have been the point: the protestors resent big tech as providing the surveillance infrastructure to the extreme anti-immigrant actions of the second Trump administration, and the cars are part of this arrangement. According to neo-luddite journalist Brian Merchant who reported from the scene, the cars were destroyed to 'punish collaborators' with the authorities:

'Protestors were reportedly calling them "spy cars" as they were vandalized and set ablaze, and some noted how the cars can share data with the LAPD' (Merchant 2025, n.p.).

This visceral scene of resistance illuminates a fundamental transformation in how movement and surveillance have become inseparable in the age of digital mapping. The burning Waymos represent more than vandalized property; they embody the violent rejection of infrastructural surveillance, where the very act of movement through space requires submission to comprehensive monitoring. As explored in chapter 3, companies like Mobileye have turned connected and autonomous vehicles, which promised liberation from the drudgery of driving, into a roving network of sensors that transforms every street into a surveillance corridor. Its road experience management (REM), built on internal car sensors, or Bee Maps' similar proposition based on dashcams, points towards a purposefully depoliticized inevitability of infrastructural surveillance: one can perhaps turn off certain privacy-compromising features in one's own car, but others' cars – now increasingly equipped with cameras and computers that are *required* to operate a variety of systems from emergency breaking to fuel efficiency optimization (Hind 2019) – can still track you.

Around the world, and more so in California, where autonomous vehicles are most abundant, police have become increasingly predisposed to request data from AVs who happened to 'witness' a crime scene by virtue of driving next to one (Farivar 2018; Koebler 2025). The protesters' targeting of these vehicles reveals an emerging consciousness about how movement data operates within broader surveillance assemblages. Every Waymo, as Merchant notes, functions as a mobile sensing platform equipped with cameras, light detection and ranging (LIDAR) sensors, radar, and other sensors ostensibly for navigation but capable of far more. Combined with the growing network of licence-plate reading cameras, it can facilitate near-real-time records of movement and actions (Pereira and Raetzsch 2022). When protesters summoned these cars to their destruction, they demonstrated an (instinctive) understanding of how the infrastructure of movement has been weaponized against them.

This weaponization extends far beyond autonomous vehicles. Phones are notorious at collecting location even when users think that they shut that function off (Hern 2020; Bhuiyan 2023). Moreover, while the actual location data may be turned off, the information of using the maps app to navigate to a place or merely searching for one on a map can still be saved and accessible to others – something that Google tried to address with the shift of Timeline data to on-device storage in 2023 (Johnson 2023). This is particularly crucial when accessing places that might be socially controversial, such as certain care facilities or abortion clinics. For example, Google Maps itself has been notoriously used by 'pregnancy crisis centres' (which persuade women against abortions) to advertise themselves when users searched for the term (Alba and Gillum 2022). No matter how many privacy functions the tech giants introduce, movement patterns still train algorithms, shape traffic predictions, and inform the AI-driven traffic light systems now deployed across hundreds of cities (Mattern 2021a). These 'smart' traffic lights (Dave 2023), which Google claims reduce emissions and congestion, represent a similarly insidious form of movement surveillance that reshapes urban flows based on aggregate data while remaining invisible to those whose movements generated that data in the first place. In this way, maps contribute to 'an emergent mode of digital socio-spatiality, which remediates existing forms of socio-spatial encounter, and recalibrates the way in which we, as citizens, seek to know, interact, document and traverse' (Barns 2019, 10).

Consider the residents in a neighbourhood of the Dutch beach town Zandvoort, who got so tired of the throngs of drive-through traffic sent their way by navigational apps that they enacted a kind of a virtual sit-in: multiple residents reported a central road as closed on their Google Maps apps, and the aggregated accounts have triggered the road to be marked off as inaccessible to coming drivers (Jacobs 2025b). The municipality, in response, have put signs commanding drivers to turn off their navigation and to follow the actual physical parking signs around them, in an ironic reversal of George Orwell's The Party dictum of not believing one's eyes and ears.

The communities that (somewhat) successfully fought to remain unmapped offer a compelling counterpoint. Germany has fought for years to limit cartographic collection, but recently announced a new round of Street View photoshoots after a decade of pause following a privacy backlash when Google collection first began (Cantrill and Bodoni 2023). The Italian *vie fittizie*, or fictitious streets, are remnants of the country's early history, where transient people like travelling salesmen or circus performers needed addresses to become registered in the emerging bureaucracies, yet had no places of residence. Today, these streets are maintained as a way for the homeless to register themselves and access services which require an address (Bennett 2022). But even they reflect the logic of the flat ontology by creating cartographic spaces that – while not mapping onto physical ones – nonetheless operate to facilitate Agre's grammars of action to be enacted for people who don't fit into the world of digital maps where people belong in defined coordinates.

What the attacks on Waymos illuminate, then, is how movement-based surveillance operates through what I have identified as the four characteristics of infrastructural surveillance. The aggregation manifests in how many vehicle journeys contribute to an ever-growing dataset that exceeds any single platform's capabilities, by tracking autonomous cars, rideshares, or personal vehicles with Google Maps running. The standards appear in the protocols that determine which movements are legible to the system: the 'optimal' routes that avoid certain neighbourhoods, the left turns that algorithms discourage in areas deemed 'inefficient' (Sheng 2023), the speeds that trigger alerts to insurance companies (Hill 2024; Kravitz 2025). The distribution emerges through the multiple actors involved, including city governments licensing autonomous vehicles, tech companies processing movement data, law enforcement accessing vehicle cameras, and insurance firms adjusting premiums based on route choices. And the enclosure completes itself in the impossibility of movement without surveillance, creating what amounts to a mobility paywall where privacy becomes incompatible with participation in urban life.

The protestors who burned those Waymos understood something fundamental: in our era of infrastructural surveillance, every journey generates data, every movement becomes trackable, and every vehicle functions as a node in a vast sensory network. Their act of resistance, simultaneously summoning and destroying these 'spy cars', represents a growing awareness that the promise of frictionless, optimized movement comes at the cost of submitting to total visibility. As we have built cities that assume and require digital navigation, we have created an environment where to move is to be watched, where to travel is to be tracked, and where the simple act of getting from one place to another involves negotiating with systems that see our movements not as private choices but as data to be harvested, analysed, and monetized.

Play: gamified places and paces

When the tanks rolled towards the border, in what became the opening salvos of Russia's brutal invasion of Ukraine in February 2022, a researcher in California noticed this before any official announcement, or news outlets, by looking at Google Maps.

Jeffrey Lewis, specializing in arms control and non-proliferation at the Middlebury Institute of International

Studies was watching with a group of students live traffic data from the Russia–Ukraine border when they began noticing strange traffic jams appearing in Russia at 3:15 in the morning. Using commercially available satellite data that had shown previous troop configurations, they confirmed that an invasion was on its way (Lerman 2022). What once was the domain of spies and militaries can now be achieved by a curious map scroller. While Google was quick to pause the live traffic and busyness function for this area (Butler 2022) to prevent others from deducing troop movements or civilians fleeing, the principle remains. A few years later, during the two weeks of the Israel–Iran war in June 2025, local authorities forbade reporting the precise location of missile strikes inside Israel, and only the city names were mentioned. Yet, a quick scan of Google Maps in a city that was reported as hit showed a suspicious traffic block around a specific area (figure 6.3). Later, news sources confirmed that this was indeed the area that was hit. Features such as check-ins, traffic reports, or any other voluntary data coaxed from users – often through gamification – are becoming used for a variety of very serious activities. Despite their bright colours, user-friendly UIs, and 'fun' features, digital maps today routinely combine mundane, playful experiences with critical infrastructural tracking of life and death.

This transformation of playful mapping into intelligence gathering represents a fundamental shift in how surveillance operates through gamified interfaces. As explored in chapter 4, the integration of play into digital maps was never innocent: it served to naturalize continuous tracking by making it enjoyable. Yet the Ukrainian invasion example reveals how this playful infrastructure doubles as a global sensing network, where every traffic report, every check-in, every shared location becomes potential intelligence. The bright, game-like interfaces that encourage users to contribute data mask their function as components of what amounts to a planetary surveillance apparatus.

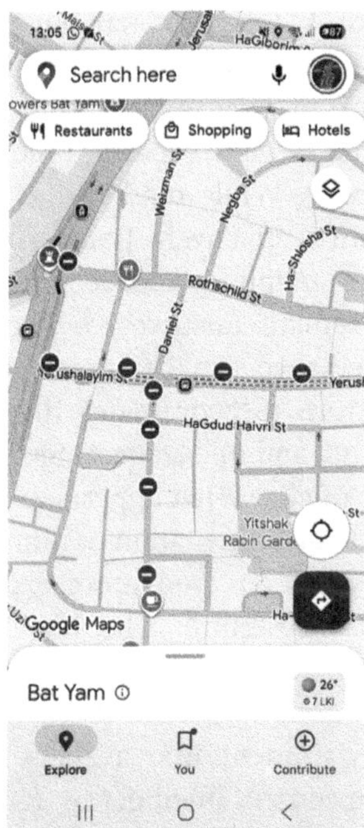

Figure 6.3: Road closures around a location in Bat Yam, Israel on 15 June 2025. It was later reported that a residential building was struck there by an Iranian ballistic missile, resulting in nine dead and hundreds wounded.

The phenomenon extends beyond military applications into increasingly strange territories. Consider Randonautica, the app that gained viral fame on TikTok in 2020 for sending users to 'random' map coordinates based on random number generation. The game is inspired in part by Guy Debord and the situationist principles of the Dérive, aiming to navigate through cities in playful, anti-utilitarian ways and by doing so to experience urban space differently from the consumerist-capitalist intention of its planners (Debord 1958; Lefebvre 1992). In fact, I was a co-designer of an educational method, later developed into an app, that used similar principles to challenge students methodologically and to re-consider the notion of fieldwork in social sciences and humanities

(Lammes et al. 2016). However, Randonautica operates not in a school setting, but in the attention economy of likes and shares. Users report discovering everything from abandoned buildings to crime scenes, sharing their adventures as content (Ankel 2020). While marketed as a game of exploration, Randonautica effectively transforms its users into distributed sensors, mapping and documenting spaces that might otherwise remain unsurveyed. The app's popularity reveals how surveillance can be repackaged as adventure: users eagerly venture to coordinates they're given, photograph what they find, and upload geotagged evidence of these locations to social media. What appears as spontaneous play becomes systematic documentation of unmapped spaces.

GeoGuessr presents an even more explicit gamification of surveillance infrastructure. The browser game, which drops players into random Google Street View locations and challenges them to determine their location, has transformed from casual entertainment into a skillset akin to serious training for open-source intelligence (OSINT) gathering. International players would scrutinize shop signs, licence plates, and architectural features to pinpoint locations, turning the casual documentation of streets into a competitive intelligence exercise. The game's most skilled players have developed techniques that border on surveillance tradecraft: identifying locations from soil types, sun angles, and electrical pylon designs (Romero 2023).

An interesting conflict has emerged around the self-uploaded images that are used in Street View in places where Google has less interest, like the ones done by RippleNami that I discussed in the previous chapter. As mentioned, non-Google images often have much lower quality than their official counterparts, and so GeoGuessr players from the Global North became angry at local uploaders for providing low-resolution images that make the game harder to play. Players indicated on Reddit that they even contacted the Tourism Council of Bhutan and users who were uploading images in Jordan and Zanzibar, asking them to cease their work so as not to 'harm the game' (Deck 2021). This highlights the tension inherent in using actual spaces, fed through cartographic translation, for playful purposes. This risks turning space into a disposable thing, to be consumed via media screens for pleasure or out of boredom. This danger is present in all forms of map-based gamification, turning *intrinsic* motivations that are about internal goals (like exploration or problem solving) and rewards into *extrinsic* ones (Fizek 2014) that are not related to the map at all and therefore alienate users from the spaces we inhabit. Such map 'players' might be indifferent to or even inscribed into surveillance apparatuses because they got used to 'getting points' from the act.

To be clear, I think that maps should be playful and fun. Maps should wink at their users, reminding them of the absurdity of trying to squish a rich, three-dimensional world into a 2D graphical representation, even if powered by some advanced algorithms and presented on pocket computers. A good digital map dispels its own cartographic illusion, reminding the user of itself being first and foremost an interface (Bolter and Gromala 2005). But contemporary algorithmic systems are often reliant on growth hacking, experience engineering, and dark patterns that mislead the users into choosing options detrimental to their own well-being (Brignull 2010; Mathur et al. 2019). Add gamification to the mix and this runs the danger of people not only accepting infrastructural surveillance but welcoming it: as a status symbol of a desire to be tracked. A timely warning is provided by China's infamous Social Credit System (or several overlapping systems, in fact) which monitors online and offline behaviour to numerically evaluate citizens within the regime. Importantly, having a high score gives one perks like expedited visa application and faster airport lanes, generating an incentive to *subscribe* to surveillance rather than just the *fear of avoiding* it. This leads to users flaunting their scores publicly: 'On its dating service Baihe, for instance, hopeful singles often post their Sesame Credit scores in the hope that it will raise their attraction' (Creemers 2018, 23).

Play does not have to be a tool of coercion, of 'gamification from above' aiming to exploit and mislead (Woodcock and Johnson 2018). The Dutch–Turkish architectural consultancy 'Play the City' (https://www.playthecity.eu/) uses collaborative and community design principles to bring multiple different stakeholders (urban planners, mayors, disenfranchised residents) together using custom games that treat each of their cases differently. They use maps and models, physical and digital, to present the complexities of cities and solutions to urban problems. Their methods resist scale: they are handcrafted for each case, built through a combination of ethnography, game design, and urban planning. They do not shun digital tools but also don't try to build 'platforms', treating each map individually. Mapping for Change in the UK (https://communitymaps.org.uk/) subscribe to similar principles. They do have their own cartographic platform, but one which is not built on data extraction, and which requires a collaboration between the organization and potential clients in defining when and how such maps are deployed. While perhaps naïve, these two examples show that we can imagine a different form of cartographic playfulness that resists data collection and surveillance.

But for the most part, infrastructural surveillance embedded in playful mapping operates through what game studies scholars term 'procedural rhetoric': the ways rules and systems make arguments about how the world works. When *Pokémon Go* players scan PokéStops to earn rewards, they're training Niantic's computer vision systems. When Snapchat users create geotagged stories, they're building a real-time intelligence feed of global activities. When amateur investigators use traffic data to track military movements, they're demonstrating that the surveillance infrastructure we've built for convenience and entertainment serves dual purposes. The same systems that help us play are indistinguishable from those that monitor, track, and analyse. Instagram's introduction of a mapped mode (figure 6.4) to promote content discovery and e-commerce shows how easy it is to introduce systems that habituate users to tracking (Clark 2022). This creates what we might term 'ambient surveillance' (cf. Monahan 2015), a constantly updating picture of global activities generated by users who think they're just sharing traffic updates or playing games. Unlike traditional intelligence gathering, which required dedicated assets and intentional collection, this new form emerges from the aggregate behaviours of millions of users engaging with gamified interfaces.

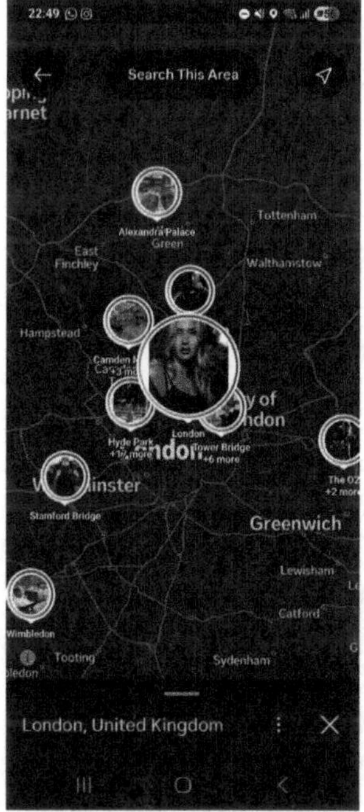

Figure 6.4: Tapping on a tagged location in Meta's popular image sharing Instagram app will lead you to discover spatially tagged content from users who might not realize they can be discovered like that. Screenshot by the author, August 2025.

Here again we see distribution and enclosure in action. Every person stuck in traffic who reports a jam, every player who captures a new location, every community member who maps their neighbourhood contributes to a surveillance apparatus they may not even realize exists.

The implications extend beyond military applications. During natural disasters, authorities increasingly rely on social media check-ins and geotagged posts to coordinate responses. Insurance companies analyse aggregated movement patterns from fitness apps to assess neighbourhood risk profiles. Real estate developers use heat maps from dating apps to identify gentrification opportunities. The playful interfaces that seemed to democratize mapping have created a new form of extractive surveillance where users enthusiastically provide the data that surveils them, motivated by points, badges, and the simple pleasure of play. As chapter 4 explored, play reambiguates the world, but in doing so, it also makes that world visible to systems of power in unprecedented ways. The question is no longer whether we're being watched, but whether we're having fun while it happens.

Work: no respite

In August 2017, the ride-hailing company Uber agreed to settle a privacy lawsuit with the US Federal Trade Commission (FTC), in its capacity as a consumer protection agency (Fung 2017). Instead of paying a fine, the company was required to hire an external firm as a privacy auditor for the duration of twenty years, making sure that the company treats its drivers' and customers' data correctly. The main cause was the infamous 'God View' mode. Simply put, the backend tool, which was available to Uber executives, some employees, and – at an earlier stage of the service – even some drivers, allowed detailed logs of a specific person's trips to be produced or they could even be tracked in real time. A male Uber executive has shown a female journalist that wrote about the company how he was keeping tabs on her without her knowledge.[1] Other reports highlighted rank-and-file employees sharing travel details of celebrities and officials around the office. A hacked version of God View's API was also available online for a while (McGuire 2014). While the callous disregard for user privacy is appalling, the company ostensibly does have a reason for the granularity of such collection: infrastructural surveillance is built into its operational logic.

When Uber began 'disrupting' transportation in the early 2010s, a chief innovation was the surge pricing, a dynamic fare mechanism that openly multiplied standard rates in specific areas during periods of high demand. The practice represented a radical departure from the fixed pricing that had governed ground transportation for over a century. Initially, Uber made surge pricing highly visible through electric-blue multiplier icons displayed prominently in the app, requiring explicit user consent before booking. This transparency, whilst often generating customer outrage over hundred-dollar rides after concerts or severe weather, served a dual purpose: it educated users to accept such supply-and-demand economics whilst providing Uber with a granular understanding of customer behaviour under varying price pressures. The system requires continuous monitoring of driver locations, passenger requests, traffic patterns, and external factors such as weather conditions, local events, and even neighbourhood demographics. This comprehensive data collection enables the algorithm to predict demand spikes and adjust pricing accordingly; a process that necessitates the very surveillance capabilities that privacy advocates found so troubling in the God View scandal.

However, the most significant evolution came in 2016 when Uber shifted from transparent surge multipliers to what it euphemistically termed 'upfront pricing' (Griswold 2023). This transition marked a fundamental change in both pricing methodology and data utilization. Rather than simply applying multipliers during high-demand periods, upfront pricing employs machine learning algorithms to calculate personalized fares based on individual users' willingness to pay. As Bloomberg reported in 2017, the system considers not merely time, distance, and demand, but also inferences about the passenger's economic status, potentially charging higher fares to riders travelling between affluent neighbourhoods than those heading to less prosperous areas, even when all other journey parameters remain identical (Newcomer 2017). The elimination of surge pricing in 2023 marked the logical conclusion of using such inference, by obfuscating the 'normal' prices altogether and showing different drivers and users a set of personalized disconnected fares for the same trip, trying to nudge riders to pay the most and find drivers who would make the trip for the lowest fare, with Uber pocketing the arbitrage. Lyft, its main competitor, soon followed suit with the same pricing scheme, leading to what Nethercote, in her analysis of the datafied real estate market, calls 'double threat enclosure' through 'the extraction of data rents alongside monetary rents' (Nethercote 2023, 14).

This progression from God View to algorithmic pricing exemplifies how the app's interfaces in work contexts operates as a one-way mirror – platforms demand total visibility of workers and users while rendering their own operations increasingly opaque. The same granular tracking that enabled executives to stalk journalists becomes repackaged as necessary infrastructure for 'efficient markets' (Rieder and Sire 2014; Fourcade and Healy 2016). According to Len Sherman, an adjunct professor at Columbia Business School, this mechanism is likely responsible for Uber's successful turnaround into a profitable company. According to him, this has enabled Uber 'to raise rider fares and cut driver pay on billions of rideshare trips, systematically, selectively, and opaquely' (Bitter 2025, n.p.) Yet this efficiency serves primarily to maximize extraction: from drivers who must accept algorithmically determined fares without understanding their calculation, from passengers who pay personalized prices based on surveillance-derived profiles, and from the urban fabric itself as platforms reshape movement patterns to optimize their revenues.

The fake appliance repair listings plaguing Google Maps represents another facet of how infrastructural surveillance creates new forms of labour exploitation. When CBC's investigation revealed that up to half of appliance repair listings in major Canadian cities were fraudulent, it exposed a parasitic ecosystem feeding on mapping infrastructure (Grundig et al. 2020). A single company took over listings of appliances in several metropolitan areas and provided fake addresses facing customers, while subcontracting local repair services without the customer's knowledge. Manufactured visibility on the map was translated into real power over local competitors. Anecdotal reports on Reddit show similar attempts in businesses naming themselves 'X Near Me' in the Google profile in an attempt to advance in ratings (dishero 2022).

What would an alternative to infrastructural surveillance-based spatial work look like? Perhaps something akin to media scholar and curator Shannon Mattern's ideas around mapping not only what is present, but also what is not. Echoing feminist GIS practitioner Mei-Po Kwan's (2002) notions of finding the data that remains underdeveloped or underexplored, or anthropologist Sally Engle Merry's (2016) work on how quantifying human rights leads aid organizations to follow the data that is available instead of the needs of the people on the ground, Mattern asks: What do maps not show? To her, the answer lies in the pandemic-era mapping of absences, particularly how race and class have been absent from many Covid maps, making it difficult to find causal links between those aspects and the spread of the virus. Yet in other cases, 'Some cartographic omissions are a conscious choice on behalf of an excluded population: a refusal to reveal protected and sacred information' (Mattern 2021b, n.p.). Requiring mapping platforms to show what data is missing or omitted, creating non-personalized versions of digital maps where information is shown equally (Gekker 2023), or perhaps the ability to log into different roles, instead of using the various spoofing and hacking techniques of rideshare drivers and couriers (van Doorn and Chen 2021) – all these could make work feel less like a digital cage (Vallas and Schor 2020), where the algorithm is the worst boss you ever had.

This totalization of work surveillance through mapping creates what we might term *cartographic precarity*, a condition where economic security depends on navigating overlapping surveillance regimes that monitor, measure, and monetize every movement. Unlike some forms of playful surveillance that users can opt out of, work-based tracking becomes mandatory for economic participation. The delivery person who touches up their appearance before approaching a doorbell camera, the Uber driver who runs multiple phones to detect fare discrimination, the field agent who rigs their mobile device to be in motion so as not to appear 'idle', all demonstrate forms of resistance that acknowledge a fundamental reality of being watched as the norm. The question then becomes not whether we can escape the cartographic panopticon of work, but whether we can collectively organize within it to demand that those who watch us from above share the value extracted from our movements below.

Conclusion

Six years after the initial Strava leak, journalists from the French daily *Le Monde* have used an update technique on Strava to uncover classified details of dozens of soldiers of the Israeli Defence Force (IDF). Instead of merely looking at the map, they used GPS spoofing to create fictitious profiles in the vicinity of existing bases, and then used that fake proximity to view details of military personnel and their training routines, both in the base and when home (Bourdon and Schirer 2024). In July 2025 the same military stopped purchasing Chinese-made electric vehicles and retroactively forbade the entrance of those already supplied to officers into high-security bases. Despite disconnecting the car's emergency e-call feature that is supposed to send out an alert in the case of a disaster, cybersecurity experts deemed it insufficient: 'I've never come across Chinese technology that doesn't transmit' (Fulton 2025, n.p.). These two short examples show that even an organization globally notorious as at the forefront of intelligence and cyber operations is not immune to data breaches from mundane objects carried by its personnel. What does it say about the rest of us?

In this chapter I have presented infrastructural surveillance as a mode through which digital maps and other spatial technologies embed tracking as a precondition for operation, depoliticizing pervasive surveillance and making it implicitly necessary. Such mode relies on the aggregation of massive amounts of data, for instance from having access to granular details about all Uber trips; creating access to this data through the setting of standards under your control, for example through providing an API to your global mapping platform; distributing the data collection to multiple parties, as done by allowing Street View upload options to amateur photographers; yet enclosing each user in a sovereign bubble that is under the mapping platform's control.

In the next and final chapter, I will examine where maps go from here, particularly with the rise of generative AI and foundation models.

7
Conclusion

Each chapter of this book began with an example, a case study, or an anecdote. Partly, this is due to my own writing style preferences, setting up an example before unpacking it conceptually. Partly, because it immediately shows the multitude of issues and complexities around digital maps that will be addressed in the chapter, going beyond 'a moving picture of some territory on a screen'. As I begin to write my concluding chapter, three tabs are open in my browser, showing two potential examples vying for the role of the final opener. Each represents a different aspect of how maps are media and what we learn from this.

The first tab is simply Google Maps, opened on the location of 'Volvo Island' in Illinois (figure 7.1). The map shows what seems like an industrial park next to some waterways. The header image depicts a car resting serenely on a small patch of soil. The designation of the landmark is 'Place of Worship' and, at the time of viewing, it scores an average of 4.9/5 with 284 contributors, depicting it as 'a breathtaking experience', or a 'stunning masterpiece ... more comparable to the Taj Mahal of Western civilization', where 'The meaning of life will be revealed to you when you visit.'

The reviews are being glib. The place is an abandoned strip mine filled with water. In 2012, a local garage proprietor placed a 2001 Volvo S80 sedan on a small peninsula protruding into the artificial lake, and then removed the connecting land, leaving the car stranded on its own little island (Wikipedia 2025d). Originally planned as part of a promotion, the car has remained there ever since, relatively intact, becoming a quirky

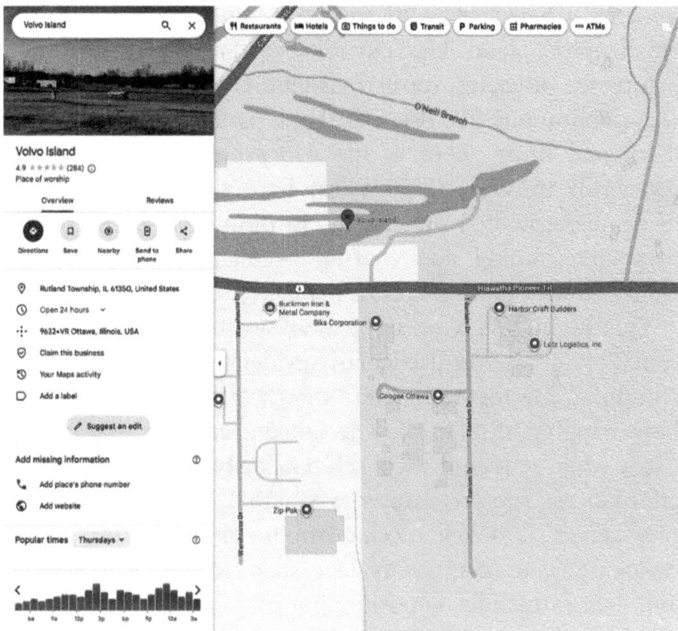

Figure 7.1: Volvo Island on Google Maps. Screenshot by the author, September 2025.

local landmark. Three years later, someone added it to Google Maps, and its fame spread. It now often appears on social media and in meme compilations, as people from outside the region come to film themselves next to it. Searching for 'Volvo Island' on video platforms like YouTube or TikTok yields content creators describing it as mysterious or claiming that 'nobody knows' how the car got there, despite the answer being one search away, on its Wikipedia page. The island's presence on Google Maps and multiple reviews give it an aura of reality that grounds it in the physical world, in a way not always present in the ephemeral meme-making complex (de Seta et al. 2025). It being a 'Place of Worship' and people reporting sublime experiences when visiting it just adds to the legend of Volvo Island and further entrenches it as a niche, if persistent, joke on the internet. There are many small, quirky places, local curiosities and urban legends. Even before the internet, travel magazines, and later dedicated web publications like Atlas Obscura, have sought to discover them and bring them to the wider public. Google Maps (especially through Street View) have allowed such places to be disseminated organically, turning them into content by people 'finding' and 'sharing' peculiar spots just as they would do with other pieces of media (John 2017).

This highlights a running theme of the book: maps are fun! This point was particularly evident in chapter 2, when I outlined my theoretical framework of *casual power*, about how mapping interfaces are designed to continuously engage users while reducing their self-reflexivity through inscribed affordances; and in chapter 4 where I demonstrated how play serves as a key mechanism for depoliticizing digital cartography, making users less suspicious of surveillance and data extraction by positioning maps as innocent, entertaining tools rather than powerful media technologies. People have been hanging maps on walls and peering over them in historical and fantasy literature precisely because they possess affective power to transport and entertain them. Volvo Island is a modern variant of a fantasy landmark – the Shire from Lord of the Rings, or a piece of Narnia – but one where users can participate and add to the mythmaking through their own reviews and share, similar to other collaborative lore platforms, which often 'harness, undermine, or even negate fan agency' (Bollmer and Tillerson 2025, 2).

The other two open tabs represent a very different case to open this concluding chapter, and they definitely show that maps can also be very not fun. The first is *Mapping the Massacres*, a map created to witness and commemorate the victims and survivors of Hamas's October 7 attack on southern Israel in 2023 (figure 7.2). The other is *Gaza Places*, a map that tracks the unimaginable devastation brought onto the strip by the Israeli retaliation (figure 7.3). The

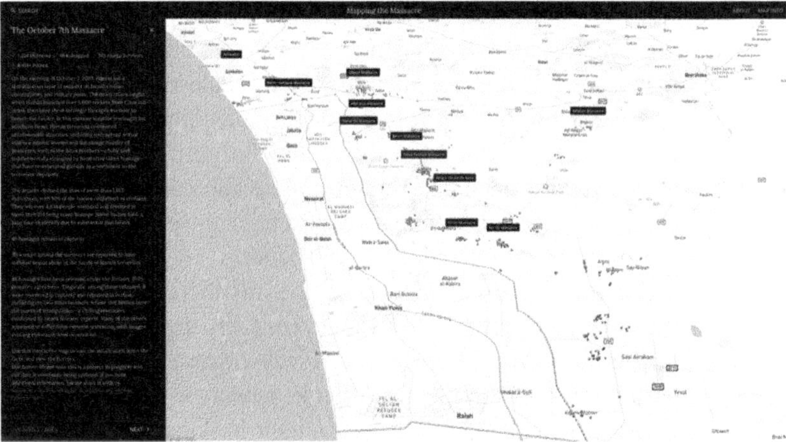

Figure 7.2: Mapping the Massacres. Screenshot by the author ('Mapping the Massacres', n.d.).

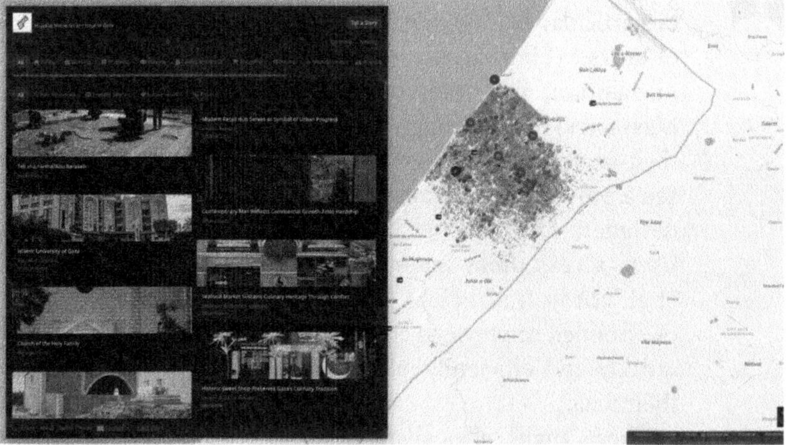

Figure 7.3: Gaza Places. Screenshot by the author ('Gaza Places (Amākin Ghazza)', n.d.).

scale, number of casualties, and nature of destruction they document differ profoundly: one mapping a few days of atrocities, the other the devastation of an entire territory over two years. The two are nonetheless eerily similar in their aesthetics, using a Mapbox base map in their depiction of red spots on white background, with the borderline of the Gaza Strip acting as a twisted mirror between them: the Israeli map does not register anything on the Palestinian side, and vice versa. Both maps are a category of digital maps that I did not cover throughout this book: story maps, specifically ones aimed to facilitate remembrance and commemoration. Obviously, both also depict war and enormous suffering, and are an (uneven) reflection of each other.

Such maps often challenge the distinction I made in the second chapter of the book between digital maps and diagrams or visualizations. As I will expand in the second part of this chapter, one difficult aspect of understanding maps is the blurred line between their backend and frontend functions: acting as a foundation behind the scenes and/or being an interface to interact with a system. In the case of the maps above, they are concerned with telling the stories of particular places, thus deliberately limiting the possibility of users to alter the map. If one wishes to issue a correction or addition, one needs to email the creators (Mapping the Massacres) or go through a separate sign-up process that will then be vetted by the administrators (Gaza Places). Here we see a purposeful creation of friction, that allows the platform designers to modulate the speed and intensity with which users access those maps (Ash et al. 2017; Ash, Anderson, et al. 2018). It stands in stark contrast to many of the maps exemplified in previous chapters, eager to onboard new users quickly and efficiently, often so that they can make use of their data.

These maps also share a lineage with crisis mapping (Specht 2020), a practice popularized by Ushahidi map (and later, platform) in the early 2000s (Okolloh 2009), with interactive web maps that allowed reports to be submitted coupled with a specific place. With the advent of mobile phones and increasing penetration of the internet, such maps offered different possibilities for various users; they allowed access to those affected on the ground, information to relief forces, as well as ways to contribute remotely to enthusiastic 'couch mappers' from around the world. Despite being celebrated as participatory and democratizing, crisis mapping experienced a high rate of failure. Asmolov (2020) puts such failures into three categories: when a map is created for a community but is not integrated into its activities; when a map is needed but there is insufficient skill to provide one that is adequate; and when the map imagined (and built) by the developers differs in scope and goals from the actual needs of those affected on the ground. Many such maps begin as committed projects by well-intending volunteers, only to be gradually abandoned over the next weeks and months. When you don't have Google's commercial juggernaut powering your map updates, the job gets hard. It's perhaps why these types of maps today most commonly crop up in relation to open-source intelligence (OSINT) tools, popularized by organizations like Bellingcat (Williams 2023) that combine OSM datasets, crisis mapping, and detective-like crowdsourced work, guided by specific goals and moderated by experienced civilian investigators. The memorial maps thus also act as spatial databases to witness – and potentially prosecute – the crimes depicted thereon.

My inability to choose between these two opening examples reveals something fundamental about digital maps as media: they resist singular interpretation precisely because they operate simultaneously across multiple registers: playful and serious, liberating and controlling, democratizing and surveilling. Volvo Island and the October 7th/Gaza memorial maps are not opposing cases but complementary manifestations of how digital cartography functions as media. The same Google Maps that enables absurdist pilgrimage to a stranded Volvo serves as infrastructure for memorial and witness; the same interfaces that gamify space also document its destruction. They can bear witness to both the sublime and the horrific, the playful and the political. This duality is not incidental but constitutive of how digital maps operate as media technologies.

Throughout this book, I have argued that understanding digital maps requires recognizing their fundamental multiplicity. Chapter 1 traced their transformation from paper to digital objects and the shift into processual understanding of mapping. Chapter 2's framework explained how this works: maps maintain their authority precisely through their ability to shift registers, appearing as neutral tools whilst shaping behaviour, presenting as entertainment whilst extracting value. The empirical chapters each revealed different facets of this multiplicity. Movement (chapter 3) showed maps simultaneously liberating and constraining mobility. Play (chapter 4) demonstrated how gamification makes map use pleasurable, transforming data extraction into entertainment. Work (chapter 5) revealed maps as sites where labour is both performed and hidden, organized and obscured. Surveillance (chapter 6) exposed how tracking becomes naturalized as the price of participation. Each chapter contributed to understanding how digital maps achieve their power not despite but through their multifaceted media characteristics – their ability to engage, entertain, and enchant users whilst simultaneously disciplining, directing, and surveilling them.

What emerges is a picture of digital maps as exemplary media objects of our current moment, operating through what I have termed *casual power*: a form of influence that works not through coercion but through engagement, not through commands but through affordances, not through ideology but through interface. The fact that both Volvo Island's whimsy and Gaza's tragedy can exist within the same mapping platforms reveals how these media objects have become infrastructure for human experience itself, illustrating the tensions embedded in contemporary mapping between profane and elated, art and science, bottom-up and top-down, controlled and open, knowable and hidden. This is why maps must be understood as media: not because they have screens or use digital technology, but because they fundamentally mediate our relationship with space, with each other, and even with relationship themselves, through the tools we use (Pettman 2019). The transformation from cartographic representation to media interfaces marks nothing less than a revolution in how space is experienced, understood, and contested in the twenty-first century.

This chapter summarizes the book in talking about the beauty and frustration of researching mapping within contemporary digital platforms configurations. In the next section, I outline the challenges of studying maps now and in the future: the blurring of boundaries, the disappearance of the interface, the encroachment of (generative) AI. In the final section, I reflect on living with and through mapping.

Challenges

The blurring of boundaries

This book has tried to walk a thin line between maps and other kinds of spatial technologies. Since the early 2000s, an explosion of mobile phones (de Souza e Silva 2006; 2023), the resulting plethora of interfaces (Farman 2012; 2021; Verhoeff 2012) and various locative social media (Evans 2015; Wilken 2019b), as well as all of the above's overall embedding in urban (Larkin 2008; Mattern 2021a; Barns 2020) and rural life (Tenhunen 2018; Ali 2021) has blurred what 'map' even means. In chapter 5, I divided work done to maintain and build maps versus work done throughout the medium of digital maps but prefaced it with a caveat that the division might be artificial. For multiple practical purposes, mapping has become synonymous with GIS and data visualization. A decade ago, Jean-Christophe Plantin already claimed that '[t]he study of online maps focuses at least as much on the data and the various stages of map production as on the maps themselves' (Plantin 2014, 146–7), due to their history being rooted in the opening of Google Maps API and the creation of the first mashups, which I detailed in chapter 1. How, then, to trace maps without hitting the long tails of adjacent spatial technologies?

Today, most maps are first and foremost *datasets*, in the way they describe and perform the world into being through a collection of discrete points that are then transformed into specific visualizations. As I highlighted in chapter 2, these datasets create *layered* maps, with different layers corresponding, for instance, to the contours of the terrain, streets, points of interest, and the like. Such layers can be added to, extracted, and recombined, resulting in radically different visual maps each time. Are these all 'different' maps? Are they a variation of the same map? In his pivotal book about digital interfaces, Alexander Galloway asks the reader to adopt two seemingly exclusive viewpoints: on the one hand, that all data visualization is meaningless, as it must invent the rules of its transformation from numerical to visual form first; on the other hand, that all data visualization share a unifying aesthetics – and through it, ontology – that says more about the visualization itself than about the underlying data. He calls this the *dilemma of unrepresentability* (2012, 86) and asserts that there is something inherent to digital interfaces that renders them unknowable to those using them. Maps are no exception.

Moreover, as discussed in the surveillance chapter, sensor technologies are becoming ubiquitous and with them mapping becomes as much about tracking entities in the world as it is about creating the rules to display them. The example of Amazon attempting to buy iRobot to incorporate its vast array of in-house maps is one clear indication of how a sensor-infused 'smart' environment lends itself to becoming mappable. But such data might become available also through software updates of existing companies. In September 2025, Signify, the former lighting division of the Philips conglomerate, introduced an update to its Philips-hue range of smart light products (Tuohy 2025). After purchasing a new 'bridge' hardware appliance, one's home lights can retroactively become motion sensors. Compatible with the second generation of its light bulbs (dating back to 2014), the new feature uses radio frequency sensing to detect shifts in signals between the lamps, thus acting as an improvised motion detector. MotionAware, as the feature is marketed, allows 'events' or 'routines' to be set up, such as turning lights on or off based on detected movement, or integrating it with Hue's security platform to set up alarms when certain conditions are met. Like any contemporary smart devices, MotionAware is integrated with a smartphone app that allows, for instance, calibration of the sensitivity of the motion or setting up various motion-sensing zones in one's home. But this leaves any Hue-connected home as a potential target for hacking, creating detailed movement maps of those inside, with security researchers previously demonstrating how these devices can be hacked remotely from a nearby car or drone (Crist 2016). The examples given in chapter 3 of hacking smart vehicles to backtrace their drivers' movement presents a similar risk. And while those technologies don't look like maps, they certainly use them or create them.

Thus, another blurred boundary is whether a map is used as an output or an input for the task at hand. Dating apps are an interesting example. Most of the mainstream ones are reluctant to include a mapping interface for obvious privacy and security purposes. Some gimmicky apps like Yando Dating Map or Mapper try to forefront a map component to facilitate dating (or new friendships), but based on their single-digit review numbers, they are not attracting users. The more mainstream Happn, which brands itself as a 'missed connections' app and bases matches between users on crossing paths or frequenting the same areas, does not display them on a map. The exception is Grindr, whose target audience is male gay users, which long experimented with various mapping features, until finally introducing a 'Live Map View' in August 2025 (Grindr 2025). This is a particularly ironic development since the company has been marred in privacy snafus for the better part of a decade, including accusations of inadvertently outing gay people in repressive regimes like Egypt or Iran, and allowing one's location to be precisely tracked even with the strictest privacy settings enabled (Duffy 2016). Several websites and social media accounts were dedicated to naming and shaming Grindr's multiple location-based breaches, often by juxtaposing (anonymized) user location overlaid on maps with the company's privacy-oriented proclamations ('GrindrMap', n.d.). Yet, following the playful surveillance developments discussed in chapters 4 and 6, and in the footsteps of the likes of Snap and Instagram, they, too, launched a mapping interface. And furthermore, all dating apps still have maps running *under the surface*, matching users based on geographical proximity and other spatial considerations. Niantic's large geospatial model (LGM) detailed in chapter 4 is another example of this blurred boundary, as their collected user data have contributed to a map-like AI construct that allows the company to expand beyond its initial gaming goals.

As a final blurring, the term *mapping* itself has long been applied to a wide variety of techniques, topics, and acts, although this might be more of a semantic problem than an epistemological one. Still, there is a plethora of visualizations, graphs, flowcharts, and the like that aim to breakdown and explain complex phenomena (Kennedy and Engebretsen 2020), and they too are sometimes referred to as maps. Not wanting to sound like a map pedant (though unfortunately often ending up like one), I try not to limit my definitions to just maps of the cartographic variety. But in doing so, I run into the problem of the too-expansive definition: if everything can be a map, then nothing is. This is why it is crucial to understand the specificity of what I consistently referred to as *the digital cartographic map*: a layered, actionable image, which is an interface to acting spatially in the world at large. Particularly, when such maps begin to escape from screens.

The disappearance of the interface

The second challenge I want to highlight in the conclusion to this book is how difficult it is to treat maps as two-dimensional representations. Much of the literature in critical cartography is rooted in the idea of maps as flat(tening) surfaces, abstracting away and simplifying the world (Della Dora 2012). While experimentation with 'digital globes' or other 3D representations (such as the zoomed-out vision of Google Earth and later Google Maps) have moved into the mainstream in the last two decades, the primacy of the screen remained. First on desktop and laptops, and today more on smartphones, a map required a clear thing to be projected upon and still operates within the traditional paradigms that drove cartographic design since at least the Second World War (see chapter 1). This might no longer be the case, due to two factors: the automation of movement through autonomous vehicles and drones, and early signs of commercially viable augmented reality.

In chapter 6, I established the idea of infrastructural surveillance that proliferates in mapping technologies today. To recap, these are the kinds of technologies that create an operational dependency between tracking the users' actions and the basic conditions of use. Under such states, one must take a drastic measure of refusal to avoid participating altogether, for instance by banning Google Street View completely by a municipal ordinance, as was done in the US town of North Oaks, MN (figure 7.4). The examples I used the most come from the world of autonomous driving, as these make a very clear connection between the ability of the vehicle to orient itself, how it plans its actions, and how it necessitates a consistent stream of sensors-enabled precise data (Hind 2024). This is especially worrying in dense urban environments, where so-called Robotaxi companies such as Waymo or Zoox are re-mapping the city by capturing it via their cars. But another aspect of such development lies in the form of the

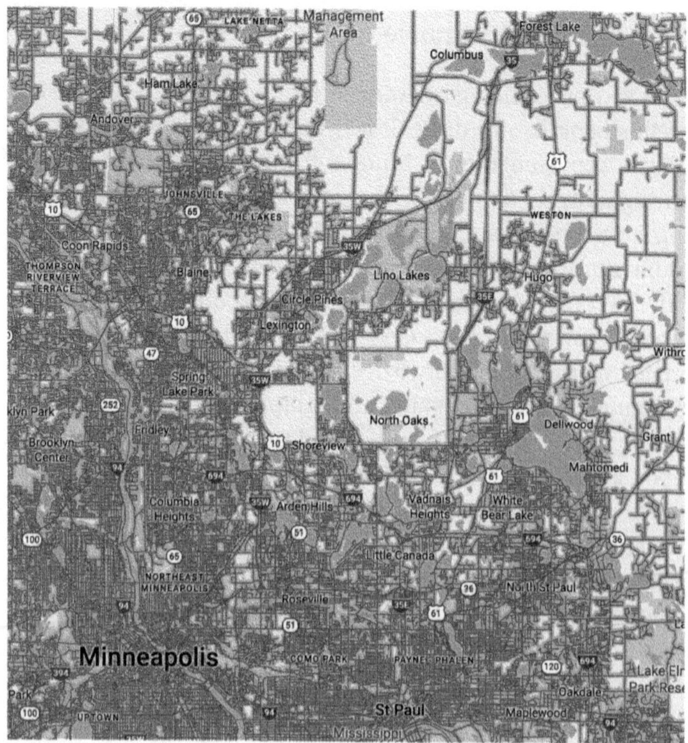

Figure 7.4: The town of North Oaks, where Street View was banned. When viewed through the Street View layer of Google Maps, it seems non-existent compared to its surroundings. Screenshot by the author, August 2025.

map itself: increasingly, digital maps are no longer intended for human consumption at all. The interfaces between such mapped data and the user comes not in the shape of screens or keyboards, but as APIs that prescribe the rules of 'data pours' (Helmond 2015) between different computerized systems. The map then becomes a background, black-boxed artifact, that depicts (and activates) the world for various types of machines that read and write on top of it. This already partially happens through the automation of various traffic and engineering aspects of cities (Coletta and Kitchin 2017), or through the secondary market of street-level data offered by the autonomous vehicles equipment manufacturer Mobileye to insurers and city officials (Hind and Gekker 2022).

This development is accelerated by the constant attempts to introduce autonomous delivery drones, of both wheeled (Koetsier 2024; Musa 2025; Hawley 2025; Khollam 2025) and airborne (Palmer 2025) variety. They add to the roster of non-human actors that operate via mapping interfaces that are invisible (or at least difficult to access) to humans. Since we have a plethora of previously documented cases of 'digital redlining' (Gilliard and Culik 2016) and other discriminatory behaviours of classification systems (O'Neil 2017; Noble 2018; Crawford 2021), including Microsoft's patent for a pedestrian routing that 'avoids ghetto' (Keyes 2012) or Google's decision to stop directing tourists through a specific neighbourhood in Cape Town (Swart 2023), this raises many potential issues. It is not a stretch to imagine a gaggle of increasingly self-reinforcing algorithmic systems both reading from and writing onto a largely invisible digital map (or multiple unified digital maps) feeding into each other through proprietary data streams.

Such Stack-like (Bratton 2015) spatial regime will be driven as much by hype and entrenched attentional inequalities as by 'facts on the ground', for instance by speculative attempts by real estate investors, realtors, and marketing agencies to position certain places as desirable (Barns 2020; Banks 2023; Boy and Uitermark 2024). Google and Apple maps have encountered and (sometimes) dealt with such manipulation (Google Transparency Report 2025) since the launch of their apps, such as the case where the *Fruit Belt District* in Buffalo, NY, suddenly becomes *Medical Park*, much to the chagrin of its residents. In parallel to the name change, the neighbourhood began to undergo rapid gentrification, with locals being pushed out financially by higher-earning newcomers most of whom came to work for the medical centre complex being built at the same time on the edge of the neighbourhood (Bacchi 2019). The name change seemingly prefigured the desired socioeconomic change, tying the area to the newly built facility instead of its historical roots. Now imagine this happening without the residents even being able to perceive that such naming change had occurred.

And even if humans remain in the loop, the critical distance between the user and the map can continue to deteriorate, further entrenching the cartographic illusion (Ingold 2000) of the world being as it is depicted on the map. Despite Facebook's rebrand into Meta, as an attempt to build on virtual reality (VR) as a new kind of technology, it failed to make it mainstream. However, by pursuing this direction, and facing competition from Snap, the first half of the 2020s saw a rapid rise of viable extended and augmented reality (XAR) technology, first through the screens of smartphones, and increasingly through wearable glasses. Currently, several high profile companies are offering wearable glasses with in-built displays and voice/wristband activation while others (such as Amazon) are reportedly developing their own versions of AR spectacles or 'smart glasses' that include voice-activated chatbots that respond to user inquiries (Ma and Osawa 2025). Augmented reality already changes the nature of map use when deployed on mobile devices. Google Maps has enabled its Live View feature on mobile devices in 2021 and further expanded it in 2023 (Phillips 2023). It allows for immersive overlaying of points of interests (such as ATMs or building exits) in select cities, and, more importantly, a new way to navigate in pedestrian mode, where shifting the phone from horizontal to vertical activates the devices camera and changes the map into a live view of where the device is pointed at, with animated arrows overlaid to direct one's journey. An earlier demo of the feature also included an animated animal (a fox) 'leading' the user towards their destination (Engadget 2019) – in a clear nod to Google's other playful tactics explored in chapter 5 – though this feature never crystallized.

Notwithstanding, whether through taking away agency from users by incorporating the map into autonomous systems that operate on the periphery of human perception or removing actionability by subsuming the map into AR: the UI disappears. Here again I refer to my chapter 2 understanding of the interface as something that is self-evident and mediating, allowing for the kinds of 'weaponized skeuomorphism' (Bratton 2015) that distinguishes physical actions in the world from those made via digital intermediation. In other words, the disappearance of the interface erodes human agency in a world increasingly dominated by mechanistic images that become their own blueprints for action. Nowhere is it clearer than when it comes to generative AI.

The encroachment of (generative) AI

At first sight, there is no obvious links between the rise of various large language models (LLMs) such as ChatGPT or Google's Gemini and mapping. While impressive at times at tasks that previously required humans (such as writing prose or code, performing qualitative analysis, or cheating on homework), maps do not seem to fall under the remit of this developing technology. However, understanding the nature of what generative AI is and how it relates to making truth-claims about the world shows that mapping will most likely also change alongside other aspects of human life. This has to do with the integration of spatial data into multimodal generative models. To appreciate this ramification, let us first establish what is different about generative AI.

Since 2021, visual diffusion models such as DALL-E and Stable Diffusion, and subsequent text models built on the revolutionary transformer architecture, such as ChatGPT, have sent shockwaves through the AI community and wider world. A key assumption until that point had been the requirement to supervise and monitor the input and output of AI training models, for instance by creating a curated dataset of images tagged manually by (often, underpaid Global South) workers to then be processed by a neural net to learn to recognize a particular object in an image (Tubaro et al. 2020; Muldoon et al. 2024). Instead, new techniques in unsupervised or self-supervised learning have allowed for the ingestion of massive amounts of unlabelled data and the subsequent creation of robust 'foundation' or general-purpose models capable of generating new outputs based on prompting – a set of instructions often given through natural language chat (Burkhardt and Rieder 2024).

A key differentiating aspect of the current generation of AI technologies is their generality. Unlike previous iterations of machine learning (ML) techniques, pre-trained on specific datasets to perform specific tasks, the transformer and attention architecture underpinning LLMs have made it applicable to a wide variety of tasks (Luitse and Denkena 2021). In fact, AI has been heralded as the next general-purpose technology (GPT), similar to electricity or the internet (Trajtenberg 2018). Previous historic examples show that such technologies can bring enormous economic value to the firms able to integrate them early on, while threatening the livelihoods and business models of those unable to compete with it. Based on empirical collection of job data, some see ML, a collection of techniques for creating new knowledge from existing datasets, already as a GPT (Goldfarb et al. 2023). Similar claims have been made more specifically about generative AI as a whole (Stackpole 2024; Steinhoff and Hind 2025) and LLMs specifically (Eloundou et al. 2024). The economic research of the so-called 'frontier' AI labs responsible for the most advanced models seemingly corroborate such claims, albeit obviously from a self-serving position (Anthropic 2025).

While evangelists claim a rapid transformation of the entire global market within a matter of several years, others show how any such changes will happen over many years if not decades (Narayanan and Kapoor 2025). One obvious – if speculative – influence of such development would be the ease of creating custom digital maps, including by those without any background in either coding or cartography.

Early anecdotal evidence shows the potential of such maps, for instance the 'Coffee in the Sun' map app I mentioned in chapter 4 was 'vibe coded' by the student originator, meaning the software was written by giving natural language commands to a ChatGPT-like agent.

However, it is the integration of mapping into existing commercial models that radically reorients the relationship between map and territory. The news website Android Authority managed to uncover an experimental feature of Gemini, Google's foundation model, showing how future versions might be able to pull spatial information, such as location, rating, and reviews directly from Google Maps and integrate it into conversation with users (Siddiqui 2025). When considering the specific characteristics of generative AI, this opens interesting possibilities for the future of digital maps. A profile story by CNBC celebrating Google's 20 years has similarly reported a wide range of future Gemini features and integrations, from summarizing the reviews of a specific POI on the map, to using AI voice mode to update the map while 'conversing' with it (Meyer et al. 2025).

Gemini, like other foundation models, as noted in a report authored by a large group of Stanford computer scientists, possesses an 'unfinished character' (Bommasani et al. 2022, 6), which highlights its role as activated and influenced by users, rather than a 'readymade' purpose-specific model optimized for a particular task (Burkhardt and Rieder 2024). Unlike previous generations of machine learning that required pre-annotated datasets for *specific* tasks, foundation models operate through prompting, allowing users to *specify* tasks through natural language queries, as demonstrated, for example, via the TomTom route-planning plugin to ChatGPT (Avery 2023) or Mapbox's voice conversation mode embedded into its MapGPT (Mapbox 2023). This shift fundamentally alters how we might interact with digital maps. Rather than navigating through predetermined interfaces with fixed affordances (as discussed in chapter 2), users could theoretically generate bespoke mapping experiences through conversational interaction. Yet this apparent democratization masks a deeper dependency on Big Tech firms already dominating both the generative AI ecosystem (Narayan 2022; van der Vlist, Helmond, and Ferrari 2024) and the digital mapping landscape (Plantin 2018; McQuire 2019).

The *multimodal* nature of these models presents particular implications for mapping. As newer versions incorporate various data types in their training corpora (Li et al. 2023), they develop unexpected capabilities. Recent demonstrations of 'video scraping', where screen recordings are fed into models like Google's Gemini 1.5 to extract structured information (Edwards 2024a) suggest that maps themselves could become training data in ways previously unimagined. OpenAI's Operator and Anthropic's Computer Use agents can already navigate online interfaces by 'reading' them visually (Anthropic 2024; OpenAI 2025). OpenAI's Atlas and Perplexity's Comet offer these capabilities inside a browser, aiming to re-capture Google's decade-old success with Chrome by using a winning product to convince users to move more of their online life into platform-controlled ecosystems. Applied to mapping, such agents could autonomously traverse digital cartographies, extracting spatial patterns and relationships without human oversight on a massive scale. Coupled with developments in autonomous driving, one can easily imagine robotic fleets writing and re-writing the map on their own. This further extends the infrastructural surveillance discussed in chapter 6 into new territories, where maps become both sources and targets of algorithmic agency.

The *tokenization* process underlying these models raises profound questions for cartographic representation. When training on datasets, developers reduce content to tokens – smallest viable units of meaning – which are then converted into numerical vectors in multidimensional space. Meaning is conveyed through performing mathematical calculation on the resulting vector strings. It is through this technology that a model can 'understand' that relationship between concepts. Simplifying, adding the vectors of 'man' and 'crown' will result in 'king', while 'woman' and 'crown' in 'queen'. Bias is an ever-present problem in tokenization, particularly as the hunger for quality human-made data drives the AI industry, after ingesting pirated books (Liedtke and O'Brien 2025) and scraping most of YouTube's videos (Reisner 2025a). Spatial data extraction is an obvious direction to supplement the dwindling troves of digitized human-made material. This 'tokenization of everything' (Foley 2025), as Nvidia positions it, transforms complex spatial phenomena into discrete, bounded units. Moreover, due to the innovation of the transformer, those are processed in parallel rather than sequentially, through the mechanism of 'attention' that radically enhances the performance of the model (Wolf et al. 2020). This is already being incorporated, for instance, into various AI companies that build artificial 'worlds' in which they continue to train their AI agents (Mitrokhov 2024). For maps, this means places, routes, and spatial relationships become abstracted tokens whose 'meaning' emerges from statistical correlations rather than geographical reality. The cartographic illusion (Ingold 2000) becomes doubly problematic: not only do users mistake the map for the territory, but the AI systems generating these maps operate on a third-order abstraction: tokens representing representations of space.

Most concerning is the resulting *epistemic agnosticism*, grounded in the foundation models' tangential relationship to truth. These systems routinely 'hallucinate' or 'confabulate' answers, presenting fundamentally untrue information convincingly. The problem is exacerbated in multi-modal or large vision models (Bai et al. 2025) that are mostly built atop tokenized text but then add visual data to establish links between the two information modalities, resulting in 'a disagreement between factual content of images and corresponding generated textual content' (Liu et al. 2024, 6). As Hicks and colleagues (2024) argue, following Frankfurt's (2009) conception of 'bullshit', model outputs remain unconcerned with truthfulness, instead reflecting correlations within training data. For mapping, this presents unique dangers. A hallucinated restaurant review might be annoying; a hallucinated street or neighbourhood could have material consequences for navigation, emergency services, or urban planning.

When models generate 'mean images' (Steyerl 2023) representing norms by signalling averages, they risk creating cartographic fictions that nonetheless shape real-world behaviours and decisions. An analysis by mapmaker and geologist James Farrell (2025) shows that the 'thinking' model from OpenAI GPT-4o can manifest proximate maps, both topographical and political, that often resemble the things that they intend to map. However, he rightfully points out that LLMs learn from scraped images, not actual data, and so even when the model produced very impressive shaded relief maps, it did so '[without] access to elevation data, it's just learned what a relief map should look like from millions of online examples' (Farrell 2025, n.p.). My personal attempts to replicate Farrell's experiment several months afterwards still shows similar results (figures 7.5 and 7.6). This does not mean that such mistakes cannot be corrected – after all, chatbots get progressively better at not generating six-fingered hands or correctly identifying the number of 'r's' in 'strawberry' – but that the underlying technology is inherently incapable of making truth claims in a way that's compatible with cartographic ground truthing.

Overall, it seems that generative AI presents both opportunities and challenges when it comes to digital mapping. The process that began with web mapping – simplifying cartography and making it accessible to the regular person – takes a giant leap with foundation models, which can make more complex actions, bracketed behind GIS and programming know-how, available to everyone (Haklay 2013). For instance, an early demo shared with the OSM community

Figure 7.5: An 'accurate' relief (topographic) map of the Netherlands, as created by ChatGPT-4o, presenting it as a mountainous archipelago. Requested by me with the prompt 'Create an accurate relief map of the Netherlands', September 2025.

sees an LLM being inserted as an intermediary in-between the user and the mapped database, with users asking questions in a natural language and the model translating it into OSM-specific commands in the background. Thus, a user might query 'An Italian restaurant near a tram stop' and the model will create a series of Overpass API queries, scanning for 'amenity=restaurant' in a proximate location next to a tag 'railway=tram_stop'. The team behind the project explains that the project was conceived to help journalists (in the vein of Bellingcat's OSM search interface I mentioned above), but the ramifications are bigger.

Figure 7.6: An actual topographic map of the Netherlands, showing much milder elevations. Wikimedia commons file by user NordNordWest, under the Creative Commons Attribution-Share Alike 3.0 German licence.

The ability to both query and generate maps using natural language descriptions – with advanced coding done in the background – opens possibilities for bespoke and unique uses, unforeseen by developers and crucial to underserved communities and financially non-viable cases. At the same time, current technology necessitates an epistemic uncertainty ever-present for each such use, twice: a mistake can happen both on the data and on the execution levels. In a departure from previous digital environments, generative models are simultaneously repositories of data and platforms that utilize it (Gorwa and Veale 2024). From a data accuracy perspective, information in the model is often degraded, a 'blurry JPEG of the web' (Chiang 2023), that cannot distinguish the Fable video-game series fantasy map of the 'Albion' from old maps that use that name for the British Isles. But even if the data is processed and interpreted accurately, the ability of the model to generate code that accesses the information is prone to bugs and issues. Combined with models' tendency towards sycophancy and misleading users (Malmqvist 2024), inaccurate results will be present with a misleading conviction. The 'death by GPS' issues I mentioned in the opening anecdotes of this book pale in comparison to an overconfident spatial foundation model ('Ah! You're correct, my mistake! It seems indeed that we are currently drowning in a river and not crossing a bridge!').

The integration of mapping data into these foundation models thus represents not merely a technical evolution but an epistemological shift. Maps have always made claims about the world: selecting, simplifying, and inevitably distorting reality for specific purposes. But they operated within established cartographic conventions and could be evaluated against ground truth, even if most users of commercial cartography trust them implicitly. Generative AI further destabilizes the world, creating maps that might be statistically plausible whilst being geographically nonsensical. As frontier labs invest heavily in 'explainability' to understand how their models arrive at answers (a tacit admission of their own ignorance), we face the prospect of maps whose logic remains opaque even to their creators. The casual power of maps becomes enmeshed with the aspect of infrastructural surveillance that reorients activities towards non-human ontologies, through increasingly opaque interfaces. Mapping moves into the domain of the unknowable.

Maps are media

It might not surprise you that I love maps. On screens and on pages of books, hanging on walls and at the entrances to metro stations, a map always catches my interest. Even though a lifetime of academic work with or about mapping tested this love at times, I always come back to them. In fact, in a personal anecdote that is completely true (even if it seemed to be custom-made for a concluding chapter of a book about digital cartography), I even developed a maps-related quirk. Sometimes, when I am absentminded or daydreaming, and I happen to have a physical keyboard in front of me, I will begin typing 'maps' into an open text field, before realizing that I'm doing that and stopping. There's probably a good metaphor here, about how – lost in thought – I reach unconsciously to a map to guide me through. But truth be told, this is probably more to do with the prevalence of Google Maps in my personal and professional life. Before beginning to use it often in a research capacity, I was an early adopter of the platform as a search and exploration device. Soon enough, whenever I had a query to do with a physical location (a shop, a restaurant), I would begin with GM, rather than the general Google search engine. Furthermore, I never bother to bookmark it – thus the typing habit.

This is one of the aspects that made writing the book both difficult and easy. I was constantly aware that my knowledge is probably underpinned by a modicum of obsession and was often reminded (including by my beloved family) that things *I* find fascinating about maps and mapping do not always appear so to others. On the other hand, it was also easy for me to adopt the point of view of the curious quotidian user: unlike many other mapping scholars, I am neither cartographer nor even really a geographer. I have very limited experience with GIS and most of my mapmaking probably took place in my childhood, using the map editor to create custom levels for the Heroes of Might and Magic 3 video game (they weren't very good maps). My entry point thus was one as a *media user*: someone who encountered them not through skill or a profession, but as things appearing progressively more on my screens, changing the way I interact with the world.

Almost a decade ago, I defended my PhD, which became the kernel that grew into this book. My friends and colleagues gifted me many maps and map-related things to commemorate the occasion. One of these was a foldable map of the Discworld – the masterpiece satirical, yet deeply humanist, book series penned by Sir Terry Pratchett – signed by the author himself and the map's designer. As a long-time fan of the books, this was truly a special gift, imbued with extra meaning due to the unique perspective the series had on cartography and worldbuilding. For years, I wanted to do the obvious: frame this map and hang it on my wall. However, a design issue prevented me from doing so. The *Discworld Mapp* was devised as an Atlas, with a short booklet containing in-fiction prefaces and explanation. The signatures were present on the first page of the booklet, not on the map itself. Framing it in a way that would render both map and signatures visible was possible, but not very aesthetically pleasing (think of a large map with a small outcropping of a booklet on its end). In other words, like so often with maps, I ran into the underlying materiality of the map, faced with an end-tail of a series of design choices I had no control over.

While digital maps at times seem much more malleable than their paper variants, they are underpinned by similar chains of cause-and-effect, dependent on particular modes of data collection and storage, platform specificities, API limits, developer ecosystem practices, and many more. When looking at the little bike icon on the map view of our food delivery app or when attempting to use a public transport app in an unfamiliar city, we rarely consider all the above, but they are there. We do, however, develop a deep, affective relationship with (some) digital maps. They comfort us in how far we've come or frustrate us with the journey time remaining. They delight us by showing the world in unexpected ways. They excite us about the possibilities of physical and virtual spaces. In this way, maps are media objects, in the traditional, McLuhanistic, sense: acting as extensions of ourselves and conveying messages more dependent on the form of the container than of what it contains.

In the case of digital maps, the message is one of possibility. In the epilogue to the third edition of his classic *How to Lie with Maps*, Mark Monmonier (2018) warns that while the cartographic language requires necessary abstractions, those can quickly grow from white lies into terrible deceptions. Though we no longer expect to find 'Here Be Dragons' inscribed onto the maps on our screens, they lurk there, nonetheless. The map as a medium speaks of facts and distortions, convincing the user that the world they see on the screen is the one that surrounds them (or close enough). And as platforms claim for themselves evermore roles in mediating the world, digital maps can act as powerful interfaces to facilitating the claims of ownership made by tech firms on our transportation, social ties, dating, and more. Maps are therefore a *medium*, and thus – to steal an old television scholars' joke – they are neither *rare* nor *well done.* Let's make sure we treat them accordingly.

Notes

Chapter 1

1 This very short story is called *On Exactitude in Science*. Its full text and additional analysis can be found through the Wikipedia page dedicated to it: https://en.wikipedia.org/wiki/On_Exactitude_in_Science.

2 This book makes few references to OSM, not because it's not important or useful (like many map geeks, I'm an avid fan), but ultimately because the book examines maps as media, and OSM simply does not function as one. With about 10 million users as of October 2025 (OSM n.d.), it does not have much impact in popular use of mapping, other than when its data is used by other companies. Like many other data commons projects, it has unfortunately been in decline for the last few years. For a good overview, see Haklay and Weber's (2008) canonical analysis of the platform, Bennett's (2010) insider journalistic account of the community, or, for a more recent review of the state of its data coverage, see Herfort et al. (2023).

Chapter 2

1 This is not to say that such activities are indeed fun for the users. As noted by Gandini (2021), there is a tendency for critical labour scholarship to frame digital activities as work, even if users themselves neither perceive it as such nor feel exploited. I explore this contradiction further in chapter 5.

Chapter 3

1 Particularly since Google has never been really threatened by Apple in the navigation and mobile categories, having more

users (O'Beirne 2021) and consistently earning four times Apple's revenue in this market segment (Statista 2023).

2 I hesitated for a while regarding the header of each column. My initial inclination was to go with 'paper maps' versus 'digital maps', but that felt like a grave oversimplification. While it is true that paper maps by definition cannot have an algorithmic interface, not all digital maps have one as well, and those that do might have varying degrees of it. So, the division is roughly between a map that you look at and a map that guides your actions. As with any generalization, this choice of definition is a necessary compromise.

Chapter 4

1 There is an interesting, if a bit insular, discussion on the correct translation of the book's original Dutch text. The concepts came into international scholarship from an English version of the book, adapted from a German translation with Huizinga rewriting parts of the book himself after the war. Subsequently, there are disparities in whether he saw play as constitutive to – or part of – various cultural forms (Frissen et al. 2015).

2 There is an extensive scholarly and industry debate across various disciplines on whether such effects can be taken outside of games and if so to what extent. Criticism is often raised against those who take the most shallow and addictive elements of gameplay in order to compel users. Yet, evidence of successful engagement under the most minimal of playful elements is also present (Lieberoth 2015). The scope of this debate is well beyond the confines of this chapter, and I suggest the edited volume by Fuchs, Fizek, Ruffino, and Schrape (2014) for further reading. However, whether one agrees or disagrees with the ethics of the move, there is a seeming consensus about the potential of such effects to affect behaviour outside of games (Johnson et al. 2016; Zainuddin et al. 2020).

3 Going DENNIS leads you to: 'Ye arrive at Dennis. He wears a sporty frock coat and a long jimberjam. He paces about nervously. Obvious exits are NOT DENNIS' (Homestar Runner 2004).

4 Android: more than ten million downloads; iOS: ranked 64th for travel apps, as of November 2024.

5 Most famously, the feature was copied by Facebook's (now

Meta's) Instagram and became a defining feature of the app. Since 2024 Instagram has also been experimenting with 'inspired' feature that strongly resembles Snap Map (Kastrenakes 2024) and launched its own map in 2025.

Chapter 5

1 For instance, Minnesota governor and 2024 US democratic vice-president nominee Tim Walz is a self-proclaimed 'GIS nerd' (Patino 2024) and is credited with introducing it into the curriculum of state school as a geography teacher and later official. He was the keynote speaker for Esri's 2024 User Conference (UC). In his speech he outlined the central role that GIS technology has played in his life and career, and it can be watched in its entirety here: https://www.esri.com/en-us/about/events/uc/plenary/sessions/tim-walz.

2 Both are freely available online, but with somewhat unwieldy URLs:
Woodstock at https://www.google.com/maps/@-33.8816841,151.1043793,3a,75y,146.85h,12.06t/data=!3m8!1e1!3m6!1sAF1QipOQLGIPW__he6Ndgc_sGdXVZgerwGdg45DbXRCV!2e10!3e11!6shttps:%2F%2Flh3.googleusercontent.com%2Fp%2FAF1QipOQLGIPW__he6Ndgc_sGdXVZgerwGdg45DbXRCV%3Dw900-h600-k-no-pi77.94-ya355.1511627197266-r00-fo100!7i12018!8i6009!5m1!1e4?entry=ttu&g_ep=EgoyMDI1MDQyOC4wIKXMDSoASAFQAw%3D%3D.
Gank at https://www.google.com/maps/@-33.8207078,151.1095972,3a,75y,56.69h,1t/data=!3m8!1e1!3m6!1sAF1QipPDRs3Sz2EbfwtdudSoM1HFo4Vay6FO1BRIyo3S!2e10!3e11!6shttps:%2F%2Flh3.googleusercontent.com%2Fp%2FAF1QipPDRs3Sz2EbfwtdudSoM1HFo4Vay6FO1BRIyo3S%3Dw900-h600-k-no-pi89-ya358.03739685058594-r00-fo100!7i7680!8i3840!5m1!1e4?entry=ttu&g_ep=EgoyMDI1MDQyOC4wIKXMDSoASAFQAw%3D%3D.
Notice the internal URL referral to GoogleUserContent.com to indicate it being an external upload.

3 Available at: https://www.pampam.city/p/AclpLBcpcoHNj1n6wYZR?52.367641,4.916569,13.58.

Chapter 6

1 This was not the last time a tech company used its location-tracking capacities to follow journalists it wanted to surveil or intimidate. TikTok's Chinese parent company, ByteDance, used IP tracking to follow a Forbes journalist who investigated them just a few years ago (Baker-White 2022).

References

Aarseth, Espen. 2000. 'Allegories of Space: The Question of Spatiality in Computer Games'. In *Cybertext Yearbook 2000*, edited by Markku Eskelinen and Raine Koskimaa. University of Jyväskylä.

Abend, Pablo. 2018. 'Seasons Change, so Do We: Heterogeneous Temporalities, Algorithmic Frames and Subjective Time in Geomedia'. In *Time for Mapping*, edited by Sybille Lammes, Chris Perkins, Alex Gekker, Sam Hind, Clancy Wilmott, and Daniel Evans. Manchester University Press.

Abt, Clark C. 2002. *Serious Games*. University Press of America.

Agre, Philip E. 1994. 'Surveillance and Capture: Two Models of Privacy'. *The Information Society* 10 (2): 101–27.

Akrich, Madeleine, and Bruno Latour. 1992. 'A Summary of a Convenient Vocabulary for the Semiotics of Human and Nonhuman Assemblies'. In *Shaping Technology/Building Society: Studies in Sociotechnical Change*, edited by Wiebe E. Bijker and John Law. MIT Press.

Alba, Davey, and Jack Gillum. 2022. 'Google Maps Is Leading Abortion Seekers to Pro-Life Religious Centers'. *Bloomberg.com*, 15 August. https://www.bloomberg.com/graphics/2022-google-search-abortion-clinic-crisis-pregnancy-center/.

Ali, Christopher. 2021. *Farm Fresh Broadband: The Politics of Rural Connectivity*. MIT Press.

Alvarez León, Luis F. 2016. 'Property Regimes and the Commodification of Geographic Information: An Examination of Google Street View'. *Big Data & Society* 3 (2): 2053951716637885.

Alvarez León, Luis F. 2019. 'Eyes on the Road: Surveillance Logics in the Autonomous Vehicle Economy'. *Surveillance & Society* 17 (1/2): 198–204.

Amoore, Louise. 2011. 'Data Derivatives: On the Emergence of a Security Risk Calculus for Our Times'. *Theory, Culture & Society* 28 (6): 24–43.

Amoore, Louise. 2020. *Cloud Ethics: Algorithms and the Attributes of Ourselves and Others*. Duke University Press.

Andrejevic, Mark. 2013. *Infoglut: How Too Much Information Is Changing the Way We Think and Know*. Routledge.

Andrejevic, Mark. 2019. 'Automating Surveillance'. *Surveillance & Society* 17 (1/2): 7–13.

Anindya, Michelle. 2024. 'Grab Built Its Own Map in Southeast Asia, and Is Now Going after Google'. Rest of World, 13 November. https://restofworld.org/2024/grab-google-maps-southeast-asia/.

Ankel, Sophia. 2020. 'A Creepy New App for Explorers Led TikTokers to a Dead Body Stuffed inside a Suitcase. Here's How Randonautica Works.' Insider, 4 July. https://www.insider.com/new-randonautica-app-is-leading-tiktokers-to-some-unusual-discoveries-2020-7.

Anthropic. 2024. 'Introducing Computer Use, a New Claude 3.5 Sonnet, and Claude 3.5 Haiku'. 22 October. https://www.anthropic.com/news/3-5-models-and-computer-use.

Anthropic. 2025. 'Anthropic Economic Index: Tracking AI's Role in the US and Global Economy'. 15 September. https://www.anthropic.com/research/economic-index-geography.

Apelberg, Shelley. 2014. 'Request for a class action lawsuit for 220 million NIS against Waze: "They stole copyrights on Freemap"'. *TheMarker*, 27 March. https://www.themarker.com/technation/2014-03-27/ty-article/0000017f-da7c-d938-a17f-fe7ed1700000.

Apperley, Thomas, and Kyle Moore. 2019. 'Haptic Ambience: Ambient Play, the Haptic Effect and Co-Presence in *Pokémon GO*'. *Convergence* 25 (1): 6–17.

Arthur, Charles. 2013. 'Apple Maps: How Google Lost When Everyone Thought It Had Won'. *The Guardian*, 11 November. https://www.theguardian.com/technology/2013/nov/11/apple-maps-google-iphone-users.

Ash, James. 2010. 'Architectures of Affect: Anticipating and Manipulating the Event in Processes of Videogame Design and Testing'. *Environment and Planning D: Society and Space* 28 (4): 653–71.

Ash, James. 2012. 'Technology, Technicity, and Emerging Practices of Temporal Sensitivity in Videogames'. *Environment and Planning A* 44 (1): 187–203.

Ash, James. 2015. *The Interface Envelope: Gaming, Technology, Power*. Bloomsbury Academic.

Ash, James. 2018. *Phase Media: Space, Time and the Politics of Smart Objects*. Bloomsbury Academic.

Ash, James, Ben Anderson, Rachel Gordon, and Paul Langley. 2017. 'Unit, Vibration, Tone: A Post-Phenomenological Method for Researching Digital Interfaces'. *Cultural Geographies* 25 (1): 165–81.

Ash, James, Ben Anderson, Rachel Gordon, and Paul Langley. 2018. 'Digital Interface Design and Power: Friction, Threshold, Transition'. *Environment and Planning D: Society and Space* 36 (6): 1136–53.

Ash, James, Rob Kitchin, and Agnieszka Leszczynski. 2018. 'Digital Turn, Digital Geographies?' *Progress in Human Geography* 42 (1): 25–43.

Asmolov, Gregory. 2020. 'The Failures of Participatory Mapping: A Mediational Perspective'. In *Mapping Crisis: Participation, Datafication and Humanitarianism in the Age of Digital Mapping*, edited by Doug Specht. University of London Press.

Avery, Rhian. 2023. 'TomTom's Location-Informed ChatGPT Plugin | TomTom Newsroom'. TomTom, 7 August. https://www.tomtom.com/newsroom/product-focus/location-informed-chatgpt-plugin/.

Bacchi, Umberto. 2019. '"Took Away Our Identity": Google Maps Puzzles Residents with New Neighborhood Names'. World. *Reuters*, 4 July. https://www.reuters.com/article/world/took-away-our-identity-google-maps-puzzles-residents-with-new-neighborhood-na-idUSKCN1TZ1ZC/.

Badger, Emily. 2013. 'The Potential Problem with Personalized Google Maps? We May Never Know What We're Not Seeing'. The Atlantic Cities, 17 May. http://www.theatlanticcities.com/technology/2013/05/potential-problem-personalized-google-maps-we-may-never-know-what-were-not-seeing/5617/.

Badger, Emily. 2014. 'What Crimea Teaches Us about the Perils of Personalized Maps'. *Washington Post*, 14 April. http://www.washingtonpost.com/blogs/wonkblog/wp/2014/04/14/what-crimea-teaches-us-about-the-perils-of-personalized-maps/.

Bai, Zechen, Pichao Wang, Tianjun Xiao, et al. 2025. 'Hallucination of Multimodal Large Language Models: A Survey'. arXiv:2404.18930. Preprint, arXiv, 1 April. https://doi.org/10.48550/arXiv.2404.18930.

Baker-White, Emily. 2022. 'EXCLUSIVE: TikTok Spied On Forbes Journalists'. Forbes, 22 December. https://www.forbes.com/sites/emilybaker-white/2022/12/22/tiktok-tracks-forbes-journalists-bytedance/.

Bakhtin, Mikhail. 1968. *Rabelais and His World*. Translated by Helene Iswolsky. MIT Press.

Banks, David A. 2023. *The City Authentic: How the Attention Economy Builds Urban America*. University of California Press.

Barns, Sarah. 2019. 'Negotiating the Platform Pivot: From Participatory Digital Ecosystems to Infrastructures of Everyday Life'. *Geography Compass* 13 (9): e12464.

Barns, Sarah. 2020. *Platform Urbanism: Negotiating Platform Ecosystems in Connected Cities*. Palgrave Macmillan.

Barr, Kyle. 2022. 'Big Tech Companies Join Linux in Effort to Kill Google Maps'. Gizmodo, 15 December. https://gizmodo.com/linux-google-maps-meta-aws-microsoft-tomtom-1849899375.

Bauman, Zygmunt, and David Lyon. 2013. *Liquid Surveillance: A Conversation*. Polity.

Beer, David. 2015a. 'Productive Measures: Culture and Measurement in the Context of Everyday Neoliberalism'. *Big Data & Society* 2 (1): 2053951715578951.

Beer, David. 2015b. 'When "Special Measures" Become Ordinary'. openDemocracy, 7 August. https://www.opendemocracy.net/ourkingdom/david-beer/when-%E2%80%98special-measures%E2%80%99-become-ordinary.

Belanger, Ashley. 2025. '"Torrenting from a Corporate Laptop Doesn't Feel Right": Meta Emails Unsealed'. Ars Technica, 6 February. https://arstechnica.com/tech-policy/2025/02/meta-torrented-over-81-7tb-of-pirated-books-to-train-ai-authors-say/.

Bemel-Benrud, Saman. 2022. 'On Leaving Mapbox after 12 Years'. 20 June. https://trashmoon.com/blog/2022/reflections-on-12-years-at-mapbox/.

Bennett, Catherine. 2022. 'The Italian Streets That Don't Exist on Any Map'. Atlas Obscura, 28 April. http://www.atlasobscura.com/articles/italian-streets-not-on-map.

Bennett, Jonathan. 2010. *OpenStreetMap: Be Your Own Cartographer*. Packt Publishing.

Bentham, Jeremy. 2017. *The Correspondence of Jeremy Bentham. Volume 1: 1752–76*. Edited by Tymothy L.S. Sprigge and James H. Burns. UCL Press.

Bergen, Mark. 2018. 'Nobody Wants to Let Google Win the War for Maps All Over Again'. *Bloomberg.com*, 21 February. https://www.bloomberg.com/news/features/2018-02-21/nobody-wants-to-let-google-win-the-war-for-maps-all-over-again.

Bernevega, Alexander, and Alex Gekker. 2022. 'The Industry of Landlords: Exploring the Assetization of the Triple-A Game'. *Games and Culture* 17 (1): 47–69.

Berry, David M. 2014. *Critical Theory and the Digital*. Bloomsbury.

Bhattacharya, Ananya. 2025. 'Is Google Maps Fatally Misleading Drivers in India? It's Complicated'. Rest of World, 5 February. https://restofworld.org/2025/google-maps-india-misdirection-fatal-accidents/.

Bhuiyan, Johana. 2023. 'Google to Pay $93m in Settlement over

Deceptive Location Tracking'. *The Guardian*, 14 September. https://www.theguardian.com/technology/2023/sep/14/google-location-tracking-data-settlement.

Birch, Kean, and Fabian Muniesa, eds. 2020. *Assetization: Turning Things into Assets in Technoscientific Capitalism*. MIT Press.

Bishop, Sophie. 2019. 'Managing Visibility on YouTube through Algorithmic Gossip'. *New Media & Society* 21 (11–12): 2589–606.

Bishop, Sophie. 2020. 'Algorithmic Experts: Selling Algorithmic Lore on YouTube'. *Social Media + Society* 6 (1): 2056305119897323.

Bissell, David. 2018. 'Automation Interrupted: How Autonomous Vehicle Accidents Transform the Material Politics of Automation'. *Political Geography* 65: 57–66.

Bitter, Alex. 2025. 'Uber Made a Big Change to How It Prices Trips. It Might Be the Real Secret to the Company's Turnaround.' *Business Insider*, 25 June. https://www.businessinsider.com/why-uber-upfront-pricing-could-be-key-to-business-turnaround-2025-6.

Bittner, Christian, Georg Glasze, and Cate Turk. 2013. 'Tracing Contingencies: Analyzing the Political in Assemblages of Web 2.0 Cartographies'. *GeoJournal* 78 (6): 935–48.

Blake, Willa, and Isabel Sunderland. 2024. 'Snap Inc. Under Fire in New Mexico's Unredacted Lawsuit, Reveals Need for Kids' Safety Legislation'. Tech Policy Press, 8 October. https://techpolicy.press/snap-inc-under-fire-in-new-mexicos-unredacted-lawsuit-reveals-need-for-kids-safety-legislation.

Bogost, Ian. 2006. *Unit Operations: An Approach to Videogame Criticism*. MIT Press.

Bogost, Ian. 2007. *Persuasive Games: The Expressive Power of Videogames*. MIT Press.

Bogost, Ian. 2011a. *How to Do Things with Videogames*. University of Minnesota Press.

Bogost, Ian. 2011b. 'Persuasive Games: Exploitationware'. *Gamasutra*, 3 May. http://www.gamasutra.com/view/feature/6366/persuasive_games_exploitationware.php.

Bogost, Ian. 2012. *Alien Phenomenology, Or What It's Like to Be a Thing*. University of Minnesota Press.

Bogost, Ian, and Nick Montfort. 2009. 'Platform Studies: Frequently Questioned Answers'. *Digital Arts and Culture 2009, Irvine, CA, 12 December*. http://escholarship.org/uc/item/01r0k9br.

Bollmer, Grant, and Bethany Tillerson. 2025. 'Platform Fandom: Weverse and the Technological Domestication of Fan Community'. *Social Media + Society* 11 (2): 20563051251326689.

Bolter, Jay David, and Diane Gromala. 2005. *Windows and Mirrors:*

Interaction Design, Digital Art, and the Myth of Transparency. MIT Press.

Bommasani, Rishi, Drew A. Hudson, Ehsan Adeli, et al. 2022. 'On the Opportunities and Risks of Foundation Models'. arXiv:2108.07258. Preprint, arXiv, 12 July. https://doi.org/10.48550/arXiv.2108.07258.

Boria, Edoardo, and Tania Rossetto. 2017. 'The Practice of Mapmaking: Bridging the Gap between Critical/Textual and Ethnographical Research Methods'. *Cartographica* 52 (1): 32–48.

Bounegru, Liliana, Melody Devries, and Esther Weltevrede. 2022. 'The Research Persona Method: Figuring and Reconfiguring Personalised Information Flows'. In *Figure Concept and Method,* edited by Celia Lury, William Viney, and Scott Wark. Palgrave Macmillan.

Bourdon, Sébastien, and Antoine Schirer. 2024. *StravaLeaks: Thousands of Israeli Soldiers Identifiable through Workout App.* 4 November. https://www.lemonde.fr/en/international/article/2024/11/04/stravaleaks-thousands-of-israeli-soldiers-identifiable-through-workout-app_6731532_4.html.

Bowker, Geoffrey C., and Susan Leigh Star. 2000. *Sorting Things Out: Classification and Its Consequences.* MIT Press.

Boy, John D., and Justus Uitermark. 2024. *On Display: Instagram, the Self, and the City.* Oxford University Press.

Brachmann, Eric, and Victor Adrian Prisacariu. 2024. 'Building a Large Geospatial Model to Achieve Spatial Intelligence'. Niantic News, 12 November. https://nianticlabs.com/news/largegeospatialmodel/.

Bratton, Benjamin H. 2015. *The Stack: On Software and Sovereignty.* MIT Press.

Brignull, Harry. 2010. 'Dark Patterns'. https://www.darkpatterns.org/.

Brown, Barry, and Eric Laurier. 2005. 'Maps & Journeying: An Ethnographic Approach'. *Cartographica* 4 (3): 17–33.

Bruns, Axel. 2007. 'Produsage'. *Proceedings of the 6th ACM SIGCHI Conference on Creativity & Cognition,* 99–106. http://dl.acm.org/citation.cfm?id=1254975.

Bryant, Levi R. 2010. 'Flat Ontology'. *Larval Subjects,* 24 February. https://larvalsubjects.wordpress.com/2010/02/24/flat-ontology-2/.

Bucher, Taina. 2017. 'The Algorithmic Imaginary: Exploring the Ordinary Affects of Facebook Algorithms'. *Information, Communication & Society* 20 (1): 30–44.

Bucher, Taina. 2018. *If ... Then: Algorithmic Power and Politics.* Oxford University Press.

Bucher, Taina, and Anne Helmond. 2018. 'The Affordances of Social Media Platforms'. In *The SAGE Handbook of Social Media,* edited by Jean Burgess, Alice E. Marwick, and Thomas Poell. Sage.

Buczkowski, Aleks. 2025. 'Street-Level Imagery by Bee Maps Is Redefining Mapmaking'. *Geoawesome*, 20 April. https://geoawesome.com/street-level-imagery-of-bee-maps-is-redefining-mapmaking/.

Burkhardt, Sarah, and Bernhard Rieder. 2024. 'Foundation Models Are Platform Models: Prompting and the Political Economy of AI'. *Big Data & Society* 11 (2): 20539517241247839.

Butler, Gavin. 2022. 'Google Turns Off Maps Features in Ukraine That Inadvertently Showed Russia's Invasion'. *VICE*, 28 February. https://www.vice.com/en/article/google-maps-ukraine-live-traffic-russia-invasion/.

Caillois, Roger, and Meyer Barash. 1961. *Man, Play, and Games.* University of Illinois Press.

Campanella, Thomas J. 2017. 'The True Measure of Robert Moses (and His Racist Bridges)'. *Bloomberg.com*, 9 July. https://www.bloomberg.com/news/articles/2017-07-09/robert-moses-and-his-racist-parkway-explained.

Cantrill, Aggi, and Stephanie Bodoni. 2023. 'Google Street View to Post First New Pictures from Germany in a Decade'. *Bloomberg.com*, 25 July. https://www.bloomberg.com/news/articles/2023-07-25/google-street-view-to-post-first-new-german-pictures-in-a-decade.

Carr, Constance, Desmond Bast, Karinne Madron, and Ahmad Mafaz Syrus. 2022. 'Mapping the Clouds: The Matter of Data Centers'. *Journal of Maps* 18 (1): 106–13.

Carton, Linda J. 2007. 'Map Making and Map Use in a Multi-Actor Context. Spatial Visualizations and Frame Conflicts in Regional Policymaking in the Netherlands.' Thesis, TU Delft.

Cartwright, William, Jeremy Crampton, Georg Gartner, et al. 2001. 'Geospatial Information Visualization User Interface Issues'. *Cartography and Geographic Information Science* 28 (1): 45–60.

Castells, Manuel. 2001. *The Internet Galaxy: Reflections on the Internet, Business and Society.* Oxford University Press.

Celis Bueno, Claudio. 2017. *The Attention Economy: Labour, Time and Power in Cognitive Capitalism.* Rowman & Littlefield International.

Cheney-Lippold, John. 2017. *We Are Data: Algorithms and The Making of Our Digital Selves.* NYU Press.

Chesher, Chris. 2012. 'Navigating Sociotechnical Spaces: Comparing Computer Games and Sat Navs as Digital Spatial Media'. *Convergence* 18 (3): 315–30.

Chiang, Ted. 2023. 'ChatGPT Is a Blurry JPEG of the Web'. Annals of Artificial Intelligence. *The New Yorker*, 9 February. https://www.newyorker.com/tech/annals-of-technology/chatgpt-is-a-blurry-jpeg-of-the-web.

Christin, Angèle. 2020. 'The Ethnographer and the Algorithm: Beyond the Black Box'. *Theory and Society* 49 (5): 897–918.

Clark, Mitchell. 2022. 'Instagram's Trying to Make It Easier to Find Nearby Businesses'. The Verge, 19 July. https://www.theverge.com/2022/7/19/23270510/instagram-searchable-map-nearby-business.

Clarke, Roger. 1988. 'Information Technology and Dataveillance'. *Communications of ACM* 31 (5): 498–512.

Ćmielová, Beata, and Jiří Pánek. 2016. 'Visual Comparison of Web Map Changes of Openstreetmap and Commercial Online-Map Providers: A Research Note'. *International Journal of E-Planning Research* 5 (2): 40–54.

Cohan, Peter. 2012. 'Apple Maps' Six Most Epic Fails'. *Forbes*, 27 September. http://www.forbes.com/sites/petercohan/2012/09/27/apple-maps-six-most-epic-fails/.

Coldewey, Devin. 2019. 'Apple and Google Maps Accommodate Russia's Annexation of Crimea'. *TechCrunch*, 27 November. https://techcrunch.com/2019/11/27/apple-and-google-maps-accommodate-russias-annexation-of-crimea/.

Coletta, Claudio, and Rob Kitchin. 2017. 'Algorhythmic Governance: Regulating the "Heartbeat" of a City Using the Internet of Things'. *Big Data & Society*, 4 (2): 2053951717742418.

Colley, Ashley, Jacob Thebault-Spieker, Allen Yilun Lin, et al. 2017. 'The Geography of Pokémon GO: Beneficial and Problematic Effects on Places and Movement'. *Proceedings of the 2017 CHI Conference on Human Factors in Computing Systems, New York, NY*, 2 May, 1179–92.

Counter Cartographies Collective, Craig Dalton, and Liz Mason-Deese. 2012. 'Counter (Mapping) Actions: Mapping as Militant Research'. *ACME: An International Journal for Critical Geographies* 11 (3): 439–66.

Craib, Raymond B. 2000. 'Cartography and Power in the Conquest and Creation of New Spain'. *Latin American Research Review* 35 (1): 7–36.

Crampton, Jeremy W. 2001. 'Maps as Social Constructions: Power, Communication and Visualization'. *Progress in Human Geography* 25 (2): 235–52.

Crampton, Jeremy W. 2002. 'Thinking Philosophically in Cartography: Toward a Critical Politics of Mapping'. *Cartographic Perspectives* 12: 12–32.

Crampton, Jeremy W. 2003. *The Political Mapping of Cyberspace*. University of Chicago Press.

Crampton, Jeremy W., and John Krygier. 2005. 'An Introduction to

Critical Cartography'. *ACME: An International E-Journal for Critical Geographies* 4 (1): 11–33.

Crary, Jonathan. 2014. *24/7: Late Capitalism and the Ends of Sleep*. Verso.

Crawford, Kate. 2021. *The Atlas of AI: Power, Politics, and the Planetary Costs of Artificial Intelligence*. Yale University Press.

Creemers, Rogier. 2018. 'China's Social Credit System: An Evolving Practice of Control'. https://doi.org/10.2139/ssrn.3175792.

Crist, Ry. 2016. 'New Study Details a Security Flaw with Philips Hue Smart Bulbs'. CNET, 3 November. https://www.cnet.com/home/kitchen-and-household/new-study-details-a-security-flaw-with-philips-hue-smart-bulbs/.

Crogan, Patrick, and Samuel Kinsley. 2012. 'Paying Attention: Toward a Critique of the Attention Economy'. *Culture Machine* 13: 1–29.

Cross, Gary S. 2018. *Machines of Youth: America's Car Obsession*. University of Chicago Press.

Dalton, Craig M. 2012. 'Mashing-up Maps: Google Geo Services and the Geography of Ubiquity'. PhD thesis, University of North Carolina – Chapel Hill.

Dalton, Craig M. 2015. 'For Fun and Profit: The Limits and Possibilities of Google-Maps-Based Geoweb Applications'. *Environment and Planning A* 47 (5): 1029–46.

Dalton, Craig M. 2018. 'Big Data from the Ground Up: Mobile Maps and Geographic Knowledge'. *The Professional Geographer* 70 (1): 157–64.

Darlington, Joseph. 2018. 'Introduction'. *Information, Communication & Society* 21 (9): 1187–92.

Dave, Paresh. 2023. 'Google's AI Is Making Traffic Lights More Efficient and Less Annoying'. *Wired*, 10 October. https://www.wired.com/story/googles-ai-traffic-lights-driving-annoying/.

Davies, John, and Alexander Kent. 2017. *The Red Atlas: How the Soviet Union Secretly Mapped the World*. University of Chicago Press.

Davies, William. 2015. '7. Living in the Lab'. In *The Happiness Industry: How the Government and Big Business Sold Us Well-Being*. Verso Books.

de Seta, Gabriele, Idil Galip, Lucie Chateau, and Gunseli Yalcinkaya. 2025. 'Groundhog Day| Memes Are New'. *International Journal of Communication* 19: 7.

de Souza e Silva, Adriana. 2006. 'From Cyber to Hybrid: Mobile Technologies as Interfaces of Hybrid Spaces'. *Space and Culture* 9: 261–78.

de Souza e Silva, Adriana. 2023. 'Hybrid Spaces 2.0: Connecting Networked Urbanism, Uneven Mobilities, and Creativity, in a (Post) Pandemic World'. *Mobile Media & Communication* 11 (1): 59–65.

de Souza e Silva, Adriana, and Larissa Hjorth. 2009. 'Playful Urban

Spaces: A Historical Approach to Mobile Games'. *Simulation & Gaming* 40 (5): 602–25.

de Souza e Silva, Adriana, and Mimi Sheller. 2015. 'Introduction: Moving toward Adjacent Possibles'. In *Mobility and Locative Media: Mobile Communication in Hybrid Spaces*, edited by Adriana de Souza e Silva and Mimi Sheller. Routledge.

De Zeeuw, Daniël, and Alex Gekker. 2023. 'A God-Tier LARP? QAnon as Conspiracy Fictioning'. *Social Media + Society* 9 (1): 205630512311573.

Debord, Guy. 1958. 'Theory of the Dérive'. *Internationale Situationniste* 2: 50–4.

Deck, Andrew. 2021. 'Zanzibar's Project to Put Itself on Google Street View Has Angered a Legion of European Video Game Streamers'. Rest of World, 8 April. https://restofworld.org/2021/zanzibar-google-street-view-geoguessr/.

Deck, Andrew. 2022. 'The Zenly Implosion: Inside 6 Months of Tension, Culture Clash, and Conflict'. Rest of World, 20 September. https://restofworld.org/2022/fearing-competition-snap-decided-to-shut-down-zenly-rather-than-sell-it/.

Del Casino, V., and S.P. Hanna. 2006. 'Beyond the "Binaries": A Methodological Intervention for Interrogating Maps as Representational Practices'. *ACME: An International E-Journal for Critical Geographies* 4 (1): 34–56.

Deleuze, Gilles. 1992. 'Postscript on the Societies of Control'. *October* 59: 3–7.

Della Dora, Veronica. 2012. 'A World of "Slippy Maps": Google Earth, Global Visions, and Topographies of Memory'. *Transatlantica* 2012 (2). http://transatlantica.revues.org.proxy.library.uu.nl/6156.

Dent, Steve. 2018. 'Here Attacks Google Maps with New Freemium Website Plan'. Engadget, 6 August. https://www.engadget.com/2018-08-06-here-attacks-google-maps-with-new-freemium-website-plan.html.

Deterding, Sebastian. 2015. 'The Ambiguity of Games: Histories and Discourses of a Gameful World'. In *The Gameful World. Approaches, Issues, Applications*, edited by Stephen P. Walz and Sebastian Deterding. MIT Press.

Diefenbach, Sarah, Nina Kolb, and Marc Hassenzahl. 2014. 'The "Hedonic" in Human-Computer Interaction: History, Contributions, and Future Research Directions'. *Proceedings of the 2014 Conference on Designing Interactive Systems – DIS '14*, 305–14.

Dieter, Michael. 2015. 'Dark Patterns: Interface Design, Augmentation and Crisis'. In *Postdigital Aesthetics: Art, Computation and Design*, edited by David M. Berry and Michael Dieter. Palgrave Macmillan.

Dilke, Oswald Ashton Wentworth. 1987a. 'Itineraries and Geographical Maps in the Early and Late Roman Empires'. In *The History of Cartography Volume 1: Cartography in Prehistoric, Ancient, and Medieval Europe and the Mediterranean*, edited by J.B. Harley and David Woodward. University of Chicago Press.

Dilke, Oswald Ashton Wentworth. 1987b. 'The Culmination of Greek Cartography in Ptolemy'. In *The History of Cartography Volume 1: Cartography in Prehistoric, Ancient, and Medieval Europe and the Mediterranean*, edited by J.B. Harley and David Woodward. University of Chicago Press.

Dillet, Romain. 2022. 'Zenly Was the Best Social App and It Will (Sadly) Shut down on February 3'. *TechCrunch*, 5 December. https://techcrunch.com/2022/12/05/zenly-was-the-best-social-app-and-it-will-sadly-shut-down-on-february-3rd/.

dishero. 2022. '"Breakfast Restaurant Near Me," This restaurant set their name in google maps to game search results'. Reddit Post. R/Assholedesign, 28 December. https://www.reddit.com/r/assholedesign/comments/zxh88r/breakfast_restaurant_near_me_this_restaurant_set/.

Drucker, Johanna. 2011. 'Humanities Approaches to Interface Theory'. *Culture Machine* 12: 1–20. http://culturemachine.net/index.php/cm/article/view/434.

Duffy, Brooke Erin, and Ngai Keung Chan. 2019. '"You Never Really Know Who's Looking": Imagined Surveillance across Social Media Platforms'. *New Media & Society* 21 (1): 119–38.

Duffy, Nick. 2016. 'Grindr Leaks Your EXACT Location Even If You Turn "Location Privacy" on, Cybersecurity Experts Warn'. *PinkNews*, 20 May. https://www.thepinknews.com/2016/05/20/grindr-leaks-your-exact-location-even-if-you-turn-location-privacy-on-cybersecurity-experts-warn/.

Duggan, Mike. 2024. *All Mapped Out: How Maps Shape Us*. Reaktion Books.

Easterling, Keller. 2016. *Extrastatecraft: The Power of Infrastructure Space*. Verso.

Edney, Matthew H. 2005. *The Origins and Development of J.B. Harley's Cartographic Theories*. Cartographica Monograph 54. University of Toronto. http://works.bepress.com/matthew_edney/13.

Edwards, Benj. 2024a. 'Cheap AI "Video Scraping" Can Now Extract Data from Any Screen Recording'. Ars Technica, 17 October. https://arstechnica.com/ai/2024/10/cheap-ai-video-scraping-can-now-extract-data-from-any-screen-recording/.

Edwards, Benj. 2024b. 'Niantic Uses Pokémon Go Player Data to

Build AI Navigation System'. Ars Technica, 19 November. https://arstechnica.com/ai/2024/11/niantic-uses-pokemon-go-player-data-to-build-ai-navigation-system/.

Elden, Stuart. 2007. 'There Is a Politics of Space Because Space Is Political: Henri Lefebvre and the Production of Space'. *Radical Philosophy Review* 10 (2): 101–16.

Elias, Jennifer. 2025. 'Google Reclassifies U.S. as "Sensitive Country" alongside China, Russia after Trump's "Gulf of America" Comments'. CNBC, 28 January. https://www.cnbc.com/2025/01/28/google-reclassifies-us-as-sensitive-country-like-china-russia-.html.

Eloundou, Tyna, Sam Manning, Pamela Mishkin, and Daniel Rock. 2024. 'GPTs Are GPTs: Labor Market Impact Potential of LLMs'. *Science* 384 (6702): 1306–8.

Engadget, dir. 2019. *Google Maps AR First Look: Helping You Navigate the City*. https://www.youtube.com/watch?v=XWbY5jdJnHg.

Eubanks, Virginia. 2017. *Automating Inequality: How High-Tech Tools Profile, Police, and Punish the Poor*. St. Martin's Press.

European Commission. 2024. 'Statement on Announcement by Amazon'. European Commission, 29 January. https://ec.europa.eu/commission/presscorner/detail/en/statement_24_521.

Evans, Elizabeth. 2016. 'The Economics of Free Freemium Games, Branding and the Impatience Economy'. *Convergence* 22 (6): 563–80.

Evans, Leighton. 2015. *Locative Social Media: Place in the Digital Age*. Palgrave Macmillan.

Farivar, Cyrus. 2013. 'Germany Fines Google a Paltry $189,000 over Street View Wi-Fi Scanning'. Ars Technica, 22 April. http://arstechnica.com/tech-policy/2013/04/germany-fines-google-a-paltry-189000-over-street-view-wi-fi-scanning/.

Farivar, Cyrus. 2018. 'Why Cops Won't Need a Warrant to Pull the Data off Your Autonomous Car'. Ars Technica, 2 March. https://arstechnica.com/tech-policy/2018/02/why-self-driving-cars-may-be-heaven-for-investigating-crimes-and-accidents/.

Farman, Jason. 2010. 'Mapping the Digital Empire: Google Earth and the Process of Postmodern Cartography'. *New Media & Society* 12 (6): 869–88.

Farman, Jason. 2012. *Mobile Interface Theory: Embodied Space and Locative Media*. Routledge.

Farman, Jason. 2015. 'Infrastructures of Mobile Social Media'. *Social Media + Society* 1 (1): 2056305115580343.

Farman, Jason. 2021. *Mobile Interface Theory: Embodied Space and Locative Media*, 2nd edn. Routledge.

Farrell, James. 2025. 'OpenAI Can Now Make Accurate Maps ... Sort

Of'. East Of Nowhere, 26 March. https://eastofnowhere.co/blogs/news/openai-can-now-make-accurate-maps-sort-of.

Fisher, Adam. 2013. 'Google's Road Map to Global Domination'. *The New York Times*, 11 December. http://www.nytimes.com/2013/12/15/magazine/googles-plan-for-global-domination-dont-ask-why-ask-where.html.

Fisher, Eran. 2022. 'Do Algorithms Have a Right to the City? Waze and Algorithmic Spatiality'. *Cultural Studies* 36 (1): 74–95.

Fizek, Sonia. 2014. 'Why Fun Matters: In Search of Emergent Playful Experiences'. In *Rethinking Gamification*, edited by Mathias Fuchs, Sonia Fizek, Paolo Ruffino, and Niklas Schrape. Meson Press.

Flink, James J. 1976. *The Car Culture*. MIT Press.

Folding Ideas, dir. 2022. *Contrepreneurs: The Mikkelsen Twins*. https://www.youtube.com/watch?v=biYciU1uiUw.

Foley, John. 2025. *Nvidia Is a $3tn Bet on the Tokenisation of Everything*. 29 May. https://www.ft.com/content/0f6b115e-0d2c-4dd7-8aa5-a031b7cd4bf3.

Foucault, Michel. 1977. *Discipline and Punish*. Pantheon.

Foucault, Michel. 1995. 'Panopticism'. In *Discipline and Punish: The Birth of the Prison*. Translated by Alan Sheridan. Vintage Books.

Fourcade, Marion, and Kieran Healy. 2016. 'Seeing like a Market'. *Socio-Economic Review* 15 (1): 9–29.

Foxman, Maxwell. 2014. 'How to Win Foursquare: Body and Space in a Gamified World'. In *Rethinking Gamification*, edited by Mathias Fuchs, Sonia Fizek, Paolo Ruffino, and Niklas Schrape. Meson Press.

Frank, Allegra. 2017. 'Pokémon Go's Maps Now Look a Lot Different'. *Polygon*, 4 December. https://www.polygon.com/2017/12/4/16725748/pokemon-go-map-changes-openstreetmap.

Frankfurt, Harry G. 2009. *On Bullshit*. Princeton University Press.

Frissen, Valerie, Sybille Lammes, Michiel de Lange, Jos de Mul, and Joost Raessens. 2015. 'Homo Ludens 2.0: Play, Media, and Identity'. In *Playful Identities: The Ludification of Digital Media Cultures*. Amsterdam University Press.

Fuchs, Mathias, Sonia Fizek, Paolo Ruffino, and Niklas Schrape. 2014. *Rethinking Gamification*. Meson Press.

Fulton, Jonathan. 2025. 'Israeli Concerns about PRC Surveillance via Smart Devices, Chinese Companies in Egypt Registering to Use Renminbi in Local Transactions, Wang Yi Comments on Iran and Israel'. Substack newsletter. *The China-MENA Newsletter*, 6 July. https://chinamenanewsletter.substack.com/p/israeli-concerns-about-prc-surveillance?utm_campaign=post&triedRedirect=true.

Fung, Brian. 2017. 'Uber Settles with FTC over "God View" and

Some Other Privacy Issues'. *Los Angeles Times*, 15 August. https://www.latimes.com/business/technology/la-fi-tn-uber-ftc-20170815-story.html.

Galloway, Alexander R. 2004. *Protocol: How Control Exists After Decentralization*. MIT Press.

Galloway, Alexander R. 2012. *The Interface Effect*. Polity.

Gandini, Alessandro. 2021. 'Digital Labour: An Empty Signifier?': *Media, Culture & Society* 43 (2): 369–80.

Gartner, Georg, David A. Bennett, and Takashi Morita. 2007. 'Towards Ubiquitous Cartography'. *Cartography and Geographic Information Science* 34 (4): 247–57.

Gayle, Damien. 2012. 'Sandy Island Tracked down to 1908 Admiralty Chart: Librarian Locates Earliest Mention yet Found of the Island That Wasn't'. *Mail Online*, 4 December. http://www.dailymail.co.uk/sciencetech/article-2242767/Sandy-Island-tracked-1908-admiralty-chart-Librarian-locates-earliest-mention-island-wasnt.html.

'Gaza Places (Amākin Ghazza)'. n.d. https://gazaplaces.com/.

Geens, Stefan. 2012. 'Apple Maps and the Diaoyu/Senkaku Islands'. Ogle Earth, 25 September. http://ogleearth.com/2012/09/apple-maps-and-the-diaoyusenkaku-islands/.

Gekker, Alex. 2016a. 'Casual Power: Understanding User Interfaces through Quantification'. *Digital Culture & Society* 2 (1): 107–22.

Gekker, Alex. 2016b. 'Uniquitous Cartography: Casual Power in Digital Maps'. PhD thesis, Utrecht University.

Gekker, Alex. 2018. 'Let's Not Play: Interpassivity as Resistance in "Let's Play" Videos'. *Journal of Gaming & Virtual Worlds* 10 (3): 219–42.

Gekker, Alex. 2019. 'Playing with Power: Casual Politicking a New Frame for Political Analysis'. In *The Playful Citizen: Civic Engagement in a Mediatized Culture*, edited by Sybille Lammes, René Glas, Michiel de Lange, Joost Raessens, and Imar de Vries. Amsterdam University Press.

Gekker, Alex. 2023. 'Google Maps' COVID-19 Layer as an Interface for Pandemic Life'. *Mobile Media & Communication* 11 (2): 193–212.

Gekker, Alex, and Anat Ben David. 2020. 'Data Cudgel or how to Generate Corona-Compliance in Israel'. In *COVID-19 from the Margins: Pandemic Invisibilities, Policies and Resistance in the Datafied Society*. Amsterdam University Press.

Gekker, Alex, and Daniel Joseph. 2021. 'Selling Elysium: The Political Economy of Radical Game Distribution'. *Baltic Screen Media Review* 9 (1): 20–31.

Gekker, Alex, and Sam Hind. 2020. 'Infrastructural Surveillance'. *New Media & Society* 22 (8): 1414–36.

Gentzel, Peter, Jeffrey Wimmer, and Ruben Schlagowski. 2021. 'Doing Google Maps: Everyday Use and the Image of Space in a Surveillance Capitalism Centrepiece'. *Digital Culture & Society* 7 (2): 159–84.

Gerlach, Joe. 2010. 'Vernacular Mapping, and the Ethics of What Comes Next'. *Cartographica* 45 (3): 165–8.

Gerlach, Joe. 2015. 'Editing Worlds: Participatory Mapping and a Minor Geopolitics'. *Transactions of the Institute of British Geographers* 40 (2): 273–86.

Gibbs, Martin, James Meese, Michael Arnold, Bjorn Nansen, and Marcus Carter. 2015. '#Funeral and Instagram: Death, Social Media, and Platform Vernacular'. *Information, Communication & Society* 18 (3): 255–68.

Gibson, James J. 1977. 'The Concept of Affordances'. In *Perceiving, Acting, and Knowing: Toward an Ecological Psychology*, edited by Robert Shaw and John Bransford. Lawrence Erlbaum Associates.

Gibson, James J. 1986. *The Ecological Approach To Visual Perception.* Psychology Press.

Gilbert, Ben. 2016. 'Pokémon Go Has Been Downloaded over 500 Million Times'. Business Insider, 7 September. https://www.businessinsider.com/pokemon-go-500-million-downloads-2016-9.

Gil-Fournier, Abelardo, and Jussi Parikka. 2021. 'Ground Truth to Fake Geographies: Machine Vision and Learning in Visual Practices'. *AI & Society* 36 (4): 1253–62.

Gillespie, Tarleton. 2010. 'The Politics of "Platforms"'. *New Media & Society* 12 (3): 347–64.

Gillespie, Tarleton. 2017. 'Governance of and by Platforms'. In *The SAGE Handbook of Social Media*, edited by Jean Burgess, Alice E. Marwick, and Thomas Poell. Sage.

Gilliard, Chris, and Hugh Culik. 2016. 'Digital Redlining, Access, and Privacy'. Common Sense Education, 24 May. https://web.archive.org/web/20190331024731/https://www.commonsense.org/education/privacy/blog/digital-redlining-access-privacy.

Gilliard, Chris, and David Golumbia. 2021. 'Luxury Surveillance'. Real Life, 6 July. https://reallifemag.com/luxury-surveillance/.

Gitelman, Lisa, ed. 2013. *'Raw Data' Is an Oxymoron*. MIT Press.

Goichman, Rafaela. 2020. 'Copyright lawsuit against Google, and Waze founder that "appropriated" app'. *TheMarker*, 29 January. https://www.themarker.com/law/2020-01-29/ty-article/0000017f-e327-d568-ad7f-f36f09ba0000.

Goldfarb, Avi, Bledi Taska, and Florenta Teodoridis. 2023. 'Could Machine Learning Be a General Purpose Technology? A Comparison of Emerging Technologies Using Data from Online Job Postings'. *Research Policy* 52 (1): 104653.

Goodin, Dan. 2024. 'Spies Hack Wi-Fi Networks in Far-off Land to Launch Attack on Target next Door'. Ars Technica, 23 November. https://arstechnica.com/security/2024/11/spies-hack-wi-fi-networks-in-far-off-land-to-launch-attack-on-target-next-door/.

Google. n.d.-a. 'Create and Publish Your Own Street View Images'. Google Maps Street View. https://www.google.com/streetview/contribute/.

Google. n.d.-b. 'Google-Contributed Street View Imagery Policy'. Google Maps Street View. https://www.google.com/streetview/policy/.

Google Maps, dir. 2022. *Meet the 2022 Guiding Stars of Our Local Guides Community*. https://www.youtube.com/watch?v=dsBXJrN-Gw8.

Google Transparency Report. 2025. 'Google Maps Content Trust & Safety Report'. https://transparencyreport.google.com/maps-content/enforcement.

Gorwa, Robert, and Michael Veale. 2024. 'Moderating Model Marketplaces: Platform Governance Puzzles for AI Intermediaries'. arXiv:2311.12573. Preprint, arXiv, 15 February. https://doi.org/10.48550/arXiv.2311.12573.

Gray, Mary L., and Siddharth Suri. 2019. *Ghost Work: How to Stop Silicon Valley from Building a New Global Underclass*. Houghton Mifflin Harcourt.

Gregg, Aaron, Trisha Thadani, and Tatum Hunter. 2025. 'Waymo Suspends Service in Parts of L.A. after Its Robotaxis Are Set on Fire'. *The Washington Post*, 9 June. https://www.washingtonpost.com/business/2025/06/09/waymo-cars-burned-los-angeles-protest/.

Grindr. 2025. 'Discover Live View on Right Now: Connect Instantly with Nearby Users'. 14 August. https://www.grindr.com/blog/introducing-map-view-a-new-way-to-see-whos-on-right-now.

'GrindrMap'. n.d. https://grindrmap.neocities.org/.

Griswold, Alison. 2023. 'The Devilish Change Uber and Lyft Made to Surge Pricing'. *Slate*, 23 August. https://slate.com/technology/2023/08/lyft-uber-surge-prime-time-upfront-pricing.html.

Grohmann, Rafael. 2025. 'Free Labor and Data Labor in the Digital Economy'. In *The Sage Handbook of Data and Society*, edited by Tommaso Venturini, Amelia Acker, Jean-Christophe Plantin, and Tone Walford. Sage.

Gross, Jenny. 2023. 'He Drove Into a Creek and Died. His Family Blames Google Maps'. *The New York Times*, 21 September. https://www.nytimes.com/2023/09/21/us/google-maps-lawsuit-collapsed-bridge.html.

Grosser, Benjamin. 2014. 'What Do Metrics Want? How Quantification Prescribes Social Interaction on Facebook'. *Computational Culture* 4 (November). http://computationalculture.net/article/what-do-metrics-want.

Grundig, Tyana, Makda Ghebreslassie, and Greg Sadler. 2020. 'Looking for Local Appliance Repair? Why You Can't Always Trust What You Find on Google Maps'. *CBC News*, 16 October. https://www.cbc.ca/news/canada/appliance-repair-industry-online-listings-1.5762489.

Hadler, Florian. 2018. 'Beyond UX'. *Interface Critique Journal* 1, https://interfacecritique.net/journal/volume-1/editorial/.

Haggerty, Kevin D., and Richard V. Ericson. 2000. 'The Surveillant Assemblage'. *British Journal of Sociology* 51 (4): 605–22.

Haklay, Mordechai. 2013. 'Neogeography and the Delusion of Democratisation'. *Environment and Planning A* 45 (1): 55–69.

Haklay, Mordechai, and Patrick Weber. 2008. 'OpenStreetMap: User-Generated Street Maps'. *IEEE Pervasive Computing* 7 (4): 12–18.

Halder, Subir, Amrita Ghosal, and Mauro Conti. 2020. 'Secure Over-the-Air Software Updates in Connected Vehicles: A Survey'. *Computer Networks* 178: 107343.

Hall, Stuart. 1980. 'Encoding/Decoding'. In *Culture, Media, Language: Working Papers in Cultural Studies, 1972–79*, edited by Stuart Hall, Dorothy Hobson, Andrew Lowe, and Paul Willis. Hutchinson.

Hancock, Edith. 2025. 'Google Offers to Tweak Automotive Services, Maps Contracts to Appease German Regulator'. *Wall Street Journal*, 9 April. https://www.wsj.com/tech/google-offers-to-tweak-automotive-services-maps-contracts-to-appease-german-regulator-fdb8cc3d.

Harley, J.B. 1987. 'The Map and the Development of the History of Cartography'. In *The History of Cartography Volume 1: Cartography in Prehistoric, Ancient, and Medieval Europe and the Mediterranean*, edited by J.B. Harley and David Woodward. University of Chicago Press.

Harley, J.B. 1988a. 'Maps, Knowledge and Power'. In *The Iconography of Landscape*, edited by Denis Cosgrove and Stephen Daniels. Cambridge University Press.

Harley, J.B. 1988b. 'Silences and Secrecy: The Hidden Agenda of Cartography in Early Modern Europe'. *Imago Mundi* 40 (1): 57–76.

Harley, J.B. 1989. 'Deconstructing the Map'. *Cartographica* 26 (2): 1–20.

Harley, J.B. 2001. 'Text and Contexts in the Interpretation of Early Maps'. In *The New Nature of Maps: Essays in the History of Cartography*, edited by J.H. Andrews. Johns Hopkins University Press.

Harman, G. 2010. *Towards Speculative Realism: Essays and Lectures*. John Hunt Publishing.

Hassenzahl, Marc. 2008. 'User Experience (UX): Towards an Experiential Perspective on Product Quality'. *Proceedings of the 20th Conference on L'Interaction Homme-Machine, New York, NY*, 11–15. https://doi.org/10.1145/1512714.1512717.

Hassenzahl, Marc, and Noam Tractinsky. 2006. 'User Experience – a Research Agenda'. *Behaviour & Information Technology* 25 (2): 91–7.

Hawkins, Andrew J. 2018. 'Inside the Lab Where Waymo Is Building the Brains for Its Driverless Cars'. The Verge, 9 May. https://www.theverge.com/2018/5/9/17307156/google-waymo-driverless-cars-deep-learning-neural-net-interview.

Hawkins, Andrew J. 2022a. 'Intel's Mobileye Announces New EyeQ Ultra System-on-a-Chip for Autonomous Driving'. The Verge, 4 January. https://www.theverge.com/2022/1/4/22865488/intel-mobileye-eyeq-ultra-soc-autonomous-driving.

Hawkins, Andrew J. 2022b. 'Mobileye and Geely Team up to Build a Self-Driving Car You Can Buy'. The Verge, 4 January. https://www.theverge.com/2022/1/4/22866100/mobileye-geely-zeekr-autonomous-vehicle-personally-owned.

Hawkins, Andrew J. 2023. 'Google Maps Tweaks Transit Directions, Adds Emoji Reactions and Collaborative Lists'. The Verge, 15 November. https://www.theverge.com/2023/11/15/23962007/google-maps-transit-collaborative-list-emoji-reactions.

Hawley, Kristen. 2025. 'DoorDash Is Now Sending Food in Delivery Robots. That's as Good and Bad as You Think'. Fast Company, 12 April. https://www.fastcompany.com/91315775/doordash-coco-food-delivery-robots-good-and-bad-as-you-think.

Hayles, N. Katherine. 2002. 'Flesh and Metal: Reconfiguring the Mindbody in Virtual Environments'. *Configurations* 10 (2): 297–320.

Hayles, N. Katherine. 2006. 'Unfinished Work: From Cyborg to Cognisphere'. *Theory, Culture & Society* 23 (7–8): 159–66.

Helles, Rasmus, and Mikkel Flyverbom. 2019. 'Meshes of Surveillance, Prediction, and Infrastructure: On the Cultural and Commercial Consequences of Digital Platforms'. *Surveillance & Society* 17 (1/2): 34–9.

Helmond, Anne. 2015. 'The Platformization of the Web: Making Web Data Platform Ready'. *Social Media + Society* 1 (2): 2056305115603080.

Herfort, Benjamin, Sven Lautenbach, João Porto de Albuquerque, Jennings Anderson, and Alexander Zipf. 2023. 'A Spatio-Temporal Analysis Investigating Completeness and Inequalities of Global Urban Building Data in OpenStreetMap'. *Nature Communications* 14 (1): 3985.

Hern, Alex. 2020. 'Apple Faces Privacy Case in Europe over iPhone

Tracking ID'. *The Guardian*, 17 November. https://www.theguardian.com/technology/2020/nov/17/apple-faces-privacy-case-in-europe-over-iphone-tracking-id.

Hicks, Michael Townsen, James Humphries, and Joe Slater. 2024. 'ChatGPT Is Bullshit'. *Ethics and Information Technology* 26 (2): 38.

Hill, Kashmir. 2024. 'How G.M. Tricked Millions of Drivers Into Being Spied On (Including Me)'. *The New York Times*, 23 April. https://www.nytimes.com/2024/04/23/technology/general-motors-spying-driver-data-consent.html.

Hind, Sam. 2019. 'Digital Navigation and the Driving-Machine: Supervision, Calculation, Optimization, and Recognition'. *Mobilities* 14 (4): 401–17.

Hind, Sam. 2020. 'Between Capture and Addition: The Ontogenesis of Cartographic Calculation'. *Political Geography* 78: 102147.

Hind, Sam. 2024. *Driving Decisions: How Autonomous Vehicles Make Sense of the World*. Springer Nature.

Hind, Sam, and Alex Gekker. 2014. '"Outsmarting Traffic, Together": Driving as Social Navigation'. *Exchanges: The Warwick Research Journal* 1 (2): 165–80.

Hind, Sam, and Alex Gekker. 2019. 'On Autopilot: Towards a Flat Ontology of Vehicular Navigation'. In *Media's Mapping Impulse*, edited by Chris Lukinbeal, Laura Sharp, Elisabeth Sommerlad, and Anton Escher. Frantz Steiner Verlag.

Hind, Sam, and Alex Gekker. 2022. 'Automotive Parasitism: Examining Mobileye's "Car-Agnostic" Platformisation'. *New Media & Society*, July 11, 14614448221104209.

Hind, Sam, Max Kanderske, and Fernando van der Vlist. 2022. 'Making the Car "Platform Ready": How Big Tech Is Driving the Platformization of Automobility'. *Social Media + Society* 8 (2): 20563051221098697.

Hind, Sam, and Sybille Lammes. 2016. 'Digital Mapping as Double-Tap: Cartographic Modes, Calculations and Failures'. Global Discourse. *Global Discourse* 6 (1–2): 79–97.

Hind, Sam, and Tatjana Seitz. 2024. 'Cynical Technical Practice: From AI to APIs'. *Convergence* 30 (1): 29–48.

Hjorth, Larissa, and Sarah Pink. 2014. 'New Visualities and the Digital Wayfarer: Reconceptualizing Camera Phone Photography and Locative Media'. *Mobile Media & Communication* 2 (1): 40–57.

Homestar Runner. 2004. 'Thy Dungeonman! Thy Hunger!' http://www.homestarrunner.com/dungeonman.html.

Hookway, Branden. 2014. 'The Forming of the Interface'. In *Interface*. MIT Press.

Hu, Yu. 2025. 'Governing Mobility through Aggregation: Platform Urbanism of Gaode Ride-hailing'. Master's thesis, University of Amsterdam.

Huizinga, Johan. 1970. *Homo Ludens: A Study of the Play Element in Culture*. Temple Smith.

Human, Soheil, and Florian Cech. 2021. 'A Human-Centric Perspective on Digital Consenting: The Case of GAFAM'. In *Human Centred Intelligent Systems*, edited by Alfred Zimmermann, Robert J. Howlett, and Lakhmi C. Jain. Springer.

Imaoka, Laura Beltz. 2017. 'Selling the Conceptual and Computational Value of Esri's ArcGIS Platform'. Preprint, SocArXiv, 2 July. https://doi.org/10.31235/osf.io/tzewh.

Imaoka, Laura Beltz. 2021. 'Branding the Geospatial Industry'. *Communication, Culture and Critique* 14 (1): 109–26.

Information Commissioner's Office. 2025. 'The Lawful Basis for Web Scraping to Train Generative AI Models'. ICO, 6 February. https://ico.org.uk/about-the-ico/what-we-do/our-work-on-artificial-intelligence/response-to-the-consultation-series-on-generative-ai/the-lawful-basis-for-web-scraping-to-train-generative-ai-models/.

Ingold, Tim. 2000. *The Perception of the Environment: Essays on Livelihood, Dwelling and Skill*. Routledge.

Intel Newsroom, dir. 2021. *CES 2021: Under the Hood with Professor Amnon Shashua*. https://www.youtube.com/watch?v=B7YNj66GxRA.

Iyengar, Rishi. 2022. 'Why Ukraine Is Stuck With Elon (for Now)'. *Foreign Policy*, 22 November. https://foreignpolicy.com/2022/11/22/ukraine-internet-starlink-elon-musk-russia-war/.

Jacobs, Simone. 2025a. 'This Dutch Website Helps Find Sunny Terraces near You'. IamExpat in the Netherlands, 22 May. https://www.iamexpat.nl/lifestyle/lifestyle-news/this-dutch-website-helps-find-sunny-terraces-near-you.

Jacobs, Simone. 2025b. 'Zandvoort Residents Fake Road Closures on Google Maps to Deter Tourists'. IamExpat in the Netherlands, 2 August. https://www.iamexpat.nl/lifestyle/lifestyle-news/zandvoort-residents-fake-road-closures-google-maps-deter-tourists.

Jacoby, Larry L. 1991. 'A Process Dissociation Framework: Separating Automatic from Intentional Uses of Memory'. *Journal of Memory and Language* 30 (5): 513–41.

Jacoby, Larry L., Colleen Kelley, Judith Brown, and Jennifer Jasechko. 1989. 'Becoming Famous Overnight: Limits on the Ability to Avoid Unconscious Influences of the Past'. *Journal of Personality and Social Psychology* 56 (3): 326–38.

Jenkins, Henry. 2004. 'Game Design as Narrative Architecture'. *First Person: New Media as Story, Performance, and Game* 118.

Jethani, Suneel, and Dale Leorke. 2013. 'Ideology, Obsolescence and Preservation in Digital Mapping and Locative Art'. *International Communication Gazette* 75 (5–6): 484–501.

John, Nicholas A. 2017. *The Age of Sharing.* Polity.

Johnson, Allison. 2023. 'Google Maps Gives You More Control from the Blue Dot'. The Verge, 12 December. https://www.theverge.com/2023/12/12/23997581/google-maps-timeline-location-history-activity-blue-dot.

Johnson, Daniel, Sebastian Deterding, Kerri-Ann Kuhn, Aleksandra Staneva, Stoyan Stoyanov, and Leanne Hides. 2016. 'Gamification for Health and Wellbeing: A Systematic Review of the Literature'. *Internet Interventions* 6: 89–106.

Johnson, Garf. 2012. 'Apple Maps Trying To Make "LoDel" Neighborhood Happen'. Gothamist, 23 November. http://gothamist.com/2012/11/23/apple_maps_is_trying_to_make_lodel.php.

Johnson, Khari. 2022. 'The iRobot Deal Would Give Amazon Maps Inside Millions of Homes'. *Wired*, 5 August. https://www.wired.com/story/amazon-irobot-roomba-acquisition-data-privacy/.

Jonty. 2025. 'Hub and Spoke'. https://jonty.github.io/pret-a-spider/.

Juul, Jesper. 2013. *The Art of Failure: An Essay on the Pain of Playing Video Games.* MIT Press.

Kabir, Omer. 2022. 'You Have Reached Your Destination: Google Elegantly Says Goodbye to Waze'. Ctech, 8 December. https://www.calcalistech.com/ctechnews/article/g092isunj.

Kale, Sirin. 2021. 'Memory Lanes: Google's Map of Our Lives'. *The Observer*, 30 October. https://www.theguardian.com/technology/2021/oct/30/memory-lanes-googles-map-of-our-lives-street-view-is-a-portal-on-forgotten-places-secret-moments.

Kang, Lei. 2024. 'Zeekr to Integrate Mobileye Tech into Next-Gen Models as Partnership Deepens'. *CnEVPost*, 2 August. https://cnevpost.com/2024/08/02/zeekr-to-integrate-mobileye-tech-next-gen-models/.

Kastrenakes, Jacob. 2024. 'Instagram Is Testing Its Own Take on Snap Map'. The Verge, 9 August. https://www.theverge.com/2024/8/9/24217027/instagram-snap-map-style-feature-testing.

Keates, John S. 1996. *Understanding Maps.* 2nd edn. Longman.

Kemper, Jakko. 2024. *Frictionlessness: The Silicon Valley Philosophy of Seamless Technology and the Aesthetic Value of Imperfection.* Bloomsbury Academic.

Kennedy, Helen, and Martin Engebretsen. 2020. 'Introduction:

The Relationships between Graphs, Charts, Maps and Meanings, Feelings, Engagements'. In *Data Visualization in Society*, edited by Helen Kennedy and Martin Engebretsen. Amsterdam University Press.

Keyes, Allison. 2012. 'This App Was Made For Walking – But Is It Racist?' *NPR*, 19 January. https://www.npr.org/2012/01/25/145337346/this-app-was-made-for-walking-but-is-it-racist.

Khollam, Aamir. 2025. 'Robomart's Shuttle-Sized RM5 Offers Autonomous Grocery Shopping'. Interesting Engineering, 26 August. https://interestingengineering.com/photo-story/robomart-rm5-autonomous-grocery.

Kingsbury, Paul, and John Paul Jones. 2009. 'Walter Benjamin's Dionysian Adventures on Google Earth'. *Geoforum* 40 (4): 502–13.

Kitchin, Rob, and Martin Dodge. 2007. 'Rethinking Maps'. *Progress in Human Geography* 31 (3): 331–44.

Kitchin, Rob, and Martin Dodge. 2011. *Code/Space: Software and Everyday Life*. MIT Press.

Kitchin, Rob, Justin Gleeson, and Martin Dodge. 2013. 'Unfolding Mapping Practices: A New Epistemology for Cartography'. *Transactions of the Institute of British Geographers* 38 (3): 480–96.

Koebler, Jason. 2025. 'LAPD Publishes Crime Footage It Got from a Waymo Driverless Car'. 404 Media, 16 April. https://www.404media.co/lapd-publishes-crime-footage-it-got-from-a-waymo-driverless-car/.

Koetsier, John. 2024. 'This On-Road Delivery Robot Carries 100 Pounds At 20 MPH'. Forbes, 23 July. https://www.forbes.com/sites/johnkoetsier/2024/07/23/worlds-first-on-road-delivery-robot-carries-100-pounds-at-20-mph/.

Kokkinidis, Tasos. 2025. 'Viral Greek Cat Chonkus Maximus Finds Peace After Fame Nearly Broke Her'. *GreekReporter.com*, 31 July. https://greekreporter.com/2025/07/31/viral-greek-cat-chonkus-maximus-peace-fame/.

Korosec, Kirsten. 2022. 'With Intel Mobileye's Newest Chip, Automakers Can Bring Automated Driving to Cars'. *TechCrunch*, 4 January. https://techcrunch.com/2022/01/04/intels-mobileye-autonomous-driving-chip-for-consumer-vehicles/.

Kotliar, Dan M. 2021. 'Who Gets to Choose? On the Socio-Algorithmic Construction of Choice'. *Science, Technology, & Human Values* 46 (2): 346–75.

Kraak, Menno-Jan. 2003. 'The Space-Time Cube Revisited from a Geovisualization Perspective'. *Proceedings of the 21st International Cartographic Conference*, 1988–95.

Kraak, Menno-Jan. 2006. 'Visualization Viewpoints: Beyond Geovisualization'. *IEEE Computer Graphics and Applications* 26 (4): 6–9.

Kravitz, Derek. 2025. 'Your Car May Be Spying On You. Here's How to Get It to Stop'. Consumer Reports, 4 March. https://www.consumerreports.org/electronics/personal-information/how-to-stop-your-car-from-collecting-sharing-driving-data-a1233378612/.

Krygier, John, and Denis Wood. 2005. *Making Maps: A Visual Guide to Map Design for GIS*. Guilford Press.

Kücklich, Julian. 2005. 'FCJ-025 Precarious Playbour: Modders and the Digital Games Industry'. *The Fibreculture Journal*, no. 5. http://five.fibreculturejournal.org/fcj-025-precarious-playbour-modders-and-the-digital-games-industry/.

Kumparak, Greg. 2013. 'Google Maps Easter Egg Lets You Explore The TARDIS'. *TechCrunch*, 13 August. https://techcrunch.com/2013/08/13/google-maps-doctor-who-tardis-easter-egg/.

Kurgan, Laura. 2013. *Close up at a Distance: Mapping, Technology, and Politics*. Zone Books.

Kwan, Mei-Po. 2002. 'Feminist Visualization: Re-Envisioning GIS as a Method in Feminist Geographic Research'. *Annals of the Association of American Geographers* 92 (4): 645–61.

Kwan, Mei-Po. 2016. 'Algorithmic Geographies: Big Data, Algorithmic Uncertainty, and the Production of Geographic Knowledge'. *Annals of the American Association of Geographers* 106 (2): 274–82.

Lammes, Sybille. 2011. 'The Map as Playground: Location-Based Games as Cartographical Practices.' *Think Design Play: The Fifth International Conference of the Digital Research Association, Hilversum.* http://www.academia.edu/925304/The_map_as_playground_Location-_based_games_as_cartographical_practices.

Lammes, Sybille. 2016. 'Digital Mapping Interfaces: From Immutable Mobiles to Mutable Images'. *New Media & Society* 19 (7): 1019–33.

Lammes, Sybille, and Chris Perkins. 2016. 'An Introduction to Playful Mapping in the Digital Age'. In *Playful Mapping in the Digital Age*. Institute of Network Cultures.

Lammes, Sybille, Chris Perkins, Alex Gekker, Sam Hind, Clancy Wilmott, and Daniel Evans. 2018. *Time for Mapping: Cartographic Temporalities*. Manchester University Press.

Lammes, Sybille, Chris Perkins, and Clancy Wilmott. 2016. 'GoGoGozo: The Magic of Playful Mapping Moments'. *Playful Mapping in the Digital Age*, Institute of Network Cultures, 28–43.

Lampland, Martha, and Susan Leigh Star, eds. 2009. *Standards and*

Their Stories: How Quantifying, Classifying, and Formalizing Practices Shape Everyday Life. Cornell University Press.

Land, Franky. 2025. 'Coffee in the Sun – Apps on Google Play'. https://play.google.com/store/apps/details?id=nl.franklyland.coffeeinthesun&hl=en.

Landow, George P. 2006. *Hypertext 3.0: Critical Theory and New Media in an Era of Globalization*. Johns Hopkins University Press.

Lange, Ryan L., Nicholas Bowman, Jaime Banks, and Amanda J. Lange. 2015. 'Grand Theft Auto(Mation): Travel Mode Habits and Video Games'. *International Journal of Technology and Human Interaction* 11 (3): 35–50.

Larkin, Brian. 2008. *Signal and Noise: Media, Infrastructure, and Urban Culture in Nigeria*. Duke University Press.

Latour, Bruno. 1986. 'Visualization and Cognition: Drawing Things Together'. *Knowledge and Society Studies in the Sociology of Culture Past and Present* 6: 1–40.

Latour, Bruno. 1987. *Science in Action*. Harvard University Press.

Latour, Bruno. 1990. 'Visualisation and Cognition: Drawing Things Together'. In *Representation in Scientific Practice*, edited by Michael Lynch and Steve Woolgar. MIT Press.

Latour, Bruno. 1999. *Pandora's Hope: Essays on the Reality of Science Studies*. Harvard University Press.

Latour, Bruno. 2005. *Reassembling the Social: An Introduction to Actor-Network-Theory*. Oxford University Press.

Law, John. 1992. 'Notes on the Theory of the Actor-Network: Ordering, Strategy, and Heterogeneity'. *Systems Practice* 5 (4): 379–93.

Lawler, John. 2020. 'What Volkswagen's Investment in Argo AI Means for Ford's Self-Driving Vehicle Business'. *Self-Driven*, 2 June. https://medium.com/self-driven/what-volkswagens-investment-in-argo-ai-means-for-ford-s-self-driving-vehicle-business-556472221dee.

Learish, Jessica. 2019. 'Crazy Images Caught on Google Street View'. CNET, 18 November. https://www.cnet.com/pictures/crazy-images-caught-on-google-street-view/.

Lefebvre, Henri. 1992. *The Production of Space*. Wiley-Blackwell.

Leorke, Dale. 2019. *Location-Based Gaming: Play in Public Space*. Palgrave Macmillan.

Lerman, Rachel. 2022. 'On Google Maps, Tracking the Invasion of Ukraine'. *Washington Post*, 28 February. https://www.washingtonpost.com/technology/2022/02/25/google-maps-ukraine-invasion/.

Lessin, Jessica E. 2012. 'An Apple Exit Over Maps'. *Wall Street Journal*, 29 October. http://online.wsj.com/article/SB10001424052970204840504578087192497916304.html.

Leszczynski, Agnieszka. 2020. 'Glitchy Vignettes of Platform Urbanism'. *Environment and Planning D: Society and Space* 38 (2): 189–208.

Li, Chunyuan, Zhe Gan, Zhengyuan Yang, et al. 2023. 'Multimodal Foundation Models: From Specialists to General-Purpose Assistants'. arXiv:2309.10020. Preprint, arXiv, 18 September. https://doi.org/10.48550/arXiv.2309.10020.

Lialina, Olia. 2018a. 'Once Again, The Doorknob. On Affordance, Forgiveness and Ambiguity in Human Computer and Human Robot Interaction'. Conference Talk. 8 June. http://contemporary-home-computing.org/affordance/.

Lialina, Olia. 2018b. 'Rich user experience, ux and desktopization of war'. *Interface Critique* 1: 176–93.

Lieberoth, Andreas. 2015. 'Shallow Gamification Testing Psychological Effects of Framing an Activity as a Game'. *Games and Culture* 10 (3): 229–48.

Liedtke, Michael, and Matt O'Brien. 2025. 'Judge Skewers $1.5B Anthropic Settlement with Authors in Pirated Books Case over AI Training'. AP News, 8 September. https://apnews.com/article/anthropic-authors-book-settlement-ai-copyright-claude-b282fe6153 38bf1f98ad97cb82e978a1.

Light, Ben, Jean Burgess, and Stefanie Duguay. 2018. 'The Walkthrough Method: An Approach to the Study of Apps'. *New Media & Society* 20 (3): 881–900.

Liu, Hanchao, Wenyuan Xue, Yifei Chen, et al. 2024. 'A Survey on Hallucination in Large Vision-Language Models'. arXiv:2402.00253. Preprint, arXiv, 6 May. https://doi.org/10.48550/arXiv.2402.00253.

Love, Julia. 2021. 'Silicon Valley Workers Vote Down Union at SoftBank-Backed Mapbox'. *Reuters*, 6 August. https://www.reuters.com/technology/silicon-valley-workers-vote-down-union-softbank-backed-mapbox-2021-08-05/.

Luitse, Dieuwertje, and Wiebke Denkena. 2021. 'The Great Transformer: Examining the Role of Large Language Models in the Political Economy of AI'. *Big Data & Society* 8 (2): 20539517211047734.

Ma, Wayne, and Juro Osawa. 2025. 'Amazon Is Developing AR Glasses in Challenge to Meta'. The Information, 10 September. https://www.theinformation.com/articles/amazon-developing-ar-glasses-challenge-meta.

MacEachren, Alan M. 1994. 'Visualization in Modern Cartography'. In *Visualization in Modern Cartography*, edited by Alan M. MacEachren and D.R. Fraser Taylor. Pergamon.

MacEachren, Alan M. 1995. *How Maps Work: Representation, Visualization, and Design*. Guilford Press.

MacEachren, Alan M. 1998. 'Visualization-Cartography for the 21st Century'. *Proceedings of the Polish Spatial Information Association Conference, Warsaw, Poland*, May.

MacEachren, Alan M., and Menno-Jan Kraak. 2001. 'Research Challenges in Geovisualization'. *Cartography and Geographic Information Science* 28 (1): 3–12.

Madrigal, Alexis C. 2013. 'The Machine Zone: This Is Where You Go When You Just Can't Stop Looking at Pictures on Facebook'. The Atlantic, 31 July. http://www.theatlantic.com/technology/archive/2013/07/the-machine-zone-this-is-where-you-go-when-you-just-cant-stop-looking-at-pictures-on-facebook/278185/.

Mainemelis, Charalampos, and Sarah Ronson. 2006. 'Ideas Are Born in Fields of Play: Towards a Theory of Play and Creativity in Organizational Settings'. *Research in Organizational Behavior* 27: 81–131.

Malaby, Thomas M. 2007. 'Beyond Play'. *Games and Culture* 2 (2): 95–113.

Malmqvist, Lars. 2024. 'Sycophancy in Large Language Models: Causes and Mitigations'. arXiv:2411.15287. Preprint, arXiv, 22 November. https://doi.org/10.48550/arXiv.2411.15287.

Manovich, Lev. 2006. 'The Poetics of Augmented Space'. *Visual Communication* 5 (2): 219–40.

Manovich, Lev. 2013. *Software Takes Command*. Bloomsbury Academic.

Mapbox. 2023. 'Mapbox MapGPT | AI Assistant with Location Intelligence'. October. https://www.mapbox.com/mapgpt.

'Mapping the Massacres'. n.d. https://oct7map.com/.

Marres, Noortje. 2020. 'Co-Existence or Displacement: Do Street Trials of Intelligent Vehicles Test Society?' *The British Journal of Sociology* 71 (3): 537–55.

Marwick, Alice E. 2015. 'Instafame: Luxury Selfies in the Attention Economy'. *Public Culture* 27: 137–60.

Marx, Paris. 2022. *Road to Nowhere: What Silicon Valley Gets Wrong about the Future of Transportation*. Verso.

Masek, Leland, and Jaakko Stenros. 2021. 'The Meaning of Playfulness: A Review of the Contemporary Definitions of the Concept across Disciplines'. *Eludamos. Journal for Computer Game Culture* 12 (1): 1.

Mathayomchan, Boonyanit, and Viriya Taecharungroj. 2020. '"How Was Your Meal?" Examining Customer Experience Using Google Maps Reviews'. *International Journal of Hospitality Management* 90: 102641.

Mathur, Arunesh, Gunes Acar, Michael J. Friedman, et al. 2019. 'Dark Patterns at Scale: Findings from a Crawl of 11K Shopping Websites'.

Proceedings of the ACM on Human-Computer Interaction 3 (CSCW): 1–32. https://doi.org/10.1145/3359183.
Mattern, Shannon. 2017. 'Mapping's Intelligent Agents'. *Places Journal*, September. https://doi.org/10.22269/170926.
Mattern, Shannon. 2018. 'Maintenance and Care'. *Places Journal*, November. https://doi.org/10.22269/181120.
Mattern, Shannon. 2021a. *A City Is Not a Computer: Other Urban Intelligences*. Princeton University Press.
Mattern, Shannon. 2021b. 'How to Map Nothing'. *Places Journal*, March. https://doi.org/10.22269/210323.
Mäyrä, Frans. 2008. *An Introduction to Game Studies*. Sage Publications.
McCosker, Anthony. 2017. 'Data Literacies for the Postdemographic Social Media Self'. *First Monday* 22 (10). https://doi.org/10.5210/fm.v22i10.7307.
McCosker, Anthony, and Rowan Wilken. 2014. 'Rethinking "Big Data" as Visual Knowledge: The Sublime and the Diagrammatic in Data Visualisation'. *Visual Studies* 29 (2): 155–64.
McCosker, Anthony, and Rowan Wilken. 2020. *Automating Vision: The Social Impact of the New Camera Consciousness*. Routledge.
McGonigal, Jane. 2011. *Reality Is Broken: Why Games Make Us Better and How They Can Change the World*. Penguin.
McGuire, Patrick. 2014. 'Uber's "God View" Was Once Available to Drivers'. *VICE*, 20 November. https://www.vice.com/en/article/ubers-god-view-was-once-available-to-drivers/.
McKelvey, Fenwick, and Joshua Neves. 2021. 'Introduction: Optimization and Its Discontents'. *Review of Communication* 21 (2): 95–112.
McLuhan, Marshall. 1994. *Understanding Media: The Extensions of Man*. MIT Press.
McQuire, Scott. 2019. 'One Map to Rule Them All? Google Maps as Digital Technical Object': *Communication and the Public* 4 (2): 150–65.
Melnick, Kyle. 2024. 'A Priest Sues Grindr after He Was Outed, His Lawsuit Says'. *The Washington Post*, 27 July. https://www.washingtonpost.com/nation/2024/07/27/priest-grindr-privacy-lawsuit/.
Merchant, Brian. 2025. 'The Weaponization of Waymo'. 2 May. https://www.bloodinthemachine.com/p/the-weaponization-of-waymo.
Merry, Sally Engle. 2016. *The Seductions of Quantification: Measuring Human Rights, Gender Violence, and Sex Trafficking*. University of Chicago Press.
Meyer, Hans, Kate Flewelling, and Chris Hayes. 2025. 'Twenty Years in Google Maps Turns to AI to Maintain Dominance'. CNBC, 18

January. https://www.cnbc.com/video/2025/01/18/twenty-years-in-google-maps-turns-to-ai-to-maintain-dominance.html.

Michael, David, and Sandra Chen. 2005. *Serious Games: Games That Educate, Train, and Inform*. Course Technology.

Miller, Greg. 2014. 'Autonomous Cars Will Require a Totally New Kind of Map'. *Wired*, 15 December. http://www.wired.com/2014/12/nokia-here-autonomous-car-maps/.

Milner, Greg. 2016. 'Death by GPS: Are Satnavs Changing Our Brains?' *The Guardian*, 25 June. https://www.theguardian.com/technology/2016/jun/25/gps-horror-stories-driving-satnav-greg-milner.

Mitrokhov, Konstantin. 2024. 'Between World Models and Model Worlds: On Generality, Agency, and Worlding in Machine Learning'. *AI & Society* 40: 5087–99.

Mobileye, dir. 2022. *CES 2022 Under the Hood An Hour with Amnon*. https://www.youtube.com/watch?v=1mXy0oi8d6o.

Mobileye. n.d.-a. 'Mobileye REM™ – Road Experience Management'. Mobileye. https://www.mobileye.com/technology/rem/.

Mobileye. n.d.-b. 'Real-Time Collision Avoidance System for Fleets | Mobileye UK'. https://ims.mobileye.com/fleets/uk/.

Mohlmann, Mareike, and Lior Zalmanson. 2017. 'Hands on the Wheel: Navigating Algorithmic Management and Uber Drivers' Autonomy'. *ICIS 2017 Proceedings*, 10 December. https://aisel.aisnet.org/icis2017/DigitalPlatforms/Presentations/3.

Monahan, Torin. 2015. 'The Right to Hide? Anti-Surveillance Camouflage and the Aestheticization of Resistance'. *Communication and Critical/Cultural Studies* 12 (2): 159–78.

Monmonier, Mark S. 2018. *How to Lie with Maps*, 3rd edn. University of Chicago Press.

Moore, Kyle. 2015. 'Playing with Portals: Rethinking Urban Play with Ingress'. *Analog Game Studies* 2 (7). https://analoggamestudies.org/2015/11/playing-with-portals-rethinking-urban-play-with-ingress/.

Morozov, Evgeny. 2013. 'My Map or Yours?' *Slate*, 28 May. http://www.slate.com/articles/technology/future_tense/2013/05/google_maps_personalization_will_hurt_public_space_and_engagement.html.

Muehrcke, Phillip C. 1990. 'Cartography and Geographic Information Systems'. *Cartography and Geographic Information Systems* 17 (1): 7–15.

Muldoon, James, Callum Cant, Boxi Wu, and Mark Graham. 2024. 'A Typology of Artificial Intelligence Data Work'. *Big Data & Society* 11 (1): 20539517241232632.

Mull, Amanda. 2023. 'Push Notifications Are Out of Control'. *The Atlantic*, 25 May. https://www.theatlantic.com/technology/archive/2023/05/too-many-push-notifications-apps-phone/674178/.

Murakami Wood, David, and Torin Monahan. 2019. 'Editorial: Platform Surveillance'. *Surveillance & Society* 17 (1/2): 1–6.

Musa, Sela. 2025. 'Foodora Calls for Drones and Delivery Robots to Improve Road Safety of Logistics'. *Zag Daily*, 15 May. https://zagdaily.com/trends/foodora-calls-for-drones-and-delivery-robots-to-improve-road-safety-of-logistics/.

Nagy, Peter, and Gina Neff. 2015. 'Imagined Affordance: Reconstructing a Keyword for Communication Theory'. *Social Media + Society* 1 (2): 2056305115603385.

Narayan, Devika. 2022. 'Platform Capitalism and Cloud Infrastructure: Theorizing a Hyper-Scalable Computing Regime'. *Environment and Planning A: Economy and Space* 54 (5): 911–29.

Narayanan, Arvind, and Sayash Kapoor. 2025. 'AI as Normal Technology'. Knight First Amendment Institute, 15 April. http://knightcolumbia.org/content/ai-as-normal-technology.

Nethercote, Megan. 2023. 'Platform Landlords: Renters, Personal Data and New Digital Footholds of Urban Control'. *Digital Geography and Society* 5: 100060.

Newcomer, Eric. 2017. 'Uber Starts Charging What It Thinks You're Willing to Pay'. *Bloomberg.com*, 19 May. https://www.bloomberg.com/news/articles/2017-05-19/uber-s-future-may-rely-on-predicting-how-much-you-re-willing-to-pay.

Newlands, Gemma. 2021. 'Algorithmic Surveillance in the Gig Economy: The Organization of Work through Lefebvrian Conceived Space'. *Organization Studies* 42 (5): 719–37.

Niccolini, Alyssa D. 2018. 'The Education of Feeling: Wearable Technology and Triggering Pedagogies'. In *Affect and Social Media: Emotion, Mediation, Anxiety and Contagion*, edited by Tony D. Sampson, Stephen Maddison, and Darren Ellis. Rowman & Littlefield.

Nieborg, David B. 2015. 'Crushing Candy: The Free-to-Play Game in Its Connective Commodity Form'. *Social Media+ Society* 1 (2): 2056305115621932.

Nieborg, David B., and Thomas Poell. 2018. 'The Platformization of Cultural Production: Theorizing the Contingent Cultural Commodity'. *New Media & Society* 20 (11): 1461444818769694.

Noble, Safiya Umoja. 2018. *Algorithms of Oppression: How Search Engines Reinforce Racism*. NYU Press.

Norman, Donald A. 1988. *The Psychology of Everyday Things*. Basic Books.

Norman, Donald A. 2002. *The Design of Everyday Things*. Basic Books.

November, Valérie, Eduardo Camacho-Hübner, and Bruno Latour. 2010.

'Entering a Risky Territory: Space in the Age of Digital Navigation'. *Environment and Planning D: Society and Space* 28 (4): 581–99.

O'Beirne, Justin. 2018. 'Google Maps's 2017 Redesign'. Justinobeirne.com. https://www.justinobeirne.com/google-maps-2017-redesign.

O'Beirne, Justin. 2021. 'How Many People Use Google Maps Compared to Apple Maps?' Justinobeirne.com, July. https://www.justinobeirne.com/how-many-people-use-google-maps-compared-to-apple-maps.

O'Brien, Kevin J., and David Streitfeld. 2012. 'Swiss Court Orders Modifications to Google Street View'. *The New York Times*, 8 June. https://www.nytimes.com/2012/06/09/technology/09iht-google09.html.

O'Brien, Matt, and Frank Bajak. 2021. 'Priest Outed via Grindr App Highlights Rampant Data Tracking'. *AP News*, 22 July. https://apnews.com/article/technology-europe-business-religion-data-privacy-97334ed1aca5bd363263c92f6de2caa2.

Odell, Jenny. 2019. *How to Do Nothing: Resisting the Attention Economy*. Melville House.

O'Donnell, Casey. 2012. 'This Is Not a Software Industry'. In *The Video Game Industry: Formation, Present State, and Future*, edited by Peter Zackariasson and Timothy Wilson. Routledge.

Oeldorf-Hirsch, Anne, and German Neubaum. 2025. 'What Do We Know about Algorithmic Literacy? The Status Quo and a Research Agenda for a Growing Field'. *New Media & Society* 27 (2): 681–701.

Okolloh, Ory. 2009. 'Ushahidi, or "Testimony": Web 2.0 Tools for Crowdsourcing Crisis Information'. *Participatory Learning and Action* 59: 65–70.

O'Leary, Martin. 2016a. 'Generating Fantasy Maps'. https://mewo2.com/notes/terrain/.

O'Leary, Martin. 2016b. 'Generating Naming Languages'. https://mewo2.com/notes/naming-language/.

O'Neil, Cathy. 2017. *Weapons of Math Destruction: How Big Data Increases Inequality and Threatens Democracy*. Broadway Books.

OpenAI. 2025. 'Introducing Operator'. 17 July. https://openai.com/index/introducing-operator/.

OpenStreetMap US, dir. 2022. *Parks, Spawns, Nests & Pikachu: OpenStreetMap & Pokemon GO Players – Christopher Greene-Szmadzinski*. https://www.youtube.com/watch?v=WktLRXejcao.

OpenStreetMap Wiki. 2024. 'Tips for New (Pokemon Go) Mappers'. https://wiki.openstreetmap.org/wiki/Tips_for_new_(Pokemon_Go)_mappers.

OSM. n.d. 'Stats – OpenStreetMap Wiki'. https://wiki.openstreetmap.org/wiki/Stats.

Palmer, Annie. 2025. 'Amazon Resumes Drone Deliveries after Two-Month Pause'. CNBC, 1 April. https://www.cnbc.com/2025/03/31/amazon-resumes-drone-deliveries-after-two-month-pause.html.

Parikka, Jussi. 2010. *Insect Media: An Archaeology of Animals and Technology*. University of Minnesota Press.

Parks, Lisa. 2005. *Cultures in Orbit: Satellites and the Televisual*. Duke University Press.

Parks, Lisa. 2009. 'Digging into Google Earth: An Analysis of "Crisis in Darfur"'. *Geoforum* 40 (4): 535–45.

Parks, Lisa, and Nicole Starosielski. 2015. 'Introduction'. In *Signal Traffic*, edited by Lisa Parks and Nicole Starosielski. University of Illinois Press.

Patino, Marie. 2024. 'Tim Walz Knows the Power of Maps'. *Bloomberg.com*, 14 August. https://www.bloomberg.com/news/newsletters/2024-08-14/tim-walz-gis-nerd-elevates-the-power-of-maps-as-vp-candidate.

Pereira, Gabriel, and Christoph Raetzsch. 2022. 'From Banal Surveillance to Function Creep: Automated License Plate Recognition (ALPR) in Denmark'. *Surveillance & Society* 20 (3): 265–80.

Perkins, Chris. 2009a. 'Mapping Agencies'. In *International Encyclopedia of Human Geography*, edited by Nigel Thrift. Elsevier.

Perkins, Chris. 2009b. 'Playing with Maps.' In *Rethinking Maps: New Frontiers in Cartographic Theory*, edited by Martin Dodge, Rob Kitchin, and Chris Perkins. Routledge.

Perkins, Chris, and Martin Dodge. 2008. 'The Potential of User-Generated Cartography: A Case Study of the OpenStreetMap Project and Mapchester Mapping Party'. *North West Geography* 8 (1): 19–32.

Perkins, Chris, and Martin Dodge. 2009. 'Satellite Imagery and the Spectacle of Secret Spaces'. *Geoforum* 40 (4): 546–60.

Peters, Jay, and Jon Porters. 2023. 'More than 7,000 Subreddits Have Gone Dark to Protest Reddit's API Changes'. The Verge, 12 June. https://www.theverge.com/2023/6/12/23755974/reddit-subreddits-going-dark-private-protest-api-changes.

Pettman, Dominic. 2019. 'The Species Without Qualities: Critical Media Theory and the Posthumanities'. *Boundary 2*, 23 April. http://www.boundary2.org/2019/04/the-species-without-qualities-critical-media-theory-and-the-posthumanities/.

Phillips, Chris. 2022. '4 New Updates That Make Maps Look and Feel More like the Real World'. Google, 28 September. https://blog.google/products/maps/4-new-updates-maps-searchon-2022/.

Phillips, Chris. 2023. 'New Ways Maps Is Getting More Immersive and Sustainable'. Google, 8 February. https://blog.google/products/maps/sustainable-immersive-maps-announcements/.

Pickles, John, ed. 1994. *Ground Truth: The Social Implications of Geographic Information Systems*. Guilford Press.

Pickles, John. 2004. *A History of Spaces: Cartographic Reason, Mapping and the Geo-Coded World*. Routledge.

Pine, B. Joseph, and James H. Gilmore. 1998. 'Welcome to the Experience Economy'. *Harvard Business Review* 76: 97–105.

Pine, B. Joseph, and James H. Gilmore. 2011. *The Experience Economy*. Updated edition. Harvard Business Review Press.

Pink, Sarah, Larissa Hjorth, Heather Horst, Josh Nettheim, and Genevieve Bell. 2018. 'Digital Work and Play: Mobile Technologies and New Ways of Feeling at Home'. *European Journal of Cultural Studies* 21 (1): 26–38.

Plantin, Jean-Christophe. 2014. *Participatory Mapping: New Data, New Cartography*. Wiley.

Plantin, Jean-Christophe. 2018. 'Google Maps as Cartographic Infrastructure: From Participatory Mapmaking to Database Maintenance'. *International Journal of Communication* 12: 489–506.

Plantin, Jean-Christophe, Carl Lagoze, Paul N. Edwards, and Christian Sandvig. 2018. 'Infrastructure Studies Meet Platform Studies in the Age of Google and Facebook'. *New Media & Society* 20 (1): 293–310.

Plantin, Jean-Christophe, and Aswin Punathambekar. 2019. 'Digital Media Infrastructures: Pipes, Platforms, and Politics'. *Media, Culture & Society* 41 (2): 163–74.

Playful Mapping Collective. 2016. *Playful Mapping in the Digital Age*. Institute of Network Cultures.

Postman, Neil. 1986. *Amusing Ourselves to Death: Public Discourse in the Age of Show Business*. Penguin.

Prey, Robert. 2018. 'Nothing Personal: Algorithmic Individuation on Music Streaming Platforms'. *Media, Culture & Society* 40 (7): 1086–100.

Proven, Liam. 2024. 'Foursquare to Close, but Swarm Game Lives On'. The Register, 27 November. https://www.theregister.com/2024/11/27/foursquare_to_close/.

Quinn, James Brian. 1992. *Intelligent Enterprise: A Knowledge and Service Based Paradigm for Industry*. Free Press.

Rankin, William J. 2011. 'After the Map: Cartography, Navigation, and the Transformation of Territory in the Twentieth Century'. PhD thesis, Harvard University.

Rankin, William. 2016. *After the Map: Cartography, Navigation, and the Transformation of Territory in the Twentieth Century*. University of Chicago Press.

Recinos, Alec. 2018. 'Towards a Postinternet Sublime, Jon Rafman's Street View Romanticism'. Rhizome, 4 January. https://rhizome.org/editorial/2018/jan/04/towards-a-post-internet-sublime/.

Regulation (EU) 2015/758 of the European Parliament and of the Council of 29 April 2015 Concerning Type-Approval Requirements for the Deployment of the eCall in-Vehicle System Based on the 112 Service and Amending Directive 2007/46/EC, 123 OJ L (2015). http://data.europa.eu/eli/reg/2015/758/oj/eng.

Reisner, Alex. 2024a. 'Generative AI Is Challenging a 234-Year-Old Law'. *The Atlantic*, 29 February. https://www.theatlantic.com/technology/archive/2024/02/generative-ai-lawsuits-copyright-fair-use/677595/.

Reisner, Alex. 2024b. 'There's No Longer Any Doubt That Hollywood Writing Is Powering AI'. *The Atlantic*, 18 November. https://www.theatlantic.com/technology/archive/2024/11/opensubtitles-ai-data-set/680650/.

Reisner, Alex. 2025a. 'AI Is Coming for YouTube Creators'. *The Atlantic*, 10 September. https://www.theatlantic.com/technology/archive/2025/09/youtube-ai-training-data-sets/684116/.

Reisner, Alex. 2025b. 'Search LibGen, the Pirated-Books Database That Meta Used to Train AI'. *The Atlantic*, 20 March. https://www.theatlantic.com/technology/archive/2025/03/search-libgen-data-set/682094/.

Rettberg, Jill Walker. 2020. 'Ways of Knowing with Data Visualizations'. In *Data Visualization in Society*, edited by Martin Engebretsen and Helen Kennedy. Amsterdam University Press.

Rieder, Bernhard. 2020. *Engines of Order: A Mechanology of Algorithmic Techniques*. Amsterdam University Press.

Rieder, Bernhard, and Guillaume Sire. 2014. 'Conflicts of Interest and Incentives to Bias: A Microeconomic Critique of Google's Tangled Position on the Web'. *New Media & Society* 16 (2): 195–211.

Rogers, Richard. 2013. *Digital Methods*. MIT Press.

Rogers, Richard. 2018. 'Otherwise Engaged: Social Media from Vanity Metrics to Critical Analytics'. *International Journal of Communication* 12: 450–72.

Romero, Pedro. 2023. 'This 31-Year-Old Dutch Player Won the GeoGuessr World Cup. Here's How He Got It Done (Part 1)'. *Medium*, 5 November. https://medium.com/@romeroesports/this-31-year-old-dutch-player-won-the-geoguessr-world-cup-heres-how-he-got-it-done-part-1-02371б2a62b1.

Rosemain, Mathieu. 2022. 'Google Hit with 150 Mln Euro French Fine for Cookie Breaches'. *Reuters*, 6 January. https://www.reuters.com/world/europe/france-imposes-fines-facebook-ireland-google-2022-01-06/.

Rossetto, Tania. 2019. *Object-Oriented Cartography: Maps as Things*. Routledge.

Rundle, Michael. 2012. '10 Funniest Fails in Apple's iOS Maps App'. The Huffington Post UK, 20 September. http://www.huffingtonpost.co.uk/2012/09/20/apples-ios-6-maps-app-fails_n_1899603.html.

Ruppert, Evelyn, Engin Isin, and Didier Bigo. 2017. 'Data Politics'. *Big Data & Society* 4 (2): 2053951717717749.

Ruppert, Evelyn, and Stephan Scheel. 2019. 'The Politics of Method: Taming the New, Making Data Official'. *International Political Sociology* 13 (3): 233–52.

Sadowski, Jathan. 2020. 'The Internet of Landlords: Digital Platforms and New Mechanisms of Rentier Capitalism'. *Antipode* 52 (2): 562–80.

Sadowski, Jathan, and Roy Bendor. 2019. 'Selling Smartness: Corporate Narratives and the Smart City as a Sociotechnical Imaginary'. *Science, Technology, & Human Values* 44 (3): 540–63.

Sampson, Tony D. 2017. *The Assemblage Brain: Sense Making in Neuroculture*. University of Minnesota Press.

Sandvig, Christian. 2014. 'Corrupt Personalization'. *Social Media Collective*, 26 June. http://socialmediacollective.org/2014/06/26/corrupt-personalization/.

Scholz, Trebor. 2008. 'Market Ideology and the Myths of Web 2.0'. *First Monday* 13 (3): 3.

Schüll, Natasha Dow. 2005. 'Digital Gambling: The Coincidence of Desire and Design'. *The Annals of the American Academy of Political and Social Science* 597 (1): 65–81.

Schüll, Natasha Dow. 2014. *Addiction by Design: Machine Gambling in Las Vegas*. Princeton University Press.

Seaver, Nick. 2015. 'The Nice Thing about Context Is That Everyone Has It'. *Media, Culture & Society* 37 (7): 1101–9.

Seaver, Nick. 2017. 'Algorithms as Culture: Some Tactics for the Ethnography of Algorithmic Systems'. *Big Data & Society* 4 (2): 2053951717738104.

Seaver, Nick. 2019. 'Captivating Algorithms: Recommender Systems as Traps'. *Journal of Material Culture* 24 (4): 421–36.

Shakir, Umar. 2023. 'Reddit's Upcoming API Changes Will Make AI Companies Pony Up'. The Verge, 18 April. https://www.theverge.com/2023/4/18/23688463/reddit-developer-api-terms-change-monetization-ai.

Shakir, Umar. 2024. 'Google Maps Is Getting Even More like Waze'. The Verge, 31 July. https://www.theverge.com/2024/7/31/24209969/google-maps-destination-guidance-waze-camera-events.

Shalev-Shwartz, Shai, Shaked Shammah, and Amnon Shashua. 2018a. 'Vision Zero: Can Roadway Accidents Be Eliminated without Compromising Traffic Throughput'. https://static.mobileye.com/website/corporate/rss/vision_zero_with_map.pdf.

Shalev-Shwartz, Shai, Shaked Shammah, and Amnon Shashua. 2018b. 'On a Formal Model of Safe and Scalable Self-Driving Cars'. arXiv:1708.06374. Preprint, arXiv, 27 October. https://doi.org/10.48550/arXiv.1708.06374.

Shapiro, Aaron, and M.C. Forelle. 2024. 'Driving into a Paywall: The Subscriptionization of Consumer Vehicles'. *Engaging Science, Technology, and Society* 10 (3): 3.

Sheng, Robert. 2023. 'Google Maps: About That Left Turn'. Medium, 18 July. https://uxdesign.cc/google-maps-about-that-left-turn-34953cdc204.

Sicart, Miguel. 2011. 'Against Procedurality'. *Game Studies* 11 (3). https://gamestudies.org/1103/articles/sicart_ap

Sicart, Miguel. 2014. *Play Matters*. MIT Press.

Sicart, Miguel. 2022. 'Playthings'. *Games and Culture* 17 (1): 140–55.

Siddiqui, Aamir. 2025. 'Gemini Live's Camera Sharing Could Soon Work Better with Google Maps (APK Teardown)'. Android Authority, 11 September. https://www.androidauthority.com/gemini-live-camera-sharing-google-maps-info-cards-apk-teardown-3596946/.

Silberling, Amanda. 2025. 'Amazon Acquires Bee, the AI Wearable That Records Everything You Say'. *TechCrunch*, 22 July. https://techcrunch.com/2025/07/22/amazon-acquires-bee-the-ai-wearable-that-records-everything-you-say/.

Silverstone, Roger. 1999. *Why Study the Media?* Sage.

Simondon, Gilbert. 1992. 'The Genesis of the Individual'. In *Incorporations*, edited by Jonathan Crary and Sanford Kwinter. Zone Books.

Simonite, Tom. 2017. 'Google's New Street View Cameras Will Help Algorithms Index the Real World'. *Wired*, 5 September. https://www.wired.com/story/googles-new-street-view-cameras-will-help-algorithms-index-the-real-world/.

Sinders, Caroline. 2022. 'What's In a Name?' *Medium*, 22 June. https://medium.com/@carolinesinders/whats-in-a-name-unpacking-dark-patterns-versus-deceptive-design-e96068627ec4.

Singh, Jagmeet, and Ivan Mehta. 2024. 'Google Maps Adds a Slew of Features to Entice Indian Drivers, Commuters and Travelers'.

TechCrunch, 25 July. https://techcrunch.com/2024/07/25/google-maps-adds-features-to-improve-navigating-flyovers-and-narrow-roads-in-india/.

Sisco, Josh. 2023. 'DOJ Pushes Ahead with Google Maps Antitrust Probe'. Politico, 22 February. https://www.politico.com/news/2023/02/22/doj-google-maps-antitrust-probe-00084058.

Sly, Liz. 2018. 'U.S. Soldiers Are Revealing Sensitive and Dangerous Information by Jogging'. *The Washington Post*, 28 January. https://www.washingtonpost.com/world/a-map-showing-the-users-of-fitness-devices-lets-the-world-see-where-us-soldiers-are-and-what-they-are-doing/2018/01/28/86915662-0441-11e8-aa61-f3391373867e_story.html.

Smith, Catherine Delano. 1987. 'Prehistoric Maps and the History of Cartography'. In *The History of Cartography Volume 1: Cartography in Prehistoric, Ancient, and Medieval Europe and the Mediterranean*, edited by J.B. Harley and David Woodward. University of Chicago Press.

Smythe, Dallas W. 1977. 'Communications: Blindspot of Western Marxism'. *CTheory* 1 (3): 3.

Specht, Doug, ed. 2020. *Mapping Crisis: Participation, Datafication and Humanitarianism in the Age of Digital Mapping*. University of London Press.

Srnicek, Nick. 2016. *Platform Capitalism*. Polity.

Stackpole, Beth. 2024. 'The Impact of Generative AI as a General-Purpose Technology'. 6 August. https://mitsloan.mit.edu/ideas-made-to-matter/impact-generative-ai-a-general-purpose-technology.

Stanfill, Mel. 2015. 'The Interface as Discourse: The Production of Norms through Web Design'. *New Media & Society* 17 (7): 1059–74.

Star, Susan Leigh. 1999. 'The Ethnography of Infrastructure'. *American Behavioral Scientist* 43 (3): 377–91.

Stark, Luke. 2018. 'Visceral Data'. In *Affect and Social Media: Emotion, Mediation, Anxiety and Contagion*, edited by Tony D. Sampson, Stephen Maddison, and Darren Ellis. Rowman & Littlefield International.

Stark, Luke. 2020. 'The Emotive Politics of Digital Mood Tracking'. *New Media & Society* 22 (11): 2039–57.

Statista. 2023. 'Navigation – Worldwide | Statista Market Forecast'. Statista, March. https://www.statista.com/outlook/dmo/app/navigation/worldwide.

Statista. 2025a. 'Biggest Social Media Platforms by Users 2025'. Statista, 26 March. https://www.statista.com/statistics/272014/global-social-networks-ranked-by-number-of-users/.

Statista. 2025b. 'China: MAU of Leading Map Apps 2024'. Statista,

3 March. https://www.statista.com/statistics/1212017/china-leading-map-apps-based-on-monthly-active-users/.

Steg, Linda. 2005. 'Car Use: Lust and Must. Instrumental, Symbolic and Affective Motives for Car Use'. *Transportation Research Part A: Policy and Practice* 39 (2): 147–62.

Steinberg, Marc. 2020. 'LINE as Super App: Platformization in East Asia'. *Social Media + Society* 6 (2): 2056305120933285.

Steinhoff, James, and Sam Hind. 2025. 'Simulation and the Reality Gap: Moments in a Prehistory of Synthetic Data'. *Big Data & Society* 12 (1): 20539517241309884.

Stevenson, Michael, and Misha Kavka. 2025. *Doing Media Research*. Sage.

Steyerl, Hito. 2023. 'Mean Images'. *New Left Review* 140/141 (April): 82–97.

Stiegler, Bernard. 2010. *Taking Care of Youth and the Generations*. Stanford University Press.

Stilgoe, Jack. 2017. 'Seeing Like a Tesla: How Can We Anticipate Self-Driving Worlds?' *Glocalism: Journal of Culture, Politics and Innovation* 3. https://doi.org/10.12893/gjcpi.2017.3.2.

Suchman, Lucy. 1995. 'Making Work Visible'. *Communications of the ACM* 38 (9): 56–64.

Sung, Morgan. 2023. 'People Are Turning to Snap Map for Firsthand Perspectives from Gaza'. *TechCrunch*, 3 November. https://techcrunch.com/2023/11/03/snapchat-snap-map-israel-hamas-war-gaza-palestine/.

SuperHumans. n.d. *Start Your Freelancing Business Today | Work on Your Terms from Anywhere*. https://superhumans.life/freelancer-freedom-blueprint-landing/.

SuperHumans.Life, dir. 2023. *I Tried Making $800 in 4 Hours with Google Maps (To See If It Works)*. https://www.youtube.com/watch?v=AoxA5vyDgzA.

Sutton-Smith, Brian. 1997. *The Ambiguity of Play*. Harvard University Press.

Sutton-Smith, Brian. 2005. 'Play and Ambiguity'. In *The Game Design Reader: A Rules of Play Anthology*, edited by Katie Salen and Eric Zimmerman. MIT Press.

Swart, Murray. 2023. 'Google Maps and Waze to Stop Directing Commuters through Nyanga'. *Cape Town ETC*, 14 November. https://www.capetownetc.com/news/google-maps-directing-through-nyanga/.

Tenhunen, Sirpa. 2018. *A Village Goes Mobile: Telephony, Mediation, and Social Change in Rural India*. Oxford University Press.

Tennant, Chris, and Jack Stilgoe. 2021. 'The Attachments of "Autonomous" Vehicles'. *Social Studies of Science* 51 (6): 846–70.

Terranova, Tiziana. 2000. 'Free Labor: Producing Culture for the Digital Economy'. *Social Text* 18 (2): 33–58.

Terranova, Tiziana. 2012. 'Attention, Economy and the Brain'. *Culture Machine* 13 (1).

Thatcher, Jim, Luke Bergmann, Britta Ricker, et al. 2016. 'Revisiting Critical GIS'. *Environment and Planning A* 48 (5): 815–24.

Thielman, Sam. 2016. 'General Motors Acquires Self-Driving Car Startup Cruise Automation'. *The Guardian*, 11 March. https://www.theguardian.com/business/2016/mar/11/general-motors-cruise-automation-self-driving-cars.

Thrift, Nigel. 2004a. 'Driving in the City'. *Theory, Culture & Society* 21 (4–5): 41–59.

Thrift, Nigel. 2004b. 'Remembering the Technological Unconscious by Foregrounding Knowledges of Position'. *Environment and Planning D: Society and Space* 22 (1): 175–90.

Tofel, Kevin C. 2012. 'Users Are Indeed Trying and Ditching Apple Maps'. *BusinessWeek: Technology*, 3 October. http://www.businessweek.com/articles/2012-10-03/users-are-indeed-trying-and-ditching-apple-maps#r=lr-fs.

Törhönen, Maria, Lobna Hassan, Max Sjöblom, and Juho Hamari. 2019. 'Play, Playbour or Labour? The Relationships between Perception of Occupational Activity and Outcomes among Streamers and YouTubers'. *Hawaii International Conference on System Sciences 2019 (HICSS-52)*, 8 January. https://aisel.aisnet.org/hicss-52/dsm/live_streaming_services/4.

Tozzi, John. 2012. 'At Least Someone's Happy About Apple Maps'. *BusinessWeek: Small_business*, 28 September. http://www.businessweek.com/articles/2012-09-28/at-least-someones-happy-about-apple-maps#r=lr-fs.

Trajtenberg, Manuel. 2018. 'AI as the Next GPT: A Political-Economy Perspective'. NBER Working Paper No. 24245. National Bureau of Economic Research. https://doi.org/10.3386/w24245.

Treisman, Rachel. 2025. 'Who Will Call It the Gulf of America? A Look at This and Other Naming Disputes'. *NPR*, 11 February. https://www.npr.org/2025/02/03/nx-s1-5281985/google-maps-gulf-of-mexico-america.

Tubaro, Paola, Antonio A. Casilli, and Marion Coville. 2020. 'The Trainer, the Verifier, the Imitator: Three Ways in Which Human Platform Workers Support Artificial Intelligence'. *Big Data & Society* 7 (1): 2053951720919776.

Tuohy, Jennifer Pattison. 2025. 'Inside Philips Hue's Plans to Make All Your Lights Motion Sensors'. The Verge, 4 September. https://www.theverge.com/smart-home/768585/philips-hue-motion-aware-rf-sensing-lights-motion-ivani.

Tuters, Marc, and Kazys Varnelis. 2006. 'Beyond Locative Media: Giving Shape to the Internet of Things'. *Leonardo* 39 (4): 357–63.

Unkelbach, Christian. 2006. 'The Learned Interpretation of Cognitive Fluency'. *Psychological Science* 17 (4): 339–45.

Vallas, Steven, and Juliet B. Schor. 2020. 'What Do Platforms Do? Understanding the Gig Economy'. *Annual Review of Sociology* 46 (1): 273–94.

van der Graaf, Shenja, and Pieter Ballon. 2019. 'Navigating Platform Urbanism'. *Technological Forecasting and Social Change* 142: 364–72.

van der Vlist, Fernando, Anne Helmond, Michael Dieter, and Esther Weltevrede. 2025. 'Super-Appification: Conglomeration in the Global Digital Economy'. *New Media & Society* 27 (6): 3314–37.

van der Vlist, Fernando, Anne Helmond, and Fabian Ferrari. 2024. 'Big AI: Cloud Infrastructure Dependence and the Industrialisation of Artificial Intelligence'. *Big Data & Society* 11 (1): 20539517241232630.

van Dijck, José. 2014. 'Datafication, Dataism and Dataveillance: Big Data between Scientific Paradigm and Ideology'. *Surveillance & Society* 12 (2): 197–208.

van Dijck, José, Thomas Poell, and Martijn de Waal. 2018. *The Platform Society*. Oxford University Press.

van Doorn, Niels. 2017. 'Platform Labor: On the Gendered and Racialized Exploitation of Low-Income Service Work in the "On-Demand" Economy'. *Information, Communication & Society* 20 (6): 898–914.

van Doorn, Niels, and Adam Badger. 2020. 'Platform Capitalism's Hidden Abode: Producing Data Assets in the Gig Economy'. *Antipode* 52 (5): 1475–95.

van Doorn, Niels, and Julie Yujie Chen. 2021. 'Odds Stacked against Workers: Datafied Gamification on Chinese and American Food Delivery Platforms'. *Socio-Economic Review* 19 (4): 1345–67.

Venturini, Tommaso, and Richard Rogers. 2019. '"API-Based Research" or How Can Digital Sociology and Journalism Studies Learn from the Facebook and Cambridge Analytica Data Breach'. *Digital Journalism* 7 (4): 532–40.

Verhoeff, Nanna. 2012. *Mobile Screens: The Visual Regime of Navigation*. Amsterdam University Press.

Verma, Inder M. 2014. 'Editorial Expression of Concern: Experimental Evidence of Massivescale Emotional Contagion through Social

Networks'. *Proceedings of the National Academy of Sciences* 111 (29): 10779–10779.

Vijay, Darsana, and Alex Gekker. 2021. 'Playing Politics: How Sabarimala Played Out on TikTok'. *American Behavioral Scientist* 65 (5): 712–34.

Whittlesea, Bruce W.A., Larry L. Jacoby, and Krista Girard. 1990. 'Illusions of Immediate Memory: Evidence of an Attributional Basis for Feelings of Familiarity and Perceptual Quality'. *Journal of Memory and Language* 29 (6): 716–32.

Wikipedia. 2025a. 'Google Street View privacy concerns: revision history'. 15 May. https://en.wikipedia.org/w/index.php?title=Google_Street_View_privacy_concerns&action=history.

Wikipedia. 2025b. 'List of Google April Fools' Day Jokes'. 28 April. https://en.wikipedia.org/w/index.php?title=List_of_Google_April_Fools%27_Day_jokes&oldid=1287845307.

Wikipedia. 2025c. 'Pokémon (video game series)'. 11 October. https://en.wikipedia.org/w/index.php?title=Pok%C3%A9mon_(video_game_series)&oldid=1256690719.

Wikipedia. 2025d. 'Volvo Island'. 23 August. https://en.wikipedia.org/w/index.php?title=Volvo_Island&oldid=1307362117.

Wilken, Rowan. 2019a. 'Communication Infrastructures and the Contest over Location Positioning'. *Mobile Media & Communication* 7 (3): 341–61.

Wilken, Rowan. 2019b. *Cultural Economies of Locative Media*. Oxford University Press.

Wilken, Rowan, and Lee Humphreys. 2021. 'Placemaking through Mobile Social Media Platform Snapchat'. *Convergence* 27 (3): 579–93.

Wilken, Rowan, and Julian Thomas. 2019. 'Maps and the Autonomous Vehicle as a Communication Platform'. *International Journal of Communication* 13: 2703–27.

Williams, James. 2018. *Stand Out of Our Light: Freedom and Resistance in the Attention Economy*. Cambridge University Press.

Williams, Logan. 2023. 'Finding Geolocation Leads with Bellingcat's OpenStreetMap Search Tool'. *Bellingcat*, 8 May. https://www.bellingcat.com/resources/how-tos/2023/05/08/finding-geolocation-leads-with-bellingcats-openstreetmap-search-tool/.

Wilmott, Clancy. 2016. 'Small Moments in Spatial Big Data: Calculability, Authority and Interoperability in Everyday Mobile Mapping'. *Big Data & Society* 3 (2): 2053951716661364.

Wilmott, Clancy. 2020. *Mobile Mapping: Space, Cartography, and the Digital*. Amsterdam University Press.

Wilmott, Clancy, and Alexis E. Wood. 2024. 'Terra Infirma: On the Base Map in Urban Cartography and GIS'. *Environment and Planning D* 42 (5–6): 734–57.
Winner, Langdon. 1980. 'Do Artifacts Have Politics?' *Daedalus* 109 (1): 121–36.
Wolf, Thomas, Lysandre Debut, Victor Sanh, et al. 2020. 'Transformers: State-of-the-Art Natural Language Processing'. In *Proceedings of the 2020 Conference on Empirical Methods in Natural Language Processing: System Demonstrations*, edited by Qun Liu and David Schlangen. Association for Computational Linguistics. https://doi.org/10.18653/v1/2020.emnlp-demos.6.
Wolford, Ben. 2019. 'What Are the GDPR Consent Requirements?' GDPR.Eu, 25 January. https://gdpr.eu/gdpr-consent-requirements/.
Wollen, Peter, and Joe Kerr. 2002. *Autopia: Cars and Culture.* Reaktion Books.
Wood, Denis. 2003. 'Cartography Is Dead (Thank God!)'. *Cartographic Perspectives* 45: 4–7.
Wood, Denis. 2010. *Rethinking the Power of Maps.* Guilford Press.
Wood, Denis, and John Fels. 2008. *The Natures of Maps: Cartographic Constructions of the Natural World.* University of Chicago Press.
Woodcock, Jamie, and Mark R. Johnson. 2018. 'Gamification: What It Is, and How to Fight It'. *The Sociological Review* 66 (3): 542–58.
Woods, Steve. 2012. 'Is Google Maps' Undiscovered Island Really Non-Existent?' *Technorati*, 26 November. http://technorati.com/technology/article/is-google-maps-undiscovered-island-really/.
Woolgar, Steve. 1990. 'Configuring the User: The Case of Usability Trials'. *The Sociological Review* 38 (S1): 58–99.
Woolgar, Steve, and Geoff Cooper. 1999. 'Do Artefacts Have Ambivalence: Moses' Bridges, Winner's Bridges and Other Urban Legends in S&TS'. *Social Studies of Science* 29 (3): 433–49.
Yeung, Karen. 2017. '"Hypernudge": Big Data as a Mode of Regulation by Design'. *Information, Communication & Society* 20 (1): 118–36.
Zainuddin, Zamzami, Samuel Kai Wah Chu, Muhammad Shujahat, and Corinne Jacqueline Perera. 2020. 'The Impact of Gamification on Learning and Instruction: A Systematic Review of Empirical Evidence'. *Educational Research Review* 30: 100326.
Zhang, Yueming, Xiaolin Song, Bing Bai, et al. 2021. '2nd Place Solution for Waymo Open Dataset Challenge – Real-Time 2D Object Detection'. arXiv:2106.08713. Preprint, arXiv, 16 June. https://doi.org/10.48550/arXiv.2106.08713.
Zheng, Yongnian, and Yanjie Huang. 2018. *Market in State: The Political Economy of Domination in China.* Cambridge University Press.

Zickuhr, Kathryn. 2013. 'Location-Based Services'. Pew Research Center: Internet, Science & Tech, 12 September. http://www.pewinternet.org/2013/09/12/location-based-services/.

Zuboff, Shoshana. 2015. 'Big Other: Surveillance Capitalism and the Prospects of an Information Civilization'. *Journal of Information Technology* 30 (1): 75–89.

Zuboff, Shoshana. 2019. *The Age of Surveillance Capitalism: The Fight for the Future at the New Frontier of Power*. Profile Books.

Index